A RISING TIDE

A RISING TIDE

Financing Strategies for Women-Owned Firms

SUSAN COLEMAN and ALICIA M. ROBB

STANFORD ECONOMICS AND FINANCE
An Imprint of Stanford University Press • Stanford, California

Stanford University Press
Stanford, California

Special discounts for bulk quantities of Stanford Economics and Finance are available to corporations, professional associations, and other organizations. For details and discount information, contact the special sales department of Stanford University Press.
Tel: (650) 736-1782, Fax: (650) 736-1784

Printed in the United States of America on acid-free, archival-quality paper

Library of Congress Cataloging-in-Publication Data
Coleman, Susan, 1951- author.
A rising tide : financing strategies for women-owned firms / Susan Coleman and Alicia M. Robb.
pages cm
Includes bibliographical references and index.
ISBN 978-0-8047-7305-8 (cloth : alk. paper)—ISBN 978-0-8047-7306-5 (pbk. : alk. paper)
1. Women-owned business enterprises—United States—Finance. 2. Businesswomen—United States. I. Robb, Alicia M., author. II. Title.
HG4061.C64 2012
658.15′2082—dc23

2011040723

Typeset by Newgen in 10/14 Minion Pro

This book is dedicated to my husband Bill—my most loyal reader, partner, and friend. I also dedicate this book to my mother, Jane Flint, who, like the entrepreneurs featured in this book, has been a model of courage, creativity, and grace. —Susan Coleman

This book is dedicated to my friends Diane, Nicole, Nancy, Helen, Brooke, Krista, and all the other women entrepreneurs out there who are making a positive difference in our world. And to Jerry—I'm still down five but getting closer. I'm waiting with much anticipation for your entrepreneurial venture that will change health care as we know it. —Alicia Robb

CONTENTS

PREFACE AND ACKNOWLEDGMENTS

One of our goals in writing this book was to tie together the research findings on financing women-owned firms with the real-world stories of a sampling of women entrepreneurs. We said to ourselves, "OK, this is what the data say, but how does it really work in practice?" In retrospect, we are so happy to have taken this approach, because it is the stories of our entrepreneurs that really make *A Rising Tide: Financing Strategies for Women-Owned Firms* come alive. To our delight, we found diverse entrepreneurs employing a diverse array of financial strategies in a broad range of industries. In other words, we found plenty to talk about and plenty to share with our readers, be they aspiring entrepreneurs, "practicing" entrepreneurs, or students of entrepreneurship.

In addition to sharing the stories of real-world entrepreneurs, we attempted to ground those stories within a framework of entrepreneurship theory and research, both past and present. In particular, we used Resource-Based Theory, Motivational Theory, and Life Cycle Theory as our guides. Resource-Based Theory contends that the resources an entrepreneur has access to in the form of financial, human, and social capital will shape the type of firm that she starts, as well as the subsequent performance of that firm. Further, human capital in the form of education and experience and social capital in the form of networks and contacts often serve as a "gateway" for sources of financing and the use of specific financial strategies. Motivational Theory suggests that entrepreneurs have different motivations for launching their firms. These, in turn, will help to determine a number of factors, such as industry selection, size, growth rate, and financial strategy. Finally, Life Cycle Theory states that firms at different stages of development have different characteristics. Thus, the financing strategies of a new or nascent firm may be very different from those of an established firm or a firm going through a period of rapid growth. In essence, firms face different types of financial challenges at different points in their development and growth.

The theme of "one size does not fit all" also serves as an underpinning for *A Rising Tide: Financing Strategies for Women-Owned Firms*. The chapters of the book are designed to illustrate many of the different types of entrepreneurial firms, including nascent, home-based, family-owned, growth-oriented, technology-based, minority-owned, and global firms. Each of these chapters gave us the opportunity to present different types of entrepreneurs and different financing strategies. In spite of these differences, however, common themes have emerged regarding the importance of developing sources of financial, human, and social capital, consistent with Resource-Based Theory.

As authors and researchers, we learned many things in the course of writing *A Rising Tide: Financing Strategies for Women-Owned Firms*. For starters, we learned that successful women entrepreneurs are a creative, energized, and proactive bunch. They are not afraid to take risks, but they do not treat risk lightly either. They are also constantly innovating to develop new products, services, delivery systems, and technologies. They are bold in seeking out and seizing opportunities. Often these opportunities require additional financial resources or new financial strategies, and our women entrepreneurs are diligent in securing those resources and creative in developing those strategies. They are the new pioneers, and they are role models for the generations of women entrepreneurs who will come after them.

In addition to blending theory and practice in each chapter, we also provided sections on "What Have We Learned?" and "What Does All This Mean for Me?" In doing so, we attempted to tie the content of the chapter to the needs and interests of our readers. We also explored issues and questions of public policy, particularly those policies that encourage entrepreneurship among women and facilitate the processes of entrepreneurship. In this era of high unemployment, rapid technological change, and growing global competition, entrepreneurship can provide a path to economic empowerment for women, as well as a means for creating new jobs, products, and services both domestically and abroad.

Many people were an integral part of writing this book, and we would like to offer our deepest thanks to just a few of them. First, we thank the wonderful women entrepreneurs who generously gave their time to share their stories with us. Without their input, this book never would have come to pass. We also thank the Kauffman Foundation for access to the invaluable Kauffman Firm Survey data that we presented and analyzed throughout the book. Further, we thank the Kauffman Foundation for its generous financial support, which allowed us to write *A Rising Tide: Financing Strategies for Women-Owned Firms* and to attend key conferences that were instrumental in the development of our ideas. We want to make it plain that although we drew heavily on the Kauffman Firm Survey data for the research contained in this book, the opinions expressed and recommendations made are our own and not necessarily those of the Kauffman Foundation.

We thank the University of Hartford's Barney School of Business for a summer research grant to support the development of later drafts of *A Rising Tide: Financing Strategies for Women-Owned Firms*. The Barney School also provided graduate assistant support that allowed us to gather and analyze earlier research and data. In particular, graduate assistants Asli Kondu, Esra Gorgulu, and Abdulla Babashov played an invaluable role in the development of individual chapters. We thank the University of Hartford's Women's Education and Leadership Fund for a grant to support data gathering and coordination with our entrepreneurs. A special thank you to our friend and colleague, Dr. Dafna Kariv at the College of Management in Israel, who conducted interviews with global entrepreneurs Gali Ross and Hilla Ovil-Brenner.

We owe a big debt of thanks to our publisher, Stanford University Press, for recognizing the need for a book of this type, and to our truly awesome editor, Margo Beth Fleming who guided us through the process and encouraged us at every step along the way. Similarly, we are indebted to our editorial assistant, Jessica Walsh, and Jay Harward, Newgen project manager, who showed unfailing patience and grace in moving us through production.

We would like to take this opportunity to also recognize and thank our three reviewers: John Becker-Blease at Washington State University, John Watson at the University of Western Australia, and Victoria Sassine at Harvard University. Their painstaking reviews of our manuscript and thoughtful recommendations and suggestions were invaluable in helping us to develop the earlier drafts of *A Rising Tide* into the later, and vastly improved, manuscript.

Last but not least, we thank our families and friends for their support, love, and patience through this process. In particular, Susan thanks her husband, Bill Coleman, for his unfailing love, encouragement, and support. She also thanks her mother, Jane Flint, and her sister, Maureen Distasio, for serving as examples of what smart women are capable of. She also expresses her thanks to the longstanding members of her book club, who rejoiced in every milestone and celebrated every victory along the road to completion. Alicia extends her thanks to all the women we interviewed for this book and all the other amazing women in her life that serve as a constant source of inspiration—especially Evelyn, Diane, Krista, Niki, Susan, Mary Ann, Julie, her aunts Barb and Brenda, and her mom, Jackie. She also thanks everyone at the Kauffman Foundation for their ongoing support and encouragement, especially E. J. Reedy, Bob Strom, Bob Litan, and Carl Schramm. Finally, we extend our appreciation to Ewing Marion Kauffman, who, through his life and through his foundation, has had an indelible impact on the world as we know it.

As we close this introductory section, we cast our lines and prepare to launch into the stories, theoretical framework, and analysis that helped us to gain a better understanding and appreciation for the rising tide of women's entrepreneurship and the financial strategies that enable women entrepreneurs to navigate vast oceans of opportunity.

INTRODUCTION

What's the "Scoop" on Women Entrepreneurs?

In recent years interest in the role of women's entrepreneurship in providing opportunities for women, economic growth, and jobs in the United States has been expanding. In *A Rising Tide: Financing Strategies for Women-Owned Firms*, we trace the increase in women's entrepreneurship and explore the financial issues and strategies that are pertinent for entrepreneurial success. We also explore the ways in which the motivations of women entrepreneurs are intertwined with the financial strategies and sources they use. Our findings suggest that women entrepreneurs have complex and distinct motivations and that growth and profits are not always the top priority. Not surprisingly, women entrepreneurs' varied motivations give rise to different types of financial strategies.

In *A Rising Tide* we build upon the findings of prior research and draw conclusions from data provided by the Kauffman Firm Survey, a longitudinal survey of over 4,000 new firms in the United States. The KFS provides detailed information on both firm and owner characteristics, as well as financing sources and amounts. We also share the experiences and insights of women entrepreneurs in a broad range of industries to illustrate the connections among motivation, the resource endowments of the entrepreneurs, and financial strategies. We take a "life cycle" approach to examining the issues and challenges that the different types of women-owned firms face by starting with nascent and home-based firms and working our way up to growth-oriented and technology-based enterprises. Finally, in each chapter we provide insights into what our findings mean for you as an entrepreneur or an aspiring entrepreneur, as well as recommendations for public policy. It is our hope that our findings will engage and inspire you as they have us.

What Do We Know About Women Entrepreneurs?

Women entrepreneurs have been growing in both number and economic importance in recent years. Table 1.1 provides data from the 2007 Survey of Business Owners conducted by the U.S. Census Bureau. It reveals that in 2007 there were 7.8 million women-owned firms in the United States, generating $1.2 trillion in revenues. This number represented an increase of 20 percent from 2002 to 2007 compared to an increase of 18 percent for all firms, indicating that the number of women-owned firms grew faster than the number of firms overall for that time period. During the same time frame, the growth rate in revenues for women-owned firms grew by 27 percent compared to a growth rate of 33 percent for all firms. Thus, although the number of

TABLE 1.1 A profile of U.S. firms by gender

	Firms (#)	*Receipts ($ millions)*
WOMEN-OWNED FIRMS		
2007	7,793,425	1,192,781
2002	6,489,259	940,775
1997	5,417,034	818,669
% change		
2002–2007	20.1	26.8
1997–2002	19.8	14.9
1997–2007	43.9	45.7
ALL U.S. FIRMS		
2007	27,110,362	30,181,461
2002	22,974,685	22,627,167
1997	20,821,934	18,553,243
% change		
2002–2007	18.0	33.4
1997–2002	10.3	22.0
1997–2007	30.2	67.7
WOMEN AS A % OF THE TOTAL		
2007	28.7	4.0
2002	28.2	4.2
1997	26.5	4.4

Sources: U.S. Census Bureau. *2007* and *2002 Survey of Business Owners* and *1997 Survey of Women-Owned Business Enterprises.*

women-owned firms grew more rapidly, their growth rate in revenues lagged those of firms overall for the five-year period. This same pattern held true for the ten-year period spanning 1997 to 2007. During those years, the number of women-owned firms increased by 44 percent compared to an increase of 30 percent for firms overall. Although women-owned firms also increased their revenues by 46 percent during this period, firms overall saw an increase of 68 percent, suggesting that the firms launched by women tended to be smaller than those started by men.

As shown in Figures 1.1 and 1.2, women are vastly underrepresented in business ownership and business receipts in the United States. Figure 1.1 shows that women represent less than one-third of all firms in each of the

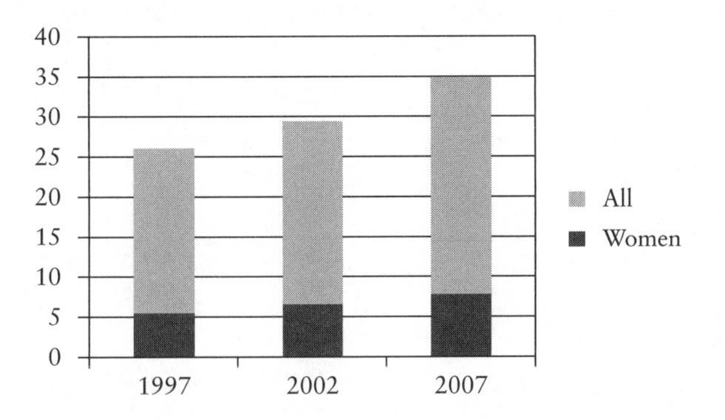

FIGURE 1.1 Number of firms in the United States (in millions)

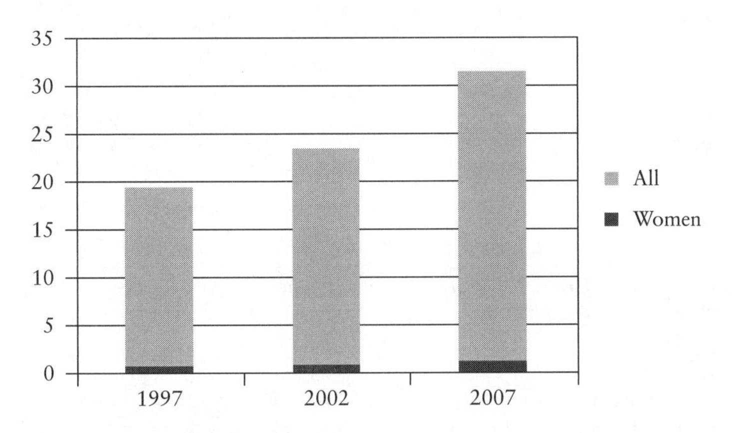

FIGURE 1.2 Business receipts in the United States (in millions of dollars)

survey years, and Figure 1.2 shows that women-owned firms represent only a tiny percentage of total receipts.

Firm Size and Numbers

Despite gains by women-owned firms in both number and revenues, their representation continues to be smaller than might be expected given the percentage of women in the population. Although the percentage of women-owned firms increased from 26.5 to 29 percent from 1997 to 2007, women-owned firms still constitute less than 30 percent of all firms, suggesting both challenges and opportunities for aspiring women entrepreneurs. Table 1.1 also reveals that women-owned firms generated only 4 percent of total firm receipts in 2007, a decline from 1997.* This finding reveals that the majority of women-owned firms are very small. Table 1.2 sheds additional light on this issue.

TABLE 1.2 Firms with paid employees only

	Firms (#)	*Receipts ($ millions)*	*Employees (#)*	*Annual payroll ($ millions)*
WOMEN-OWNED FIRMS				
2007	911,285	1,010,470	7,587,020	218,136
2002	916,768	804,097	7,146,229	173,709
1997	846,780	717,764	7,076,081	149,116
% change				
2002–2007	−0.6	25.7	6.2	25.6
1997–2002	8.3	12.0	1.0	16.5
1997–2007	7.6	40.8	7.2	46.3
ALL U.S. FIRMS				
2007	5,752,975	29,208,766	118,668,699	4,886,977
2002	5,524,813	21,859,758	110,786,416	3,813,488
1997	5,295,151	17,907,940	103,359,815	2,936,493
% change				
2002–2007	4.1	33.6	7.1	28.1
1997–2002	4.3	22.1	7.2	29.9
1997–2007	8.6	63.1	14.8	66.4
WOMEN AS A % OF THE TOTAL				
2007	15.8	3.5	6.4	4.5
2002	16.6	3.7	6.5	4.6
1997	16.0	4.0	6.8	5.1

Sources: U.S. Census Bureau. *2007 and 2002 Survey of Business Owners and 1997 Survey of Women-Owned Business Enterprises.*

* Women-owned firms are defined as sole proprietorships, partnerships, and corporations that are at least 51 percent owned by women. These data do not include firms that are jointly owned (50/50) by women and men.

Table 1.2 presents data on only firms that included paid employees in 1997, 2002, and 2007. A comparison of Tables 1.1 and 1.2 reveals that the vast majority of women-owned firms (88 percent in 2007) were sole proprietorships with no paid employees. Further, the number of women-owned firms with paid employees actually declined relative to all firms during the 2002–2007 period. Table 1.2 also shows that the growth rates for women-owned firms in terms of revenues, employment, and payroll lagged behind those of firms overall for both the five-year period of 2002–2007 and the ten-year period of 1997–2007. Table 1.2 provides evidence of the relatively small size of women-owned firms that had employees. In 2007 they accounted for only 3.5 percent of total sales, 6.4 percent of total employment, and 4.5 percent of annual payroll.

Figure 1.3 provides clear evidence of the relatively small size of women-owned firms that had paid employees. In 2007 they accounted for only 16 percent of firms, 3.5 percent of total sales, 6.4 percent of total employment, and 4.5 percent of annual payroll.

Clearly, although women-owned firms have begun to make an impact in terms of numbers, they are still in the early stages of making an economic impact on a larger scale. This is not to suggest, however, that the sole proprietorships or small firms owned by women do not have a significant economic impact on both individual households and local communities. A study conducted by George Haynes (2010) at Montana State University on behalf of the

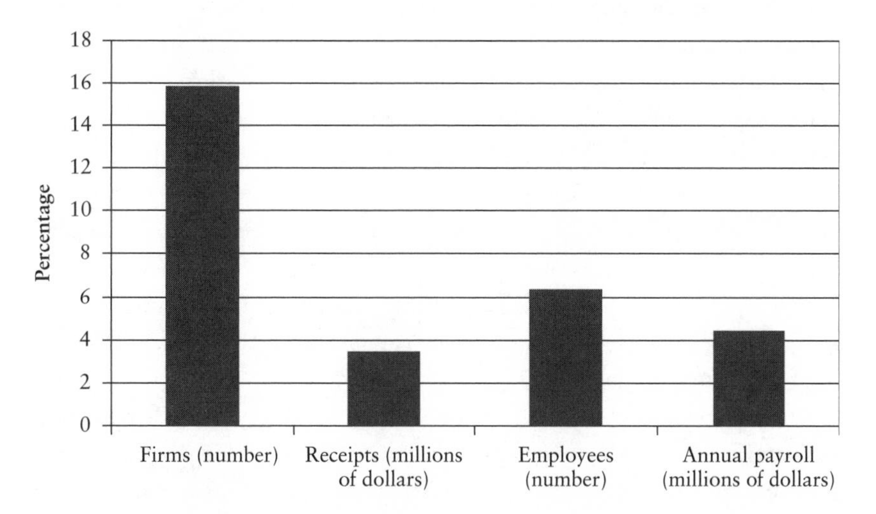

FIGURE 1.3 Percentage contributed by women-owned employer firms in 2007

U.S. Small Business Administration found that households that owned small businesses had a significantly higher probability of attaining high income and financial security (upper 50 percent) than households overall. Thus, it is very likely that many women who own businesses improve their own economic standing as well as that of their families.

Small size, however, does have implications for raising capital. Typically, owners of very small and home-based businesses rely primarily on personal savings, often supplemented by funding from family and friends, personal loans, and credit cards. They are less likely to use bank loans for their business, and they are too small to attract the interest or attention of external equity investors such as angel investors or venture capitalists. Bootstrapping (minimizing expenses) and microfinance (very small loans) also play an important role for the smallest of women-owned firms and are discussed in later chapters.

Industry Sector

Another factor that greatly impacts the financing strategies of women-owned firms is industry sector. Prior research shows that women are more likely to start firms in the retail and service industries (Coleman, 2002a; Robb and Wolken, 2002), and this is supported by data from the U.S. Census Bureau. Table 1.3 shows that women-owned firms were much more heavily represented in retail trade, health care and social assistance, and "other" services than were men-owned firms. Conversely, women played a lesser role in the construction, manufacturing, wholesale trade, and manufacturing industries. These distinctions are important because they have implications for the firm's ability to raise capital. The sectors with higher female representation—retail and service—tend to be populated by relatively small firms with few assets that could be used as collateral for loans. Similarly, many of these firms do not have growth aspirations or prospects, so they are not candidates for external equity. Manufacturing, construction, and transportation firms where men are more heavily represented, however, tend to be larger and more growth-oriented, and they typically have assets such as vehicles, equipment, and buildings that can be used as collateral for loans.

Why do women choose the industries they do? Many theories regarding the pattern of "industry segregation" shown in Table 1.3 and Figure 1.4 have been offered. One is that women have not had the opportunities to accumulate either the human capital (education and experience) or the financial capital

TABLE 1.3 Statistics for U.S. firms by gender and industry sector

Sector	*Women-owned (#)*	*Women-owned (%)*	*Men-owned (#)*	*Men-owned (%)*
Forestry, hunting, fishing, agriculture	52,115	0.71	172,790	1.30
Mining	28,615	0.39	79,636	0.60
Utilities	3,237	0.04	10,668	0.08
Construction	393,392	5.39	1,985,720	14.93
Manufacturing	179,006	2.45	453,154	3.41
Wholesale trade	186,395	2.55	501,650	3.77
Retail trade	1,133,362	15.54	1,361,735	10.24
Transportation	170,556	2.34	575,165	4.33
Information	91,457	1.25	181,131	1.36
Finance, insurance	216,346	2.97	601,462	4.52
Real estate	735,657	10.08	1,484,913	11.17
Professional, science, technical	1,043,259	14.30	2,051,541	15.43
Management	5,141	0.07	20,939	0.16
Administration and support, plus waste management and remediation	525,575	7.20	725,682	5.46
Education	185,994	2.55	160,530	1.21
Health care and social assistance	831,246	11.39	756,237	5.69
Arts, entertainment, recreation	311,480	4.27	527,546	3.97
Accommodation and food service	227,657	3.12	395,506	2.97
Other services	972,006	13.32	1,246,063	9.37
Not classified	2,960	0.04	5,590	0.04
Total	**7,295,456**	**100**	**13,297,658**	**100**

Source: U.S. Census Bureau. Characteristics of Business Owners: 2002.

(wealth) that would allow them to establish larger and more growth-oriented firms (Becker-Blease and Sohl, 2007; Marlow and Patton, 2005). Thus, they tend to gravitate toward the service and retail sectors, which do not require highly specialized skills or large amounts of capital to start.

Another theory is that women have different goals for their firms than men do, and they do not see size and growth as measures of success (Cliff, 1998; Morris et al., 2006). Alternatively, women consider their businesses an extension of their personal lives, and they manage their firms in a way that will allow them to fulfill multiple goals and objectives. These could include accumulating wealth, but they could also include "doing something I love," "being my own boss," or balancing the competing demands of home and child rearing (Boden, 1999).

In a very thought-provoking article, Helene Ahl (2006) contends that for too long women-owned businesses have been measured with the same yardstick as for men-owned businesses, so we expect to see the same size, growth

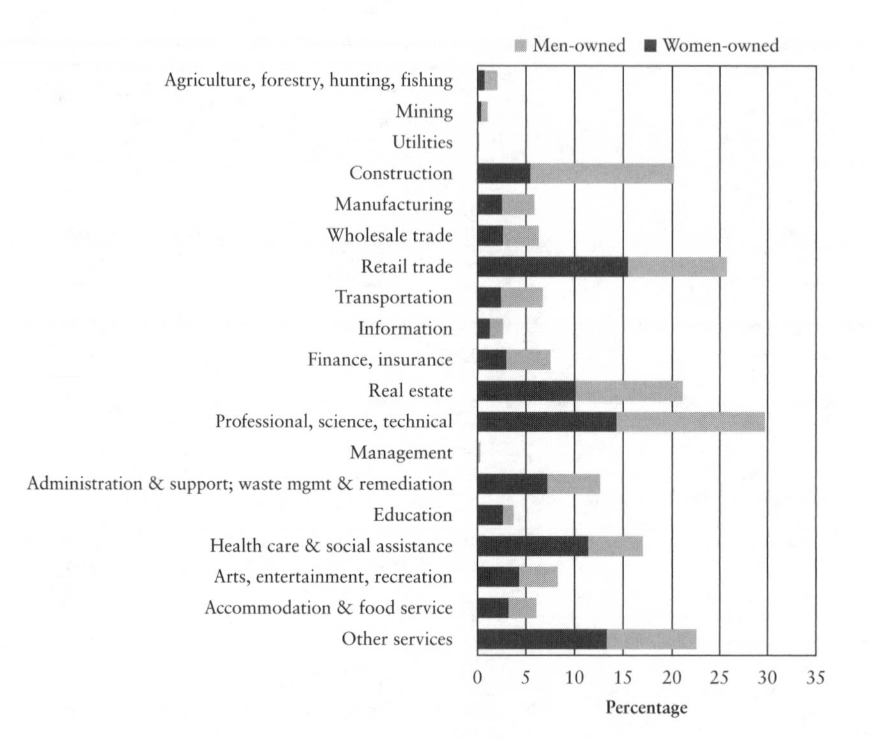

FIGURE 1.4 Industry distribution of women- and men-owned firms in 2002

rates, and standards of performance. Ahl points out in a very compelling way, however, that if women have different motivations and goals for their firms, their outcomes and measures for success will also differ. In other words, we need to use a different yardstick! Robb and Watson (2012) make some progress in this regard by measuring outcomes that are adjusted for both size and risk.

Theoretical Foundations for *A Rising Tide*

This book is based on three major theories pertaining to entrepreneurial firms. The first, Resource-Based Theory, contends that the role of the entrepreneur is to secure and transform needed resources, including financial resources, to create a competitive advantage. The second theory, which we refer to as Motivational Theory, asserts that individuals take the actions they believe will lead to desired outcomes. Thus, from the standpoint of entrepreneurial finance, entrepreneurs tend to select financial strategies in accordance with their motivations and goals. Finally, the Life Cycle Theory states that firms go through different stages as they develop and grow. This theory also contends that different financial strategies are appropriate at different stages of the life cycle. We now explore each of these theories more fully within the context of the central theme of this book: financing strategies for women-owned firms.

The Components of Entrepreneurial Success: Resource-Based Theory

Edith Penrose—an entrepreneur in the field of economics if there ever was one—was among the first economic theorists to address the links among resources, profitable growth, and competitive advantage. Penrose (1959) asserted that the entrepreneur's effective management of firm resources allows her to take advantage of productive opportunities in the marketplace to achieve profitable growth. Further, Penrose noted that the entrepreneur must continually maintain and develop the firm's resources if she is to retain a competitive advantage. In the case of small and entrepreneurial firms, Penrose observed that opportunities often emerge in segments of the market that larger, well-established firms tend to ignore or abandon. Finally, Penrose theorized that achieving profitable growth requires an optimal growth rate. In other words, growth for growth's sake alone is not necessarily the entrepreneur's objective. (This theme will come up repeatedly as we discuss the stories of successful women entrepreneurs throughout this book.) Penrose's early work is important not only in and of itself but also because she established the foundation for a Resource-Based Theory of the firm that links the fields of economics, entrepreneurship, and strategic management (Kor and Mahoney, 2000; Rugman and Verbeke, 2002).

According to the Resource-Based Theory of entrepreneurship, a firm is a collection of resources (Bergmann Lichtenstein and Brush, 2001; Brush et al., 2001; Hanlon and Saunders, 2007). The entrepreneur's tasks are to assemble, develop, and transform needed resources to generate unique capabilities that will give her a competitive advantage (Amit and Schoemaker, 1993; Wernerfelt, 1984). Resource-Based Theory also states that those firms that muster and apply their resources most effectively will also be the ones that enjoy superior performance (Brush et al., 2001; Sirmon and Hitt, 2003). The "resources" involved fall into the major categories of financial capital (debt and equity), human capital (education and experience), and social capital (networks and contacts). Following, the role and importance of each is examined, as well as some of the unique resource characteristics of women-owned firms.

Show Me the Money! The Role of Financial Capital

Since this book is about the financing strategies of women-owned firms, much of the focus is on the types and amounts of capital women entrepreneurs raise. Financial capital is one of the key inputs that make it possible for the entrepreneur to launch, develop, and grow her firm. As just mentioned, motivations and goals have an impact on the types of firms women start and the types and amounts of capital they use to finance them.

Women-owned firms and men-owned firms have several important distinctions when it comes to financial capital. First, women typically start their businesses with smaller amounts of personal financial capital. Women tend to cluster at the lower end of the compensation "food chain," and they are less likely to reach the levels of senior management. Thus, their levels of compensation and their accumulated wealth are both lower than men's. This is important because women entrepreneurs typically launch their businesses using their own money before trying to raise capital from outsiders. If women start their firms with smaller amounts of personal capital, that has implications for their ability to survive, develop new products and services, hire employees, and grow. Women are also more likely to experience career interruptions while they bear and raise children. These interruptions may slow down their ability to advance their careers and realize gains in compensation.

The good news is that women have made dramatic gains in both education and employment. Today, more women attend college than do men, and an increasing number of women are going into growth-oriented fields such as health care, bioscience, engineering, and computer science.

Women are also experiencing gains in the workplace. During the recent financial crisis, the unemployment rate for women was actually lower than the unemployment rate for men for the first time in our country's history. Further, women are advancing into positions of responsibility and power that will provide them with opportunities for higher levels of compensation and accumulated wealth. Despite these facts, however, a recent study found that executive women are more likely to leave S&P 1500 firms for both voluntary and involuntary reasons than men are (Becker-Blease et al., 2010). This suggests the existence of a potential pool of highly skilled women with executive experience who have the human, social, and financial resources to launch their own firms.

Some prior research suggests that women are more risk averse than men. "Risk aversion" means that individuals are unwilling to take bigger risks unless they can also anticipate bigger rewards for doing so. Consistent with this theory, some contend that women start smaller and more manageable businesses because they tend to be less risky (Cliff, 1998; Orser and Hogarth-Scott, 2002). Smaller firms minimize the need to raise financial capital in the form of debt or equity from external sources. External debt is borrowed money, and it increases the riskiness of the firm because it has to be paid back. Debt can also increase the risk of financial distress or bankruptcy. External equity involves sharing ownership with outsiders. From the entrepreneur's perspective, sharing ownership may increase the riskiness of the firm because the entrepreneur no longer has sole decision-making power. Thus, to summarize, the theory of risk aversion suggests that women will start firms in industries that are familiar to them (service and retail), and these firms will remain small, manageable, and largely financed with internal rather than external sources of financial capital.

Often risk aversion is presented as if it were a negative quality—as if women who start smaller firms are less "gutsy" than those who start larger, growth-oriented firms. Women-owned firms, however, need to be evaluated within the context of the motivations and goals of the entrepreneur. For example, a single mother who starts a home-based business to support her family while also being able to be in the home and attend to their needs is still an entrepreneur. Similarly, a 50-year-old woman who opts out of the corporate battlefield to start her own high-tech consulting firm is not engaging in a "lesser" form of entrepreneurship. Both women are creating economic value for their families and for the larger economy. Further, by starting their own firms, both may be pursuing personal goals that are even more important to them than the more obvious economic ones.

Another distinction between women- and men-owned firms that has implications for their ability to raise financial capital is that women are less likely to be a part of professional or social networks that could provide them access to sources of capital. The authors' research reveals that women-owned firms are significantly more likely to be sole proprietorships than are men-owned firms (Coleman and Robb, 2009). This can be a problem because it means a woman sole owner has fewer financial resources to draw upon than if she had partners or other equity investors who could also provide capital. Since women are also less likely to have had prior experience at the senior management level, they are also less likely to have friends and former associates who are capable of investing substantial amounts in their firms. Finally, women are less likely to be a part of formal networks that could provide financial capital. This is particularly true of financial capital in the form of external equity. Prior research has noted that angel investor and venture capital networks are male-dominated with few women in decision-making roles (Brush et al., 2002). Their lack of access to these important financial networks often means that women entrepreneurs do not even get on the radar screen of major equity investors. This is a structural challenge that will be discussed at length in subsequent chapters.

9 to 5 in Perspective: The Role of Human Capital

"Human capital" refers to the education and experience that individuals accumulate, and it is an essential ingredient for entrepreneurial success. Typically, before you start a business, you want to find out as much as possible about what it will involve. If you want to start a graphic design firm, for example, you would probably take some courses or get a degree in art. If you would like to open a restaurant, you might try to get a job at a restaurant and see what is involved in operating one. These types of human capital prepare you for the process of entrepreneurship. They allow you to learn from the successes (and failures) of others, so when you finally launch your own business, you will be better prepared.

Women entrepreneurs often have different types of human capital than men (Boden and Nucci, 2000; Fairlie and Robb, 2009). Although more women than men attend college (*National Center for Education Statistics Fast Facts*, 2009), women are less likely to major in business, engineering, or computer science, which are all fertile ground for aspiring entrepreneurs (Bobbitt-Zeher, 2007; Zafar, 2009). They are more likely to major in education, nursing, and the health professions, which are also fields with an abundance of entrepreneurial opportunities.

It is important to keep the doors of opportunity open for girls and young women who will be the entrepreneurs of tomorrow by encouraging them to explore and excel in a broad range of fields. Many elementary and secondary schools, as well as colleges and universities, are doing this by developing programs to attract and engage female students in the fields of science and engineering. The National Science Foundation's ADVANCE Program (http://www.nsf.gov), launched in 2001, was designed for this purpose. ADVANCE grants are intended to help colleges and universities increase the number of women faculty in the STEM fields (science, technology, engineering, and math), remove obstacles and barriers to their career advancement, and prepare them for positions of leadership. These women faculty, in turn, will serve as the teachers, role models, and mentors for generations of young women to come.

Prior studies also show that previous employment as well as managerial and entrepreneurial experience are just as important, if not more important, than education in predicting the success of new ventures (Boden and Nucci, 2000; Carter et al., 1997). It is much easier to start your own business in a particular field if you have already worked for or managed that type of business. By acquiring experience of this type, you gain an understanding of the factors that contribute to success, and you also learn about the pitfalls and "warts" of a particular business. Most important, you may learn that you actually don't want to start a business in that field after all, because it's not what you thought it would be. Those lessons learned are an important part of your entrepreneurial tool kit!

Previous entrepreneurial experience as an employee, a manager, or an entrepreneur may be especially valuable. If you have worked for an entrepreneurial venture, or if you have started one in the past, you have already experienced the "thrill of victory and the agony of defeat." You know the ups and downs that come with launching a new firm, and you have a better idea of what to expect. It's a little bit like riding a roller coaster. If you have never done it, you don't know what to expect and you may be terrified. If you have done it at least once, you may still be terrified, but at least you have a better idea of what lies ahead. From a financial perspective, investors are particularly fond of successful "serial entrepreneurs"—those individuals who have already launched and managed at least one other business. They believe that one of the best predictors of success in the future is success in the past. That's why it is often easier for serial entrepreneurs to raise capital than fledgling entrepreneurs. Investors are betting on the individual entrepreneur and her track record as well as on the new business.

Social Capital as "Glue"

In recent years researchers have devoted an increasing amount of attention to the role of social capital in the entrepreneurial process (Becker-Blease and Sohl, 2007; Brush et al., 2002; Harrison and Mason, 2007). "Social capital" refers to the networks and relationships that can provide an entrepreneur with resources or access to resources. These resources can include financial capital, key employees and advisors, linkages to suppliers or buyers, and other forms of assistance. Typically an entrepreneur does not have all the resources she will need to launch her firm. She may have an innovative product, but she lacks the financial capital to bring it to market. She may have great product development skills, but she lacks marketing expertise. She may have a company with the potential for dramatic growth, but she lacks systems and controls to ensure that the fast-moving train does not go off the tracks. All of these are opportunities for her to use social capital, networks, and contacts who can help her secure the resources and capabilities she needs to succeed.

Social capital isn't something you can just run out and buy off the shelf. Social capital is carefully built and cultivated over time, and it is something women entrepreneurs need to pay careful attention to. What or who makes up the parts of your social capital? Your social capital network can include classmates, professors, previous employers and coworkers, family, friends, and associates that you meet through clubs, organizations, or civic events. As an entrepreneur, you must develop and sustain your social capital network. Identify key players who can help you gain access to resources or give you valuable advice early in the process. Then develop these relationships over time. Don't wait until you actually need something; start now! Seek out role models and mentors, particularly those in the field you wish to enter.

This is particularly important advice for women because we all have a tendency to establish connections with people who are like us. If women entrepreneurs are seeking access to resources, however, they may have to push beyond their comfort zone to network with those who can actually provide those resources. In other words, network strategically, and if your current network does not include key types of individuals, identify and add them.

As an example, if you are launching a biotech start-up, establish linkages with local industry groups, your state department of economic development, college incubator programs, and angel investor or venture capital networks. These are all individuals who can help you on your path to entrepreneurial success. Too often we hear women entrepreneurs say, "Oh, I am so busy with the business, I just don't have time to go to meetings and events." *Make* the time! Establishing these networks and building your social capital are essential parts of the entrepreneurial process. It is just as important as developing and marketing your product. Social capital is the "glue" that helps you assemble the pieces of your business and hold them together.

Motivational Theory: The Role of Motivations and Firm Expectations

The second major theory in this book is what we refer to as "Motivational Theory." Motivational Theory is grounded in Expectancy Theory, which states that individuals will take the actions they believe will lead to expected and desired outcomes (Olson et al., 1996; Vroom, 1964). Expectancy Theory, taken from the literature of psychology, has been applied to the field of entrepreneurship to explain the motivations and behaviors of entrepreneurs. Specifically, entrepreneurs start a business to achieve expected and desired outcomes such as self-realization, status, autonomy, and financial success (Gatewood et al., 2002; Manolova et al., 2008). In the case of women entrepreneurs, researchers have noted that women and men have different expectations and desired outcomes for their firms. Thus, the actions they take to achieve those outcomes may also differ (Hughes, 2006; Manolova et al., 2008). This body of work is consistent with our Motivational Theory, which states that the diverse motivations of women entrepreneurs will give rise to different decisions and behaviors in the area of financial strategy.

As you will see throughout the book, women entrepreneurs are driven by a broad range of motivations. Some desire financial gains and rapid growth. Others want to be their own boss or do something they genuinely love. Others may seek to augment their family income while simultaneously balancing the demands of work and family. Still others may start firms because they are "pulled" into entrepreneurship by a desire to take advantage of an opportunity in the marketplace. Motivations abound, and they will determine the types of firms women start and the financing strategies they use. For example, a high-tech entrepreneur who is starting a rapid-growth business will probably have to bring in external equity investors to help finance research and development as well as firm growth. Conversely, a home-based entrepreneur may be able to start her firm with personal savings and then finance it with earnings from the business. She may never need external sources of financing at all. The point is that new entrepreneurs should evaluate their goals for the firm and be honest with themselves about what they want out of their entrepreneurial experience. Once they have taken that step, they will have a better idea about the financing strategies that will help them achieve their objectives. In essence, their motivations and expectations for the firm will shape the level and sources of financing they ultimately use.

Principles in Action: Cookies Direct LLC

When her oldest child started high school, Debbie Godowsky could just hear the clock ticking as the countdown to college tuition payments started. Debbie had been working as a substitute teacher while her children were young, but she realized that she would have to do something else to meet their college expenses. At the time, she had two goals for starting a business. First, she wanted to do something that would continue to provide flexibility while her son and daughter were still in school. Second, she wanted to start a business that would be sufficiently profitable to allow her to pay for college.

I was substitute teaching a study hall for seniors at the high school, and I asked them if they had any ideas for a home business. They said, "Why don't you do cookie care packages for kids in college?" It seemed like a good idea. I called our state's Small Business Administration—every state has one—and they said for $4 they could send me a packet on how to start a business. I brought cookies to school and tested my recipes on the students. By summer I was taking orders, and in September we started shipping. (Schillinger, 2006)

Debbie started her firm, Cookies Direct, in 1991 as a "Cookie of the Month" club, where people could have a different type of cookie shipped to college students every month. Debbie believed a cookie business had great potential because everybody loves cookies! She did not want to start a firm based on some fad or trend that would die out in a few years. She emphasizes that the business was not a hobby but started with a very specific financial goal.

A lot of people try to turn something they love to do into a business—let's say baking pies or dog walking. But I went at it from the opposite end: I thought, "What I'd love is to run a business. What will make it work?" I didn't love baking cookies. I loved being able to send my kids to college. (Schillinger, 2006)

In terms of financing, Debbie started her firm with $319 that she used to print a brochure that could be distributed in schools and colleges. She already had a kitchen, and since the cookies were made to order, she did not have to finance a large inventory of cookie supplies. Her customers prepaid for the year, and these funds provided working capital. Debbie did not use any debt to start, and only she invested capital in her business.

I was not a risk taker. I started small and grew by baby steps. Initially, and even today, I was very cost conscious, and I only bought stuff for the firm when I absolutely needed it and could not get it somewhere else.

One of the most impressive things about Debbie's financial strategies is that she became a pro at bootstrapping. "Bootstrapping" refers to techniques that allow the entrepreneur to minimize expenses as an alternative to raising additional capital. When Debbie started her firm, she used her kitchen to make the cookies and her dining room as her office. In terms of marketing, she persuaded colleges to include her brochure in mailings to prospective students and parents. They were happy to do so, since Debbie provided an added level of service they didn't have to pay for.

As her sales increased, Debbie realized that her kitchen equipment was not sufficient for the additional volume. She persuaded a local restaurant to allow her to use their industrial mixer to mix her cookie dough, and a local church charged her $10 a month for the use of their large ovens. Rather than buying a separate phone for the business, Debbie paid $6 a month to have the phone company set up her home phone with different ring tones. One ring was calls to the business, and two rings were calls to family members.

You really have to understand the financials of your business and be looking at the books constantly. You have to understand where your revenues and costs come from, particularly at a time like this when people are cutting back on expenditures. If your revenues go down, you have to be on top of that, and you have to know which expenses you can cut back without sacrificing the quality of your product.

Over time, Debbie expanded beyond the Cookie of the Month program to offer a full line of cookie gift baskets for all occasions, including shipments to military personnel. Today, Cookie of the Month makes up about 10 percent of her sales, while gift baskets for other occasions make up the other 90 percent. Debbie has her own website so people can order online now (www.mainecookies.com), and she has customers worldwide. In recent years, she started a new cookie program called "Club 9," which allowed individuals to contribute $9 to a cookie fund for soldiers in Iraq and Afghanistan. With every cookie order sent to a member of the military, Debbie included an extra dozen that was paid for by a Club 9 member. This program has been a way to share support and encouragement for troops overseas. To date, Debbie has shipped over 4,700 cookie packages to military personnel, each containing an extra dozen cookies from a Club 9 donor.

As her business continued to grow, Debbie realized that she would need more space on a permanent basis. She remodeled a spare bedroom on the ground level of her home to use for mixing, cooking, packaging, and mailing her gift baskets. Today she has six employees, all part-time, who help with the production, assembly, and shipping functions. In 2011, Debbie's business celebrated its twentieth anniversary, and she commemorated that milestone by offering a 20 percent discount for 20 days to her returning customers, since they were the people responsible for her 20 years of growth and success. Although her children have now graduated from college, entrepreneurship has become a way of life for Debbie, and she has shifted her goals from paying for college to paying for retirement and renovations on the home that she shares with her husband. Debbie is as passionate as ever about the quality of her products and services, and she is vigilant about cost control. Although she is comfortable with the current size of her firm, she is always on the lookout for opportunities to introduce new products or grow sales.

The Internet has been a blessing because it has opened up a whole new world of potential customers. At the same time, it has dramatically increased the level of competition. I need to be visible, and I need to deliver the best product out there so people will come back. I want a relationship with my customers, and I want them to think of me when they need a gift for a special occasion. Everyone likes cookies.

• Bootstrapping

Bootstrapping is one of the most frequently used—but most frequently ignored—financing techniques for entrepreneurs. Although we have introduced bootstrapping in our case study about Debbie Godowsky, the founder of Cookies Direct, it is a technique that entrepreneurs in all industries and in firms of all sizes use (Ebben, 2009; Gatewood et al., 2009; Van Auken and Neeley, 1996).

Bootstrapping is minimizing expenses as a way to minimize the amount of capital the entrepreneur needs to raise. It is a valuable financial strategy for the entrepreneur because it reduces the amount of money she has to borrow in the form of debt as well as the amount of firm ownership she must share in the form of equity. This book presents several stories of savvy women entrepreneurs using bootstrapping for their firms. In fact, a recent study found that women entrepreneurs tend to control their cash flows more carefully than men do and that during periods of declining sales, women are more aggressive in their use of bootstrapping strategies (Neeley and Van Auken, 2010).

Bootstrapping involves several techniques. One of the most obvious strategies is to start the firm out of your home rather than renting or buying office space. Other bootstrapping techniques include obtaining low-cost or no-cost services such as Debbie's use of industrial equipment at a local restaurant and church. Additional techniques include delaying compensation for the entrepreneur, sharing space or equipment, using temporary personnel to meet changing demand, securing credit from suppliers, obtaining loans from family and friends, leasing rather than buying, and bartering to obtain products and services (Ebben, 2009; Gatewood et al., 2009).

Although bootstrapping is an invaluable strategy for small and new firms, some researchers warn that it can be overused to the detriment of firm growth (Patel et al., 2011). They point out that bootstrapping can be labor intensive and typically provides resources in small increments. When a firm needs larger amounts of capital to grow, however, the entrepreneur needs to redirect her energies toward raising external sources of debt and equity or developing strategic alliances. In other words, bootstrapping will help you to get started and survive, but by itself it will not fund the growth of your firm.

Tips for Bootstrapping

1. Be proactive in your bootstrapping strategy! Don't wait until you are short of cash to explore ways to minimize expenses. By then, you are already behind the eight ball.
2. Be creative! As Debbie Godowsky shows, your local community is a wellspring of untapped bootstrapping opportunities.
3. Be frugal! Being frugal means you don't have to spend precious cash or use external sources of debt and equity.
4. Do not confuse effective bootstrapping with strategies that strangle the firm and its prospects for growth. Although bootstrapping can help you to minimize costs, do not be afraid to spend money or raise external capital when needed.

Although Debbie Godowsky continues to be a devoted bootstrapper, it can be a particularly valuable technique for new firms as well. During the early days of a business's creation, it is often especially difficult to raise funds externally. The firm may not yet be profitable, and it has no track record of success. This is a critical stage for new firms, and it is the point at which many go out of business due to the lack of capital to keep going. Debbie understood this from the earliest days of her firm, and she used bootstrapping to minimize expenses and maintain cash flows so her firm could survive and prosper.

Life Cycle Theory

The third theory in this book is Life Cycle Theory, which contends that a firm goes through different stages over the course of its life cycle, starting with the initial idea and development through to maturity. The various stages and their relative duration are illustrated in Figure 1.5.

At each of these stages the entrepreneur faces different financial issues and challenges (Berger and Udell, 1998), and she will employ different strategies and sources of financing to address them. For example, during the development stage, the entrepreneur is still working on her idea and

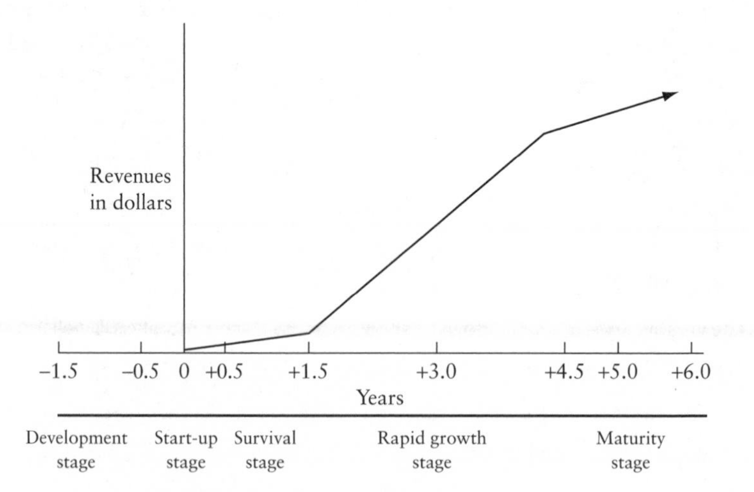

FIGURE 1.5 Life Cycle Theory stages of the successful venture
Source: From LEACH/MELICHER. *Entrepreneurial Finance,* 3rd ed. © 2009 South-Western, a part of Cengage Learning, Inc. Reproduced by permission. www.cengage.com/permissions.

getting started. Most of her financing will come from her personal savings. Family or friends may provide additional funds at the outset. At the start-up stage, she now has a product or service to sell and has begun generating revenues. At this point she may be able to attract outside investors in the form of business angels (individual investors) or venture capitalists (investment funds) if she is starting a firm that has the potential to achieve significant growth. The survival stage is a critical point because this is when the entrepreneur is generating substantial revenues. Typically, however, expenses still exceed revenues, so additional outside financing is still required to keep the company going. This may come in the form of bank loans, government assistance programs, or equity investments from angel or venture capital investors. When the company reaches the rapid growth stage, it now has a proven business model. At this stage it can secure bank loans and self-financing through the earnings it generates. At this point also, firms can secure financing from suppliers (in the form of trade credit) and from customers (in the form of accounts payable). Finally, in the maturity stage, the growth rate of the firm has leveled off, and the entrepreneur can now secure financing from a full range of debt and equity alternatives (Leach and Melicher, 2009).

When we look at it this way, the venture life cycle sounds like a nice, neat progression in terms of firm growth and financing. But in fact, many, if not most, firms do not go through all the stages of the venture life cycle. In particular, the majority of firms do not go through a period of rapid growth. Alternatively, most firms remain small or midsized, which in the case of women-owned firms is often by choice. In future chapters we examine the full spectrum of women-owned firms, including new or nascent firms, small, home-based firms, growth-oriented firms, and firms that have achieved substantial size and scope.

What Have We Learned?

In this chapter we saw that women-owned firms are growing in terms of both number and economic importance. Further, entrepreneurship has provided a pathway to economic empowerment for many women, while simultaneously allowing them to fulfill personal goals. We also saw that women have different motivations for starting businesses and that different motivations lead to different types of entrepreneurial ventures. These, in turn, necessitate different types of financial strategies.

This chapter outlined some of the differences between women and men entrepreneurs and the challenges those differences incur. Women tend to start smaller and less growth-oriented firms. Although an increasing number of women are venturing into nontraditional types of businesses, the majority of women continue to start firms in the highly competitive service and retail fields.

From a resource-based perspective, women also bring a different array of resources to their firms than men do. Women tend to have lower earnings and accumulated wealth, which poses a financial challenge. They also have different educational and experiential backgrounds. Finally, women are less likely to have well-developed social networks that could provide them access to needed resources. These are not insurmountable challenges, but they are challenges to be faced and dealt with nevertheless.

This chapter introduced Motivational Theory, which states that women entrepreneurs have a diverse array of motivations and expectations that help them to determine the types of businesses they start, their measures of success, and the financing strategies they use. Throughout this book we will see the interaction of the entrepreneur's motivations and her resources in shaping the financial strategies that she employs to achieve her goals.

What Does All This Mean for Me?

As a woman entrepreneur or an aspiring woman entrepreneur, this chapter told you the following:

1. You are not alone! There are thousands of successful women entrepreneurs out there who have followed the path you seek to follow. These women can serve as role models and mentors. Seek them out, and learn from both their successes and their mistakes. Don't be shy! Get out there and meet some people!
2. The starting point for launching a business is evaluating your personal goals and motivations. What do you want to achieve, and what measures of success are most important to you? Is it having a flexible schedule, being your own boss, rapid growth, or high earnings and wealth? Be honest with yourself, and do not shortchange this step! Your motivations should determine the type of business you start.
3. Understand that different types of firms have different characteristics and different outcomes. For example, if you open a nail salon, you will probably

have a number of competitors that could limit your prospects for growth and profits. If you open an upscale restaurant, your business may suffer during a recession. If you establish a biotech start-up, it will probably take a long time, many approvals, and large amounts of external funding before you can actually market your drug. Do your homework, and take the time to understand the dynamics of your firm and industry before you get started. This will help you to identify and plan for appropriate funding sources, and it will also help you to minimize unpleasant surprises.

4. Take an inventory of your personal resources in the form of financial capital, human capital, and social capital. Which resources can you bring to the firm yourself, and what gaps have to be filled? This will differ, depending on the type of business you start, because different industries and firms require different types of resources.
5. Recognize that different financing strategies and sources may be appropriate for different stages of firm growth. Entrepreneurs establishing new or nascent firms tend to rely heavily on personal financial resources, family, and friends. Alternatively, growth-oriented entrepreneurs need to weigh the costs and benefits of raising external capital, which may also involve sharing ownership and control. At different stages of growth, different sources of capital may be more or less available and desirable than at others.

Public Policy Implications

This chapter lays the groundwork for several public policy considerations pertaining to starting and financing women-owned firms. The first of these is recognizing that women-owned firms reflect the unique circumstances, motivations, and goals of the entrepreneurs who create them. They are not a mirror image of firms founded by men, nor should they be. Although a growing number of women are starting growth-oriented firms in nontraditional fields such as science, technology, and engineering, many other women are launching home-based firms or micro-businesses that will employ fewer than five people. We cannot evaluate these different types of firms using the same economic ruler that states "bigger is better." Women own and operate firms at all stages of the life cycle, and our measures of success need to reflect the diverse experience and goals of women entrepreneurs.

A second public policy consideration is to recognize that women often bring different resources in the form of financial, human, and social capital to the table when they establish their firms. In terms of financial capital, women, on average, have lower earnings and accumulated wealth than men, and they start their firms with smaller amounts of capital. Although women are just as likely as men to attend college, they are less likely to major in science, engineering, or computer science. Women are also less likely to have prior work experience at the senior manager level. Finally, women are less likely to be a part of networks that could provide them access to financial capital.

These resource-based differences suggest strategies to enhance the entrepreneurial opportunities for women. From an academic perspective, programs have already been designed to increase the number of women faculty and students in the STEM (science, technology, engineering, and math) disciplines. These initiatives should continue to be funded, and model programs should be replicated in multiple locations. Within the corporate sector, a growing number of firms are advancing women into the ranks of senior management. We need additional programs to identify talented women managers and provide them with the training and mentoring that will prepare them for key decision-making roles. These women leaders may become the entrepreneurs of tomorrow, or, alternatively, they may serve as role models, mentors, or investors for other aspiring women entrepreneurs. Finally, we need to further develop and expand upon networks that can provide women access to needed resources such as financial capital. Although angel and venture capital firms that actively seek out investments in women-owned firms are already in place, the majority of external equity capital still flows to firms that are owned by men. Angel and venture capital firms need to further diversify their mix of senior managers to attract, identify, and develop high-potential women-owned firms.

LAYING THE GROUNDWORK

What Do We Know About the Financing Strategies of Women-Owned Firms?

As we saw in Chapter 1, the number of women-owned businesses is increasing at a faster rate than businesses overall. Furthermore, women start or acquire their firms for many different reasons, and these motivations have an impact on the financing strategies they use. It stands to reason that a woman who starts a home-based business with the goal of balancing the competing demands of work and family will use different sources and amounts of financing than a woman who starts a rapid growth, technology-based business with the goal of eventually going public. In this chapter, we discuss some of the major financing issues and patterns among women-owned firms. We will examine barriers, constraints, and the "myths" concerning women and finance, as well as strategies for overcoming obstacles, both internal and external.

Fear of Finance

One thing we have learned from prior research is that women often lack the confidence and/or skills to deal with finances, but they do not necessarily lack the ability. In spite of that, women frequently describe themselves as having a "math phobia" or not being "good with numbers." These sentiments are partially due to the ways in which women have been socialized both within and outside the classroom, but they also arise at least partially from our preconceived notions about ourselves. We tell our undergraduate finance students, both male and female, that finance is a skill to be learned just like any other skill, such as tennis, driving, or playing video games. You learn the basics, you practice, and then you apply those skills, and over time you get to be pretty good at them. There is no magic or "voodoo economics," just practice and application.

Nevertheless, women continue to experience difficulties in the area of finance. Recent research on financial literacy reveals that women had lower levels of knowledge and confidence than men (Lusardi and Mitchell, 2006; Lusardi et al., 2009). In fact, this pattern emerges as early as junior high and high school, and it is clearly evident by the time women enter college (Altman et al., 2007; Correll, 2001; Ford and Kent, 2010; Jensen and Owen, 2001). In the realm of entrepreneurship, women also report that financial management is one of their greatest areas of concern and weakness (Brush, 1992; Hisrich and Brush, 1984; Pellegrino and Reece, 1982). A recent study on the "financial self-efficacy" of women entrepreneurs revealed that only 35 percent indicated that they were "confident" or "very confident" in their skills in the area of financial management (Amatucci and Crawley, 2010).

Not surprisingly, women's anxiety about finance affects how they run their businesses. A study of Canadian firms (Orser et al., 2000) found that women were more concerned about securing financing for their firms than with any other business problem. A later study (Coleman, 2002a) using a large sample of U.S. firms found further evidence of women's lack of confidence in the area of finance. Specifically, the U.S. study found that women business owners were just as likely to be approved for loans as men. Nevertheless, a significantly higher percentage of women did not apply for loans because they feared they would be denied. These findings are important because a reluctance to deal with financial service providers and financial priorities can deprive a firm of the capital needed to innovate, develop new products and services, hire key employees, and grow (Robb and Coleman, 2009).

This message is as relevant for women entrepreneurs as it is for undergraduate finance students, because, ultimately, the buck stops with you (whoever you are). As a business owner, you may have people to assist you with the company's finances, but you are in charge, and you need to be able to make financial decisions that are in your best interests and the best interests of your company. Fortunately, there are many sources of assistance and support to help you get over the financial "hump" if you are experiencing one. Most colleges and community colleges offer introductory courses in both accounting and finance that can introduce anyone to the basics of these disciplines. Many communities also offer adult education courses on "how to start a small business" or "financing a small business." If your community has a local chapter of SCORE (Service Corps of Retired Executives), those individuals can also be an invaluable resource. SCORE volunteers are individuals with significant managerial and entrepreneurial experience who are willing and eager to work with new entrepreneurs to help them "learn the ropes" and get off to a good start. The "Events" or "Calendar" section of your local newspaper can also provide information about low-cost and no-cost programs and groups that can help you learn the basics. If you genuinely feel that you lack math skills, find one of these programs and get yourself signed up today!

• The U.S. Small Business Administration

The U.S. Small Business Administration, or SBA, was established in 1953 as an independent agency of the federal government with the goal of helping individuals start, build, and grow their firms. The SBA provides services to new and existing business owners through a network of field offices and partnerships with both public and private organizations throughout the United States. Each state has an SBA office to provide information, advice, and support (www.sba.gov). Equally important, the SBA can direct entrepreneurs to other resources, including training, business support, sources of financing, and key networks. From the standpoint of women entrepreneurs, the SBA also maintains an Online Women's Business Center (www.onlinewbc.gov). This is a free and interactive website designed to help women expand their businesses. It provides information on business principles and practices, management techniques, networking, industry news, market research, technology training, online counseling, and links to hundreds of other sites. Your area SBA office can also put you in touch with a local chapter of the Service Corps of Retired Executives (SCORE) or with a Small Business Development Center (SBDC) in your area. SBDCs are often affiliated with universities, and they provide counseling, training, and technical assistance in all aspects of small business development. For further information on how to locate the SBA office in your area, go to www.sba.gov or call the SBA Answer Desk at 1-800-827-5722.

Sources of Financing 101

In the simplest of all possible terms, capital comes in two "flavors": debt and equity. Debt is money that you borrow. Typically it has to be paid back at some point and carries an interest rate or "cost." Providers of debt, such as banks, finance companies, and mortgage companies, do not "own" the firm but are simply lenders. In the case of small and entrepreneurial firms, borrowing may take the form of a business loan or a personal loan that is directed toward the needs of the business.

In contrast, equity represents ownership interest. Equity is capital that you or other investors put into the firm in exchange for a share of ownership. Equity is permanent capital and is not repaid. Equity holders expect to get their returns from either dividends or an increase in the value of the firm. If you reinvest earnings from your business back into the company, this is also a type of equity referred to as "retained earnings."

Just as there are two types of capital (debt and equity), there are two sources of capital: internal and external. Internal capital is debt or equity that you or other insiders (spouse, family, friends, employees) provide, while external capital is provided by outside parties such as banks, angel investors, or venture capitalists.

Both debt and equity show up on one of the firm's major financial statements: the balance sheet. The simple balance sheet in Figure 2.1 shows the assets in the first column and the liabilities (debt) and equity in the second column. Assets are used to produce goods and services. They include short-term or current assets such as cash, accounts receivable, and inventories, as well as fixed assets such as buildings, equipment, and vehicles. Every asset must be "paid for" with either a liability (money that you borrow) or equity (money that you or other owners invest). The reason we call this form the "balance" sheet is that *total assets* must equal *total liabilities* plus *equity.* (In other words, the balance sheet has to balance.). Another way of looking at it is that there is no free lunch on the balance sheet; every asset has to be "paid for" with either a liability or equity.

Looking at the year-end balance sheet for Heavenly Chocolate Company in Figure 2.1, we see that the balance sheet does indeed balance. Total assets equal total liabilities and equity. Voila! Further, we see that this company finances its assets with a combination of short-term debt ($3,000), long-term debt ($2,000), and equity ($5,000).

The mix of debt and equity that a firm uses to finance its assets is called the "capital structure." For example, we might say that a firm uses a capital structure of 40 percent debt and 60 percent equity. That means that every dollar in assets is financed by 40 cents of debt and 60 cents of equity. As you can

Assets ($ thousands)		Liabilities ($ thousands)	
Cash	1,000	Accounts payable	1,500
Accounts receivable	2,000	Short-term loans	1,500
Inventory	4,000	Current liabilities	3,000
Current assets	7,000	Long-term debt	2,000
Net fixed assets	3,000	Total liabilities	5,000
Total assets	10,000	Equity	5,000
		Total liabilities & equity	10,000

FIGURE 2.1 Heavenly Chocolate Company balance sheet, December 31, 2010

see, the percentages of debt and equity in the capital structure have to add up to 100 percent. In the case of Heavenly Chocolate Company, 50 percent of its assets are financed with debt, while the remaining 50 percent are financed with equity.

The Financing Strategies of Women-Owned Firms: Evidence from the Kauffman Firm Survey

Now that we have reviewed the basics of debt, equity, and capital structure, let's take a closer look at the patterns of financing in women-owned firms. A recent article by the authors (Coleman and Robb, 2009) used Kauffman Firm Survey (KFS) data to examine sources and amounts of financing for women- and men-owned firms at both start-up and in the early years of operation to reveal some important distinctions between the two. The KFS is a particularly rich data set that includes information on more than 4,000 U.S. firms that began operations in 2004. The intent is to track these firms over time and gather data for the 2004–2011 time period, thereby providing eight years of data—a veritable treasure trove for researchers and a valuable resource for decision makers in the area of public policy. The data include information by owner characteristics, which include gender, age, education, and prior experience, and firm characteristics, which include industry, location, revenues, profits, employment, and intellectual property. The KFS also includes information on sources and amounts of both debt and equity at start-up and over time. Table 2.1 provides a summary and comparison of financing sources and amounts for women- and men-owned firms included in the KFS.

Table 2.1 shows, first of all, that women raised less money to fund their firms than men did. This was true in the start-up year—2004—but it was also true in subsequent years. Table 2.1 also shows that, on average, women entrepreneurs started their firms with just over $71,000, compared with more than $134,000 for men. In other words, men raised over 80 percent more capital than women in the first year of operation. Moreover, Table 2.1 reveals that the gap persisted in subsequent years as women- and men-owned firms raised additional funds. For example, by 2008 men raised an additional $85,000, compared with just over $51,000 in new capital raised by women.

• Issues of Supply and Demand

Why do men raise much greater amounts of capital than women? Several theories have been put forth to address this discrepancy. The first pertains to "demand" factors, or the extent to which women seek out sources of financing. If more women launch home-based businesses or small retail or service establishments, it stands to reason that their demand for capital will be lower (Coleman, 2000; Coleman, 2002a; Cole and Wolken, 1995). A second theory contends that women are less likely to start businesses with the goal of growing them into large ventures (Cliff, 1998; Orser and Hogarth-Scott, 2002). Thus, they are less likely to launch rapid growth firms, which tend to consume large amounts of capital. A third theory asserts that women are more risk averse than men (Barber and Odean, 2001; Canizares et al., 2010; Dohmen et al., 2005; Jianakoplos and Bernasek, 1998; Powell and Ansic, 1997). Further, they are more concerned with maintaining control over their businesses (Constantinidis et al., 2006). If this is the case, women might choose to use smaller amounts of debt (because more debt increases the risk of bankruptcy), as well as smaller amounts of external equity (because external equity typically entails sharing control with outside investors).

TABLE 2.1 2004–2008 firm financing by 2004 start-ups by primary owner gender

	Initial year of operation 2004		*Second year 2005*		*Third year 2006*		*Fourth year 2007*		*Fifth year 2008*	
	Female	*Male*	*Female*	*Male*	*Female*	*Male*	*Female*	*Male*	*Female*	*Male*
FINANCIAL INJECTIONS ($)[1]										
Owner equity	23,948	36,697	9,693	19,585	8,424	14,726	8,925	10,788	7,084	12,807
Insider equity	1,876	2,088	437	1,880	587	824	733	1,720	403	602
Outsider equity	935	25,980	7,612	32,507	1,342	22,788	1,729	12,283	1,016	7,536
Owner debt	3,897	5,412	5,222	4,225	3,178	4,311	5,700	3,973	4,913	4,813
Insider debt	4,771	7,772	3,198	6,138	2,183	6,050	1,105	4,293	2,788	4,688
Outsider debt	36,057	56,191	35,959	46,863	30,908	73,144	32,702	64,336	34,980	54,459
Total financial cap	71,484	134,139	62,120	111,197	46,624	121,842	50,894	97,393	51,184	84,905
DISTRIBUTION OF INJECTIONS (%)										
Owner equity	33.5	27.4	15.6	17.6	18.1	12.1	17.5	11.1	13.8	15.1
Insider equity	2.6	1.6	0.7	1.7	1.3	0.7	1.4	1.8	0.8	0.7
Outsider equity	1.3	19.4	12.3	29.2	2.9	18.7	3.4	12.6	2.0	8.9
Owner debt	5.5	4.0	8.4	3.8	6.8	3.5	11.2	4.1	9.6	5.7
Insider debt	6.7	5.8	5.1	5.5	4.7	5.0	2.2	4.4	5.4	5.5
Outsider debt	50.4	41.9	57.9	42.1	66.3	60.0	64.3	66.1	68.3	64.1
LEVERAGE RATIOS (%)										
Debt/equity	167.1	107.1	250.1	106.0	350.3	217.8	347.0	292.9	501.9	305.4
Debt/total FK	62.6	51.7	71.4	51.5	77.8	68.5	77.6	74.5	83.4	75.3
Insider eq/total FK	2.6	1.6	0.7	1.7	1.3	0.7	1.4	1.8	0.8	0.7
Outsider eq/total FK	1.3	19.4	12.3	29.2	2.9	18.7	3.4	12.6	2.0	8.9
CREDIT CARD DEBT										
Balance of CC debt ($)	807	1,410	1,325	2,328	4,355	3,181	3,762	2,727	2,205	2,685
CC debt/total debt (%)	1.8	2.0	3.0	4.1	12.0	3.8	9.5	3.8	5.2	4.2
CC debt/total FK (%)	1.1	1.1	2.1	2.1	9.3	2.6	7.4	2.8	4.3	3.2

Source: Kauffman Firm Survey Microdata.

[1] Owner financing includes financing by any owner of the firm. Inside financing includes financing from friends, family, and employees of firm. Outsider financing includes financing from formal sources including banks, credit cards, angel investors, venture capitalists, and other firms.

A recent study by Watson, Newby, and Mahuka (2009) argues that, for women entrepreneurs, demand factors actually take precedence over supply factors in their willingness to seek out external sources of debt. In a series of focus groups involving small firm owners in Australia, they found that the issue of control was a major theme for women and affected their inclination to use external funding. In the same study, Watson and colleagues also conducted a survey of small firms, where they found no evidence of a supply gap in bank loans for either women or men, leading them to conclude that there is no evidence of lending discrimination against women in Australia by the banking sector. Rather, their findings revealed that women had less demand for external capital, at least partially due to their desire to avoid risks and maintain control.

Other researchers argue that "supply" factors play a role in the acquisition of capital as well. They assert that women face either overt or covert forms of discrimination in their attempts to secure external sources of capital (Marlow and Patton, 2005; Sabarwal and Terrell, 2008). Further, they contend that women face structural barriers in the form of networks and key contacts that deny them access to important sources of capital (Becker-Blease and Sohl, 2007; Brush et al., 2001a; Brush et al., 2004; Harrison and Mason, 2007).

The authors' interviews with women entrepreneurs suggest that both supply and demand factors are at work in their search for and uses of various types of capital. Depending on the type of firm, the industry, the entrepreneur's personal preferences, and the type of capital sought (debt versus equity), supply factors may dominate in some instances, whereas demand factors dominate in others. Although a number of recent studies, including Watson and colleagues (2009), have found that women's access to external debt in the form of bank loans is now comparable to that of men, other studies suggest that the same cannot necessarily be said for external equity (Brush et al., 2001a).

Earlier we noted that women raised smaller amounts of capital than men. This is true for both sources of debt and sources of equity. In addition to distinguishing between debt and equity, we also distinguish capital according to its source. Capital can be acquired from owners, insiders, or outsiders. The KFS is careful to distinguish owner equity from cash that a business owner obtained through, say, a home equity line of credit, which in our classification scheme would be a source of outside debt, since it was provided through a formal contract with a lending institution. Insider or informal financing channels include debt or equity from family members and personal affiliates of the firm, while outsider or formal financing channels include debt accessed through formal credit markets (banks, credit cards, lines of credit) as well as venture capital and angel financing.

In our classification of sources of debt, we followed the scheme that Alicia Robb and David Robinson (2010) used. Specifically we grouped together business bank loans and personal debt on the business owner's household balance sheet and placed them under the "outside debt" category. We did this for several reasons. First, if the business is structured as a sole proprietorship, there is no legal difference between the assets of the firm and those of the owner. Thus, for approximately 40 percent of our sample, the distinction between personal debt and business debt is meaningless. Further, research has shown that personal guarantees and personal collateral are often required to secure financing for start-ups (Avery et al., 1998; Mann, 1998; Moon, 2009). In effect, this practice circumvents the limited liability protection offered by incorporation for the remaining 60 percent of our firms. In light of this, our primary distinction in the classification of sources of debt is not whether the debt represents a claim on the business owner's household assets or her business assets but rather whether an institution or friends and family issued this debt.

Let's go back to Table 2.1 and consider the sources of financing for entrepreneurs in the KFS database. In 2004 women raised about $36,000 in external debt and about $9,000 in internal debt (owner plus insider debt). This finding suggests that, even in the start-up year, women entrepreneurs had access to substantial amounts of external debt in the form of loans and credit cards. Nevertheless, men raised more: over $56,000 in external debt and over $13,000 in internal debt. Thus, while women raised a total of $45,000 in debt during their first year of operation (internal plus external debt), men raised nearly $70,000, a difference of more than 50 percent.

Table 2.1 also reveals that while women raised relatively modest amounts of external equity in the start-up year (less than $1,000), men raised substantially more (more than $25,000). In other words, men raised 27 times more equity from outsiders during the first year of operation! Clearly these comparisons indicate that women and men entrepreneurs have different patterns of financing.

We can draw additional conclusions by examining the ways women and men use debt and equity as a percentage of total capital raised. Table 2.1 reveals that although women-owned firms used smaller amounts of external debt than men in their start-up year, they actually used a higher level of debt as a percentage of total financing (50 versus 42 percent). This would suggest that, at least in relative terms, women are as willing and as able to use external debt as a source of financing for their firms as men. This observation argues against the theories that women are more risk averse than men. To reinforce this point, the financial leverage ratios provided in Table 2.1 (debt/equity and debt/total financial capital) reveal that women-owned firms were more heavily leveraged than firms owned by men in the start-up year and in each subsequent year.

Table 2.1 also shows that women relied more heavily on credit card debt than men as an ongoing source of financing. Although the ratios of credit card to total debt were similar for women and men in 2004 and 2005, by 2006 women started to use a substantially higher percentage of credit card debt, and that pattern persisted. These findings confirm the results of an earlier study that also found that women were more heavily reliant on credit card debt than men (Robb and Wolken, 2002). From the standpoint of a borrower, credit cards are an attractive source of debt because they are readily available, easy to obtain, and help with record keeping. Nevertheless, credit cards carry a high interest rate, as well as fees and penalties, and higher levels of credit card debt can reduce the firm's chances of survival (Scott, 2009).

Although prior research confirms that women are as likely as men to secure loans (Coleman, 2002a; Fabowale et al., 1995; Haynes and Haynes, 1999; Orser et al., 2006), some researchers have found that women borrowers experience less favorable treatment in terms of loan size, interest rates, and collateral requirements (Alesina et al., 2008; Coleman, 2000; Riding and Swift, 1990; Treichel and Scott, 2006). Several studies have also found that women express dissatisfaction with their lending relationships (Constantinidis et al., 2006; Fabowale et al., 1995). Thus, although the Kauffman Firm data reveal that women are actually more reliant on debt financing than men, they may not necessarily be entirely satisfied with either the terms or conditions for borrowing.

Because a picture is worth a thousand words (or numbers), Figure 2.2 illustrates the relative use of debt and equity by women- and men-owned firms in their start-up year. These charts clearly illustrate that women entrepreneurs used a larger percentage of outside debt during their start-up year. As Table 2.1 reveals, a similar pattern of debt and equity usage continues in years 2005 through 2008. For each year, women raised more debt as a percentage of total capital than men. This pattern suggests that women entrepreneurs are not, in fact, more risk averse than men in terms of their selection of sources of capital. Since women consistently raised smaller amounts of external debt than men, however, there may still be issues of demand in the form of smaller loans requested and supply in the form of smaller loans granted.

When we look at the percentages for external equity in Figure 2.1, we see a very different pattern. Women not only used higher percentages of owner and insider equity than men, but they also used a dramatically lower percentage of external equity in the start-up year (1.3 versus 19.4 percent) and in each subsequent year. Figure 2.2 confirms this gender gap in the use of outside equity for the start-up year. This finding gives credence to the theories that women are more reluctant to share control with outsiders, that the types of businesses they start are unattractive to equity investors, or that they face structural barriers that prevent them from accessing external sources of equity. Thus, in the case of external equity, issues of both demand and supply may play a role in determining the financing strategies of women entrepreneurs.

If women do not seek external equity, their lack of demand may be consistent with the goals they have for the firm: smaller in size and scale, easier to control, and less complex. A recent study of angel investor groups found that women were much less likely to seek angel investor financing than men were (Becker-Blease and Sohl, 2007). Nevertheless, those women who did seek funding had an equal probability of receiving it. This study also found that women were more likely to seek and to receive funding from women angel investors, suggesting that women entrepreneurs may anticipate a greater

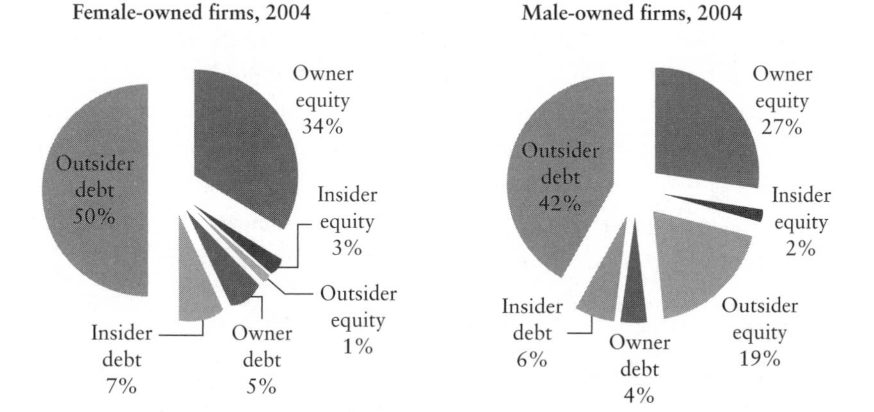

FIGURE 2.2 Debt and equity start-up capital

willingness on the part of other women to at least consider funding their firms. These findings argue for the need to increase the number of women who can serve as angel investors. Further, it is important that such women investors not be "tokens" in angel investor or venture capital firms. Research has shown that when women represent a very small percentage of investors in an angel investor group, they are actually less likely to invest than in firms that have a larger percentage of women investors, possibly due to a lack of confidence and a desire to not make mistakes in an environment dominated by men (Becker-Blease and Sohl, 2010).

Alternatively, if women seek external equity but are unable to secure it, this suggests supply side issues. As an example, the authors of the Diana Project (Brush et al., 2004) have found that the venture capital industry is a close-knit and male-dominated network. Few women venture capitalists hold key decision-making roles, and women entrepreneurs receive only a small percentage (5 percent) of venture capital funding. It stands to reason that women who are not a part of angel investor and venture capital networks will have a more difficult time penetrating those networks to secure financing. The good news, as Brush and her colleagues point out, is that a growing number of women are aspiring to and succeeding as growth-oriented entrepreneurs! This trend will help to create a cohort of women who have the education, experience, and wealth to become equity investors in future businesses, thereby increasing the number of women angel and venture capital investors.

Our results show that, overall, women entrepreneurs were more reliant on internal than external sources of financing to start their firms. If the percentages of owner and insider debt and equity for both women and men are totaled, the results are 48 percent for women and 39 percent for men in 2004. Thus, women raised approximately half of their initial funding from outside sources, while men raised roughly 60 percent. This gap lessens, but it persists into the fifth year of operation. In 2008 women relied on internal sources for 30 percent of new financing, compared with 27 percent for men. This pattern reveals that both at start-up and in subsequent years, men were willing and/or able to raise larger amounts and higher percentages of external capital.

- **SCORing for Equity**

SCOR is the acronym for Small Corporate Offering Registration, which provides smaller firms with a method for raising up to $1 million in external equity financing within a 12-month period. These offerings are also referred to as "self-underwritten" offerings or "direct public offerings." The intent of SCOR is to provide small firms with a more affordable means for going public and using their regular accountants and attorneys to do so as opposed to hiring an investment bank, which can entail higher costs. A study of SCOR offerings conducted in Washington State found that 73 percent of the firms saved on underwriting fees (Brau and Osteryoung, 2001).

A second major advantage of a SCOR offering is that it requires significantly less reporting to the Securities and Exchange Commission (SEC), the government entity that regulates publicly held firms in the United States. Further, a SCOR offering allows firms to offer their securities directly to the public through public meetings, advertisements, or the Internet. Any type of investor may purchase the shares. SCOR forms are reviewed by both the SEC and the state in which the shares will be sold. For further information on SCOR offerings, see the website for the North American Securities Administrators Association (www.nasaa.org). You should also contact the securities regulator in your state to review applicable standards. A good place to start would be the Office of the Secretary of State. He or she can direct you to the appropriate office or individual. To date, SCOR offerings have not been widely used, but they do represent one more alternative for firms desiring to raise external equity in amounts of $1 million or less.

Principles in Action: Brown & Meyers

Kate Meyers is a bundle of energy. When you sit with her, you can almost hear her brain going "snap, crackle, pop" as she thinks of new ways to improve and grow her firm, Brown & Meyers (www.brownmeyers.com), which provides web-based legal and medical transcription services. Kate worked as an executive secretary for a series of Fortune 500 companies prior to acquiring the firm in 1994.

I did not have a college education at the time, and I realized that I was never going to advance beyond a certain level in that kind of environment. When they started asking me to make coffee, that did it for me.*

* Kate Myers completed her college degree in the spring of 2010, yet another accomplishment for this "can-do" entrepreneur!

Armed with a will to achieve and advance, Kate put herself through court reporting school and joined a firm specializing in that field. Six months later, when the owner of the firm (Mr. Brown) decided to retire and offered Kate a chance to buy the company, she jumped at the opportunity. She financed the purchase with a $15,000 loan from her mother-in-law, which she subsequently repaid. She felt that she was not bankable at that point because she was new to the business and no one knew her. Following the purchase, Kate made aggressive use of bootstrapping techniques to finance the early days of her firm, which she called Brown & Meyers. She worked out of a "tiny" office (her description) and reinvested all of her earnings into the firm.

In 1997 another opportunity emerged, this time to purchase a medical transcription franchise. In light of the dramatic changes in the health care industry, Kate felt, rightly so, that this could be a significant area of growth for her firm. She financed the purchase with a $50,000 bank loan from a local bank using her home as collateral. She recognized the risk, but at that point she had enough confidence in herself and in the firm to move forward. Over time, Kate has continued to develop her relationship with that bank, and today she has both a line of credit and a commercial mortgage on her office building. Nevertheless, Kate describes herself as being "very lean on debt," and earnings from the firm are sufficient to cover operating expenses. She is not averse to using debt in the future, however, to develop new business opportunities to make strategic acquisitions. She has recently developed a new line of business to help companies learn to become more "green" by using technology and reducing their need for paper documents and files. She is also exploring the possibility of yet another line of business that would provide long-term storage for paper files while gradually converting them to electronic records over time.

The legal and medical transcription business has changed dramatically since Kate got her start, and Brown & Meyers has evolved to keep pace with changing market conditions and technologies. Today, Kate uses a web-based applications service provider (ASP). Attorneys or doctors call a designated number and then dictate their notes over the phone. This creates a voice file that is stored on the ASP. A transcriber logs on to the ASP, downloads the voice file, transcribes it into Word, and uploads the Word file onto the ASP, where it can be accessed by the client. The web-based nature of the business has allowed Kate to grow her firm and serve clients nationwide. Client files can be dictated from any location, and, in turn, they can be downloaded and transcribed from any location.

Today, Brown & Meyers employs eight people full-time at the firm's headquarters in Portland, Maine. Kate also uses a pool of 75 part-time transcribers who work from their homes. Providing employment opportunities to others as well as a family-friendly environment is an important motivation for Kate. She notes that most of her employees and many of her transcribers have young children. Full-time employees work four days, ten hours per day each week, to allow them more time with family on weekends. Transcribers work flexible schedules from their homes, which allows them to combine work with child care and family responsibilities.

In discussing the factors contributing to her firm's success, Kate stresses the importance of relationships and networks. She started one network for women business owners in Portland, and she has participated in several others. These experiences have provided not only business-specific knowledge and skills but also emotional support and a sense of community. Kate is enthusiastic in describing the benefits of owning her own firm:

I like the flexibility provided by owning my own business. I'm also the kind of person who likes to call the shots. I can see a lot of opportunity, and I know I can take this firm wherever I want.

• Bank Loans

Bank loans are one of the most frequently used sources of debt capital. From the perspective of an entrepreneur, one of the major advantages of a bank loan is that it does not necessitate giving up ownership or control of the company. Thus, entrepreneurs like Kate Meyers who are concerned with maintaining a certain culture and environment for their firm can do so. Another advantage of bank loans is that they come in a variety of shapes and sizes. Bank loans can be large or small, and they can be unsecured or secured by specific assets such as inventory or equipment. Bank loans can also be made directly to the business, or if the business is too new or not yet profitable, they can be made to the entrepreneur. Such personal loans are often secured by personal assets; a common strategy is for entrepreneurs to put up their home as collateral.

From the bank's perspective, the lender's objective is to get her money back, on time, with a reasonable return, typically in the form of interest and fees. Bank loans are granted based on the borrower's ability to satisfy the "5 Cs":

Capacity: Do you have the capacity to repay the loan? In other words, will the financial health and cash flows of your business be sufficient to guarantee repayment? This is probably the most important consideration from the lender's perspective.

Capital: Has the entrepreneur made a personal investment in the firm? Lenders want to see that you are willing to risk your own money as well as theirs. An entrepreneur who has made a personal financial commitment is more likely to be committed to the success of the firm.

Collateral: What additional guarantees can you provide to the lender? Collateral is something that the lender can take away from you if you do not repay the loan. Your willingness and ability to provide collateral reduces the risk to the lender and may increase her willingness to lend. Typical forms of collateral include business assets such as buildings, equipment, inventory, or receivables and personal assets such as your house.

Conditions: Why are you borrowing money? If you are borrowing money to finance additional inventories or to buy a building, this could be a sign of financial health and growth in sales. Alternatively, if you are borrowing money to fund operating deficits, this is a sign of financial weakness. Lenders also take the general conditions of the economy and the industry into consideration.

Character: What is your track record for being trustworthy and reliable? Lenders will look at your history of debt repayment, as well as your qualifications in the form of education and experience. This is one of the reasons it is important for you to develop a good credit history by taking out loans and repaying them on schedule. Examples of loans that will help you to build a good credit history include auto loans and mortgage loans on a house or condo. The importance of a good credit history cannot be overstated. A good history will not only increase your access to loans, but it will also make you eligible for a lower interest rate.

In spite of their many advantages, bank loans do carry some risks. Unlike equity, debt has to be repaid to the lender, and it has to be repaid on schedule. In this sense, debt repayment in the form of principle and interest increases the fixed costs of the firm. If you go through a rough patch caused by a recession or industry downturn, it may be difficult for you to make these payments. Because of this characteristic, debt increases the riskiness of the firm and increases the risk of bankruptcy, particularly if your firm carries high levels of debt. You will recall that our entrepreneur, Kate Meyers, chose to keep her firm "lean on debt" to minimize risks and have additional borrowing capacity if opportunities emerged for additional acquisitions or the creation of new profit centers.

Another risk of debt is that you can lose your collateral if you do not repay the loan on schedule. If you put up your home as collateral, as many entrepreneurs do, this can be extremely rough on both the business and your family. Nevertheless, this is a risk that many entrepreneurs are willing to take in order to secure necessary financing for their firms.

Tips on Bank Borrowing

1. You must give the bank business and possibly personal financial statements. If you do not have them, work with an accountant to prepare them before you apply for a loan.
2. Be prepared to put up collateral, either business or personal. Common forms of collateral include buildings, equipment, accounts receivable, inventory, or your personal residence.
3. Your credit history matters. If you have a track record showing missed or late payments or business or personal bankruptcy, you may be denied a loan or charged a higher interest rate.
4. Shop around! Banks vary widely in terms of rates, fees, and collateral requirements. Look for a bank that will work with you and is interested in doing business with you and your firm.

What should you look for in a lender? Several of the women entrepreneurs we interviewed for this book stressed the importance of banking relationships. You want to work with a banker over time so she will get to know you and your business. Prior research indicates that this strategy increases access to credit for smaller firms (Berger and Udell, 1995; Coleman, 2000; Peterson and Rajan, 1994). Obviously you will also want to consider factors such as the bank's location, interest rates, additional fees, and collateral requirements. These can vary widely from one lender to another. You may also wish to seek out a bank that markets to particular segments of the population, such as small business owners, firms in a particular industry, or women-owned firms. If you and your firm fit the bank's desired customer profile, you have a better chance of securing a loan.

The Elephant in the Room: The Financial Crash of 2007–2008 and the "Great Recession" of 2008–2009

This book is not about the recent financial crash and ensuing "Great Recession." It is not even about financial strategies for surviving our recent turbulent times. Rather, it is about tried-and-true financial strategies that women entrepreneurs across a broad range of firms and industries have employed successfully during good and bad economic times. With that said, however, we would be remiss if we did not at least discuss some of the effects of the recent financial crisis on financial markets and women-owned firms.

The financial crisis actually had its roots in an earlier financial crisis—specifically the recession of 2000–2001 that followed the collapse of the dot-coms and, with them, the stock market. During that time, the Federal Reserve employed the tools of monetary policy to lower interest rates and stimulate a recovery. All went as planned. Some contend, however, that the Fed kept rates low for too long, thereby stimulating a housing bubble. This paved the way for the next financial crisis. As housing values soared, individuals began to use equity in their home as a source of cash. In doing so, they increased their levels of indebtedness, which was not a problem as long as housing values continued to rise. Simultaneously, banks and other financial institutions granted mortgages to increasingly risky (subprime) borrowers who put down little or nothing in the way of a down payment. These loans were packaged into mortgage-backed securities that were sold, primarily to other financial institutions, all over the world.

In 2005 housing values peaked in the United States and began a period of decline. As borrowers with little or no equity in their homes began to default, mortgage-backed securities suffered huge losses. A series of runs on financial institutions began in 2007 and lasted into 2008. One of the more significant of these runs occurred at Bear Stearns, a U.S. investment bank, in March of 2008. This was a turning point for the financial crisis in the United States (Reinhart, 2011).

The Federal Reserve intervened to help arrange the purchase of Bear Stearns by JPMorgan Chase. As a part of that deal, the Fed actually assumed $30 billion of Bear Stearns's bad assets, thereby signaling that it would intervene to prevent the failure of large and systemically important financial institutions. In September 2008, however, when another large investment bank,

Lehman Brothers, experienced similar difficulties in the market for subprime securities, the Fed did not intervene, and Lehman filed for bankruptcy. This inconsistency and uncertainty about the Fed's willingness to rescue troubled firms led to a wave of distressed sales of mortgage-backed securities, a collapse in asset prices, and a dramatic decline in liquidity in the financial markets (Bordo and James, 2010; Mishkin, 2011).

What did all this mean for small and entrepreneurial firms? First, bank lending contracted dramatically. Since small firms are generally viewed as being more risky, they suffered the effects of this lending drought more deeply than larger, more established firms. Second, housing values declined by about 30 percent nationally and even more severely in some parts of the country. This basically eliminated the ability of business owners to use their home equity as a source of financing or their homes as collateral. Third, the stock market dropped by 50 percent, reaching its lowest point in March 2009. Angel investors who might have invested in small or new firms no longer had the capital to do so, and the volume of venture capital investing declined dramatically, with many VC firms going out of business. Last, but certainly not least, a severe recession lasting 16 months followed the financial crash. The national unemployment rate exceeded 9 percent, and almost 17 million people were either unemployed or underemployed. Both businesses and households stopped spending, and business and personal bankruptcies soared.

Figure 2.3 chronicles the decline in both number and dollar volume of bank loans in the United States from December 2007 through March 2010. Further, although the recession "officially" ended in June 2009, neither the number nor the volume of loans had regained its prerecession peak as of March 2010.

On the equity side, Figure 2.4 illustrates the virtual collapse of the venture capital industry in the United States during the Great Recession in terms of both the number of deals and dollar volume. Although venture capital firms fund a relatively tiny percentage of firms, these companies are typically growth-oriented firms with the potential to employ large numbers of individuals. Thus, a dramatic decline in venture capital funding has an impact not only on the ability of entrepreneurial firms to develop new products and services but on their ability to fund their growth and hire employees as well.

The Federal Reserve and the U.S. government responded to the financial crash and Great Recession with a number of policy measures. The Fed lowered interest rates to zero percent and resumed its intervention to prevent the

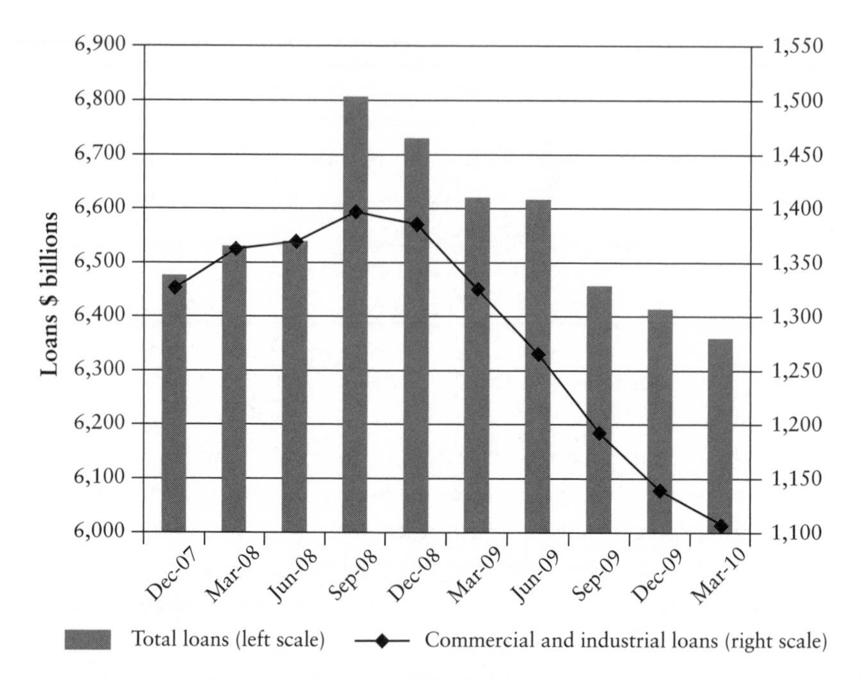

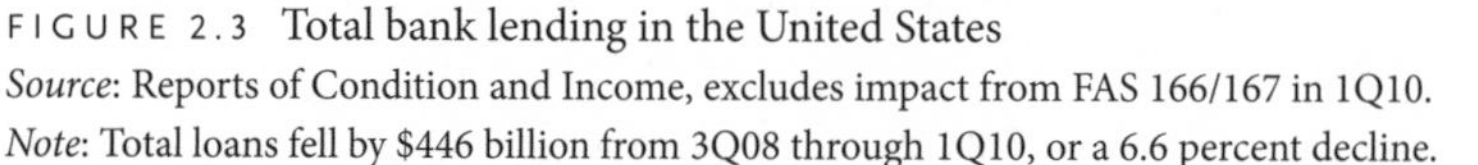

FIGURE 2.3 Total bank lending in the United States
Source: Reports of Condition and Income, excludes impact from FAS 166/167 in 1Q10.
Note: Total loans fell by $446 billion from 3Q08 through 1Q10, or a 6.6 percent decline.

failure of large financial institutions such as AIG. It also embarked on a course of "quantitative easing," which included loans to banks and other financial institutions and the purchase of large volumes of securities, including U.S. Treasury bonds and mortgage-backed securities, to restore liquidity to the financial system (Mishkin, 2011).

In 2009 the U.S. Treasury announced a series of "stress tests" for the nation's largest banks. The results of these tests provided further information to the financial markets and made it possible for these large banks to raise the additional capital required to strengthen their balance sheets. Congress, with some difficulty and delays, passed the Troubled Asset Relief Program (TARP), which authorized the expenditure of $700 billion to purchase subprime mortgage assets from troubled financial institutions. In the first few weeks of the Obama administration, Congress also passed the American Recovery and Reinvestment Act of 2009, which included a combination of tax cuts and government spending designed to stimulate the economy.

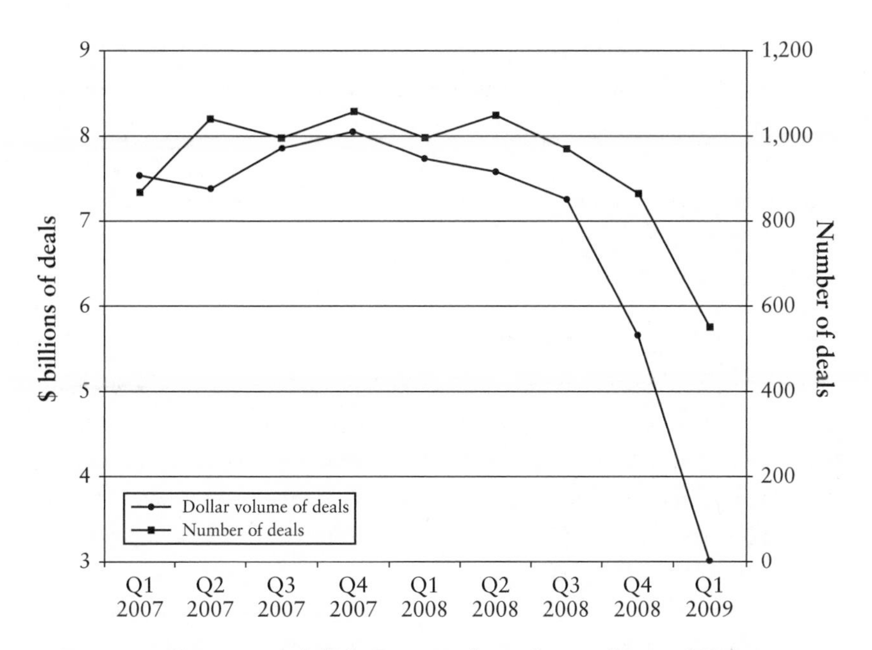

FIGURE 2.4 Venture capital deals, PricewaterhouseCoopers/National Venture Capital Association MoneyTree Report

As of the writing of this book in 2011, the U.S. economy has begun a slow process of recovery, but it is still fragile. The national unemployment rate is still over 8 percent, and millions of individuals have been out of work for months, if not years. The housing market is very weak, with thousands of homes in foreclosure. Simultaneously, however, both individuals and businesses have used the crisis as a time to repair their balance sheets and pay down debt. Corporate profits have been strong, and the stock market has rebounded strongly from its low point. Consumer and business confidence recovered somewhat in 2010 but declined sharply in the second half of 2011. Many anticipate further stimulus from both the Federal Reserve and Congress to help prevent a "double-dip" recession. The fact remains that the ways in which we have dealt with this most recent crisis have changed, perhaps permanently, the lines of demarcation between the public sector in the form of government and the Federal Reserve, and the private sector in the form of banks and other financial institutions. The direct intervention of the first to bail out larger representatives of the second that are deemed "too big to fail" creates an environment of moral hazard that could pave the way for the next crisis.

Most of the women entrepreneurs and firms that we present in this book are survivors of the Financial Crash and Great Recession. Others have launched recently, seeing opportunities in the midst of the chaos. We consider all of them pioneers—explorers in a new economic and financial galaxy that is more competitive, more global, more challenging, and less predictable than what has gone before. These are exciting stories to be told.

Principles in Actions: Equator Coffees and Teas

Helen Russell is one of the cofounders of Equator Coffees and Teas (www.equatorcoffees.com), based in Marin County, California. Equator's mission is "to be a growing, customer-centric company, dedicated to quality, environmental sustainability, and social responsibility. Our commitment is to procure distinctive coffees from growers who practice responsible land stewardship and bio-friendly farming techniques."

Helen and Brooke McDonnell cofounded the company in 1995, initially capitalizing Equator with $125,000 in cash. These start-up funds came from their personal accounts, friends, family, and credit cards. One of them sold her mother's diamond ring as a down payment on their first roaster! A good friend loaned them $35,000, which they paid back in five years at a 6 percent interest rate. Years later, that same friend gave them a second loan of $25,000.

Currently, Equator has 20 employees (in addition to the founders) and generates more than $5 million in annual sales. Nevertheless, a track record of 16 years and a good relationship with their bank did not insulate Equator from the effects of the financial crisis in terms of accessing capital. In Helen's words:

Last year, for the first time, we had to produce more documentation and show a use of the line as well as steady action of paying back the line in order for our line to renew in 2010. This will be the case again this year. If we do not pay off the LOC by June 1, 2011, it will convert to a term loan, and the LOC will not be renewed. This is a new procedure for our bank. They are willing, however, to give us a new loan of $250,000 for a retail location, but it involves tons of paperwork, tax returns, interviews, and so on.

In light of Equator's history with its bank, it may seem surprising that the bank would require so much of a long-standing customer, especially one that experienced double-digit growth every year until 2010. Equator's experience illustrates the ways in which the financial crisis has resulted in substantial changes in banks' lending policies.

Equator expects to grow at 5 to 10 percent annually over the next five years by adding more wholesale customers and opening a retail location. When asked how they will finance these expansions, Helen explained:

We just pulled $250,000 out of our house in preparation to open a new retail location. We are also actively looking to bring on a strategic financial partner as we look to grow the retail side of our business. In addition, we have lined up a seven-year term loan with our bank for $250,000.

Helen's story drives home the fact that the tradeoff between risk and reward remains up close and personal for many entrepreneurs. As this mini–case study on Equator shows, even successful and well-established entrepreneurs have to be willing to tap into their personal resources to finance the continued growth and development of their firms in these still challenging economic times.

What Have We Learned?

In this chapter, we saw that despite their progress in education, experience, and entrepreneurship, many women still have a "fear of finance" and report difficulties in dealing with financial service providers. We also discovered that women tend to finance their firms with smaller amounts of capital, on average, than men. We saw that women entrepreneurs are more reliant on internal than external sources of capital. This is particularly true for external sources of equity. Prior research suggests that the discrepancies in financing patterns between women and men may be a function of both demand and supply. A lack of demand implies that women are reluctant to seek sources of financing, or, alternatively, they believe they do not need them, possibly because of the types of firms they start. A lack of supply occurs if women encounter discrimination in the financial markets or structural barriers that reduce their access to debt or equity. Finally, we examined the importance of networks that include key advisors and contacts who can provide an entry into various sources of financing.

What Does All This Mean for Me?

As a woman entrepreneur—or perhaps as an aspiring woman entrepreneur—you have several takeaways from this chapter:

1. Recognize that the type of firm you start will largely determine the amounts and sources of financing that are appropriate for you. For example, if you start a wedding planning business that you will operate out of your home, you will probably rely heavily on your own savings, investments from family and friends, earnings from the business, bank loans, and credit cards. Alternatively, if you start a biotech firm based upon a new drug that has found a way to treat Alzheimer's, you will no doubt seek out substantial amounts of external financing in the form of angel and venture capital. Different strokes for different folks!
2. Find a way to become comfortable with finance, because if you are an entrepreneur, you will be living with it for a long time. Take a course, find a mentor, motivate yourself to learn it—whatever it takes! Although you may have trusted financial advisors and employees who handle the firm's finances, ultimately the buck stops with you. Thus, you need to understand finance well enough to ensure that your best interests are being served. Start with the basics, practice your skills, and learn as you go along. In fact, a mastery of the basics will take you a long way.
3. Typically, entrepreneurs get started by relying on their own sources of financing, as well as financing from family and friends. Take an inventory of your personal financial resources. What sources of capital do you already have that could help to finance your firm? Do you have personal savings, an inheritance, or a severance package from a former job? Do you have a home that could be used for collateral on a loan? Do you have family and friends who would be willing to lend you money or become equity investors? The more money you can raise internally, the less you have to raise externally. This can be particularly important in the firm's earliest days before it has developed a track record of profitability.
4. Debt or borrowed money is also an important source of financing for women-owned firms. You should attempt to satisfy the "5 Cs" of borrowing: capacity, capital, collateral, conditions, and character. If you needed a bank loan for your firm, would you be able to secure one? If not, evaluate where your weaknesses are, and take steps to address them. Also, remember that as borrowed money, loans have to be repaid. In this sense, debt increases the riskiness of the firm. When applying for a loan, make sure that the cash flows from your business will be sufficient to allow repayment.

5. Networks of advisors and key contacts can be instrumental in providing access to sources of both debt and equity. Take the time to develop and sustain your networks. Women are often so concerned with running their businesses that they neglect this side of the equation. Make time to attend business networking events, join a business organization, and find ways to meet individuals that you think might be helpful to your firm now or at some point in the future. Don't make excuses (we have heard all of them!), and, above all, don't isolate yourself.

Public Policy Implications

The issues raised in this chapter pave the way for at least two major types of public policy recommendations. The first pertains to women's "fear of finance," and the second pertains to women's access to key networks, particularly those involving the providers of external equity. In the case of women's "fear of finance," we need to ensure that girls and young women are not socialized to avoid or dislike math and other quantitative subjects that can be a gateway to many attractive careers, including entrepreneurial ones. Further, we need to ensure that math is taught in a gender-neutral fashion. Teaching materials and activities should highlight girls and women as often as they do boys and men. We should encourage girls and young women to pursue and excel in math and quantitative subjects, and we should recognize and reward them for doing so. These women can then serve as teachers, mentors, and role models for girls and young women who follow.

Second, prior research has clearly demonstrated that women are underrepresented in networks that provide external equity financing both as investors and as the recipients of investments. As an increasing number of women are launching technology-based and growth-oriented types of firms, we need to open up these networks in order to recognize and promote women-owned firms. Here are some ways to do that:

1. Promote the establishment of angel investor networks or VC firms that actively seek out opportunities to invest in women-owned firms. These could be privately funded, or they could be structured as public/private partnerships.
2. Identify and mobilize successful women entrepreneurs or investors who have the experience, skills, and capital to recognize high-potential firms

launched by women. Prior research suggests that women investors are more open to the possibility of funding women-owned firms, although the viability of the firm remains the deciding factor. If this is the case, identifying more women who can serve as equity investors, helping them to organize, or adding them to the ranks of existing VC firms would increase opportunities for funding women-owned ventures.

3. Highlight the growing number of women starting rapid growth firms and their success stories. This may serve to dispel the "myth" that women are only interested in starting smaller firms.

ONE SIZE DOES NOT FIT ALL

Many research articles and books on women's entrepreneurship seem to be based on the assumption that women-owned firms are homogeneous. In fact, there is a tremendous amount of diversity in the types of businesses women start and operate. Often this diversity is driven by the resources that women entrepreneurs have access to in the form of human, social, and financial capital and by their selection of industry. For example, Figure 3.1 shows that women-owned firms are heavily represented in the service, health care, and professional fields. These industries tend to be knowledge intensive rather than capital intensive. Alternatively, women are considerably less well represented in the fields of construction, transportation, and manufacturing—all industries that are highly capital intensive. As we will see, these industry concentrations have implications for the types of financing available to women entrepreneurs, as well as for the financial strategies they employ.

In other instances, diversity may be a function of different priorities and motivations. Women who launch smaller, lifestyle businesses use different financial sources and strategies than women who launch growth-oriented firms. U.S. Census data from 2007 (Figure 3.2) reveal that 41 percent of women-owned firms were indeed very small, with annual revenues of less than $25,000. In all likelihood the majority of these firms are home-based with minimal requirements for capital. Conversely, 4 percent of women-owned firms had revenues of $500,000 or more. Revenues of this magnitude suggest business owners who place greater emphasis on size and growth.

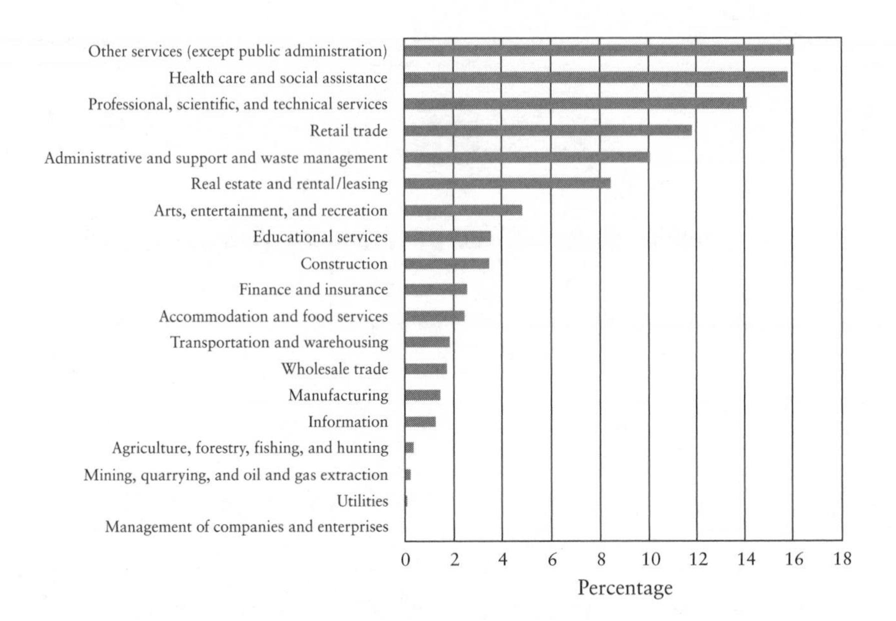

FIGURE 3.1 Distribution of women-owned firms by industry in 2007
Source: U.S. Census Bureau, 2007. *Survey of Business Owners.*

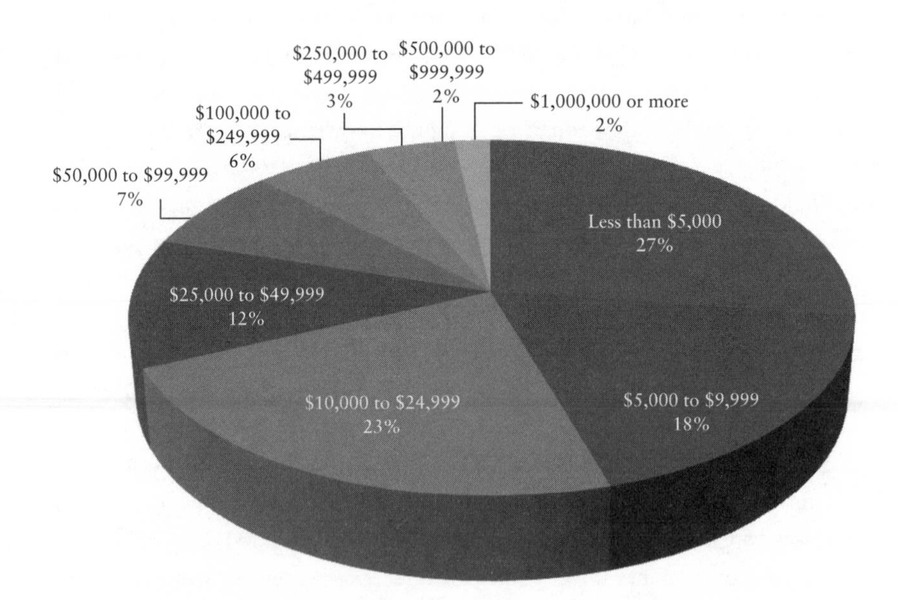

FIGURE 3.2 Distribution of women-owned firms by revenues in 2007
Source: U.S. Census Bureau, 2007. *Survey of Business Owners.*

Finally, diversity may be determined by different stages of the life cycle. Nascent (new) firms face different types of financial challenges than established firms. They are heavily dependent on the personal financial resources of the entrepreneur, whereas established firms typically have access to a much broader array of financing sources. This chapter explores some of these various sources of diversity and the links among firm type or stage, financing sources, and financing strategies. In this chapter we also briefly introduce the various firm types that are the focal point of chapters to follow. These include nascent firms, home-based firms, family-owned firms, growth-oriented firms, technology-based firms, minority-owned firms, and global firms. Each of these firm types brings with it a unique set of challenges and opportunities in terms of financing. We will touch upon these challenges here and develop them more fully in the chapters to come.

Motivation as a Driving Force

In Chapter 1 we introduced both Resource-Based Theory and Motivational Theory. Together with Life Cycle Theory, these three theories provide the theoretical foundations for this book. Resource-Based Theory states that the entrepreneur must assemble, develop, and transform needed resources in the form of financial, human, and social capital to generate unique capabilities if she is to generate a competitive advantage. Motivational Theory, however, often drives the types of businesses that individuals start, as well as their goals and aspirations for those firms. We titled this chapter "One Size Does Not Fit All" because the motivations of women entrepreneurs are as diverse as the types of firms they start. Prior research suggests that many women entrepreneurs are motivated by lifestyle factors such as personal fulfillment, flexibility in scheduling, and the ability to balance work and family (Boden, 1999; Buttner and Moore, 1997; Morris et al., 2006). Conversely, women may give less emphasis to traditional economic performance measures such as firm size, growth, and earnings (Anna et al., 1999; Cliff, 1998; Kepler and Shane, 2007; Orser and Hogarth-Scott, 2002). Nevertheless, these research findings do not negate the role and importance of the increasing number of women entrepreneurs who are launching growth-oriented and technology-based firms (Brush et al., 2001a; Gundry and Welsch, 2001). They merely illustrate that, for women entrepreneurs, "one size does not fit all."

As an example, one of our women entrepreneurs—we'll call her Sandy—started her graphic design and marketing firm after her children were born.

Her primary motivations were to have "freedom" in choosing her own clients and to have scheduling flexibility to accommodate the needs of her family. She established the firm with $8,000 in savings and has subsequently financed it with earnings from the business. Sandy explains:

Money was not my primary motivation. It was nice to have it, but my priorities were to do work I loved and take care of my family. I could have grown the business more rapidly but chose not to. In fact, recently I downsized because there was too much pressure, and I needed to spend more time with my children at this point in their life. When I started the firm, I also chose clients who were "family-friendly" because when my daughter was young, I often took her to work with me. I have also tried to have good benefits and family-friendly policies for my own employees.

In this book we take Motivational Theory a step further by asserting that motivations, in addition to determining the types of firms that women start, also largely determine the sources of financing that are available to and appropriate for women. The notion is that smaller and less complex firms like Sandy's will often rely on personal sources of financing to start and then on revenues from the business once it is up and running. Conversely, rapid growth firms in the technology or bioscience arenas will rely heavily on external sources of capital in order to finance research and development (R&D) and growth. Is this what *really* happens? Let's take a look!

Principles in Action: Nancy Ann Flowers

Nancy Hansen started her floral shop at the age of 22 because she wanted complete creative and artistic freedom. She had always been passionate about flowers, and she felt there was an unmet need for someone with her creativity and commitment to quality. She founded her firm, Nancy Ann Flowers (www.nancyannflowers.com), in Sausalito, California, with $15,000 she borrowed from her parents.

It would have been very difficult for me to borrow money at that time. I was a 22-year-old kid with no assets. My parents offered, and I was grateful.

Today, 25 years later, Nancy is still in business and has eight employees. She has never sought or needed external financing, and she finances the firm entirely with earnings from the business. She also has a couple of credit cards that she uses for business transactions, but they serve primarily as a convenience rather than as a source of financing. As promised, she paid her parents back within the first five years she was in business.

Initially, Nancy was responsible for all aspects of the business, including financial management, a skill she had to learn. Today, she is able to delegate those tasks to someone else while she concentrates on the creative side of the firm. Nevertheless, she knows the dollars and cents pertaining to her business inside and out.

Since revenues are Nancy's major source of financing today, we asked her what strategies she uses to sustain and maximize revenues.

I really focus on buying good product (flowers) and freshness. I want to make sure that my arrangements last at least five to seven days, and if they don't, I make it right. My business is primarily individual customers, and I rely heavily on repeat business. It is important to me that my customers be satisfied and happy with their orders. I am passionate about flowers and passionate about quality. So many people are in this business just for the money; they don't care about the quality. That's not how I do business. I want my customers to come back, and I want them to tell their friends. That's how I sustain and build my revenues.

Since we find ourselves in the midst of a tough economy, and California is no exception to that trend, we asked Nancy what financial strategies she uses to weather tough economic times.

We have to manage very carefully, because flowers are perishable and many people regard them as a luxury. That's why I do the buying myself: because it is so important. I not only have to ensure product quality, but I have to make sure that our product will go out the door in one to two days. If it doesn't, we eat the cost, so managing our ordering and floral inventory is a key element of success, particularly in an economy like this. There is also an element of cyclicality to my business. Obviously, Christmas, Valentine's Day, and Mother's Day are busy times, but we are usually really slow in July when people are away on vacation. During July I not only manage my inventory very carefully, but I also manage my employees' hours to make sure that our expenses do not exceed our revenues.

We had the good fortune to interview Nancy on a crystal clear, sunny day in July (her slow month). As we sat on the deck together, Nancy was beaming with happiness, pride, and excitement as she talked about her company. We asked her if she felt she had been successful and how she defined "success."

Yes, absolutely! My experience with the business has far exceeded my expectations. I have been able to support myself and contribute financially to my family. I have also been able to stay in business and retain customers through economic ups and downs. I have provided employment to other individuals, and I create products that I am proud of. To me, all of those factors are important measures of success.

Nancy's story illustrates one of our key points in this book: the connections among the entrepreneur's motivations, the type of business she starts, the financing strategies that are appropriate, and how she views success. Nancy established a small retail firm at a time when she was too young to have any personal assets or even much of a credit history. The size and nature of the business and Nancy's desire for creative freedom ruled out external equity investors. Similarly, her lack of assets and credit history would have made it difficult for her to secure a loan. She was too young to even have much in the way of personal savings. Fortunately, her parents were willing to put up financing to help Nancy get started, and she was off and running!

Once the firm was established, Nancy's primary motivation continued to be creativity and control rather than growth. Although her revenues increased and she was able to hire employees, she chose to keep the firm at a manageable size. She maximized revenues by focusing on product quality and managed the expense side of her business carefully. This combination of strategies eliminated any need for her to raise either external debt or equity. To summarize, her motivations and goals matched her financing strategies.

Nancy's story illustrates an important point. For many women entrepreneurs, although financial success is important, it is typically not the only motivation or goal, or even the most important one. Nonfinancial factors such as creativity, product quality, and good relationships with customers and employees are often equally important from the entrepreneur's perspective. We will encounter this theme repeatedly in our interviews with women entrepreneurs throughout this book.

What's in Store?

The many different types of businesses that women entrepreneurs have started are a reflection of the motivations and goals of their founders, and they have allowed women to experience fulfillment and success as they define it. In addition to data-driven findings, we are fortunate to be able to share more stories like Nancy's with you in the chapters that follow.

The entrepreneurs we will see throughout these pages of this book are thoughtful and deliberate. Most have thought about their personal motivations and goals for the firm. They have also been astute in matching their financing strategies to those motivations and goals. They are not "accidental entrepreneurs," and the fact that so many of them have survived and prospered through economic ups and downs is a testament to their dedication.

The chapters that follow weave a tapestry that tells the story of women's entrepreneurship. They come in different sizes, colors, and shapes, but it all comes together to make a picture that has meaning for today's women entrepreneurs and for those yet to come. For so many of our women entrepreneurs, entrepreneurship and the financial strategies that help them launch and sustain their ventures represent a path to independence, empowerment, creativity, financial gain, and the opportunity to set the priorities that are important to them. They are all wonderful stories, and we are happy to share them with you.

Each chapter focuses on a particular type of entrepreneurship. We will examine the motivations, the characteristics, and the potential financial strategies of each type of entrepreneurial venture at various stages of development. These will include personal financing and bootstrapping; financing provided by family and friends (F&F); external debt, including bank loans and lines of credit; and external equity in the form of angel or venture capital.

Nascent Firms

Nascent firms are start-up or early-stage firms. These types of firms face special financing challenges because they have no track record of performance or accomplishments. Further, they may be started by inexperienced entrepreneurs who lack skills in the area of financial management as well as a network of financing sources. Start-up firms often make the mistake of not raising enough money to launch the business, resulting in a relatively high failure rate. In Chapter 4 we discuss sources of start-up capital, with particular emphasis on the entrepreneur's personal sources of capital and bootstrapping (minimizing expenses). We also address the important roles of both human capital (education and experience) and social capital (networks and contacts) in securing early-stage financing.

Home-Based Firms

Increasingly, prior research attests to the fact that women entrepreneurs may have different goals from men. In particular, flexibility and the need to balance work and family may be more important than firm size, growth, and profits. This difference leads many women to launch home-based businesses, which allows them to fulfill both economic and personal goals. Chapter 5 discusses some of the benefits of starting a home-based business, including lower capital requirements, flexibility, and the ability to balance work and family. It will also address some of the disadvantages, such as the difficulty of raising external sources of capital, the challenge of maintaining a professional environment, the need to establish boundaries, dealing with professional isolation, and the continued need to resolve child care issues.

Family-Owned Firms

Chapter 6, which deals with family-owned firms, discusses the benefits and challenges of establishing a family business. Many people think of family-owned firms as small, low-growth firms and similar to home-based businesses, but many of the largest firms in this country started out as, and are still, family-owned or family-controlled. Think of Ford Motors, Dupont, and L.L. Bean, to name a few. Family businesses are unique in that they often have different motivations from other types of firms. Specifically, the goals of the firm may include the ability to employ and spend time with family members or a desire to continue a family legacy. In fact, these goals may be just as important as more traditional financial and economic measures of success. The advantages of a family-owned business include the ability to employ family members, greater loyalty, and a shared history. Challenges can include succession planning, the willingness or need to bring in nonfamily talent, and conflicting attitudes toward growth, change, and the necessity of bringing in external sources of capital.

High-Growth Firms

In Chapter 7 we focus on the financial challenges associated with rapid firm growth. Prior research suggests that an increasing number of women entrepreneurs are taking the plunge and starting firms in rapid growth sectors or industries. Typically rapid growth necessitates the use of external sources of both debt and equity. This can entail higher levels of risk, since bank loans are frequently secured by personal assets. The entrepreneur must also be willing to share control with new equity investors such as angel investors or venture capitalists. In Chapter 7 we discuss the importance of social capital in penetrating the "old boys" financing network and accessing external sources of capital.

We also address the topic of negotiating with outsiders to preserve a reasonable share of ownership.

We also examine some of the mistakes that the owners of rapid growth firms make. These include not developing a management team to delegate leadership tasks, not raising enough money, and not having the proper systems and controls in place to manage working capital (cash, receivables, and inventory).

Technology-Based Firms

Chapter 8 addresses the challenges and opportunities of starting a technology-based business. Traditionally firms in this sector have been heavily male-dominated, but as women have accumulated education and experience in these fields, a growing number are starting firms in this sector as well. Typically technology-based firms have long lead times, necessitating multiyear sources of funding. External funding sources may have a difficult time evaluating firms based on new and innovative products, services, or technologies. Many of the funding sources for technology-based firms, such as venture capital and angel investor networks, are male-dominated, which poses special challenges for women entrepreneurs. Nevertheless, these firms and industries offer the promise for substantial growth and profits.

We will examine the extent to which women are currently participating in high-tech entrepreneurship, as well as some of the barriers they face. Technology-based entrepreneurship poses significant demands in the form of human capital. The entrepreneur needs education and training in specialized areas of technology or bioscience, and she will be required to interact and have credibility with scientists and technology types on a regular basis. Aside from these challenges, starting a technology-based firm can have substantial benefits in terms of a more diverse array of potential funding sources. In addition to more traditional sources of debt and equity, funding sources may include grants, government funding, and strategic alliances with larger and wealthier firms seeking to develop or acquire new technologies. Chapter 8 also discusses the importance of intellectual capital in creating a source of competitive advantage, as well as strategies for protecting intellectual capital.

Minority-Owned Firms

Chapter 9 focuses on the growth rates and economic impact of firms owned by minority women, including their impact on urban areas through the provision of needed products and services. Prior research reveals that minority women entrepreneurs are often less dependent on traditional sources of financing and more dependent on informal sources such as personal financing and financing provided by family and friends. Both language and cultural differences may discourage minority entrepreneurs from pursuing more traditional sources. Chapter 9 reviews the sources of financing, both formal and informal, including domestic microfinancing programs, and addresses the role of various networks and agencies in providing training, counseling, and funding for minority-owned firms.

A Global Perspective

Chapter 10 provides a global perspective on financing women-owned firms using data and research from the Global Entrepreneurship Monitor (GEM). It demonstrates that the growth of women's entrepreneurship is a global phenomenon and that women around the world are turning to entrepreneurship as a path to economic and personal empowerment. In Chapter 10, we focus on three different types of "global" entrepreneurs: women business owners in the United States who are involved in exporting, immigrant entrepreneurs who operate firms in the United States, and women entrepreneurs in other countries. We highlight the fact that many of the financial challenges faced by women entrepreneurs in the United States are not unique to our country. Further, we explore some of the creative solutions developed in other countries to address the financing needs of women entrepreneurs.

Principles in Action: Telesis

When Patty Sue Williams established her software testing firm, Telesis (www.telesisllc.com), in 1997, she had 20 years of software testing and development experience in major firms behind her. This experience allowed Patty to develop a new system for software testing that could be applied across all industries. Initially, Patty tried to get one of the major insurance firms that she had worked for to establish a software testing unit. When the insurance companies didn't bite, she decided to establish her own firm to develop the idea. In doing so, one of her motives was to achieve the creative freedom to develop her software products and services as she saw fit in order to take advantage of opportunities in the marketplace. A second was to create an organization that would allow her to protect her intellectual capital and to reap the financial rewards associated with it. Realizing that her firm had the potential to achieve significant growth, and armed with her industry experience and an extensive network of contacts, Patty set about the process of looking for a venture capital firm to provide funding.

That was a rude awakening! I looked for about a year and a half! I did find venture capital firms that were interested in my idea, but they wanted to take a major portion of equity. The best offer I got would have left me with only about 40 percent of the firm.

Like Nancy Hansen, Patty turned to her family as a source of financing. Specifically, her parents offered to lend her $300,000 to launch her firm.

I had the loan structured as a formal agreement, and I put up my house as collateral. I even used an attorney to draw up the agreement. I knew my parents were taking a risk, and I was determined that they were going to get their money back, one way or the other. As it happened, the loan was structured as a three-year loan, and I repaid it in full one day shy of the first year. That loan allowed me to retain the equity in my firm, and it also allowed me to develop the firm in accordance with my goals and vision.

Patty's parents were also her greatest cheerleaders during those stressful early days, continually urging her, "Come on! Come on! You can do it!" Their emotional support and confidence in her was as important as the loan they provided.

Today, Telesis has 38 employees and revenues of $3 million. In 2008, Telesis was ranked fifty-seventh out of the top one hundred computer and electronics companies in *Inc. Magazine*'s "Inc. 5000" ranking of the fastest-growing companies in the United States. The following year it received an Innovation Pipeline Award from the Connecticut Technology Council. Patty's clients include both large and small companies in a broad range of industries. She also counts among her clients the large insurance companies in Hartford, which is where she got her start. Today, funding for Telesis comes from earnings. In addition, Patty secured a line of credit as "insurance."

We had no problem getting our line of credit because we were very profitable and have a good reputation. We don't use it very often, but I thought it would be good to have it should the need arise. Also, I felt that it was important to establish a track record of securing and repaying debt. It's good business practice.

Having her own firm has given Patty the opportunity to develop the products and services she wants to provide to her clients, as well as financial freedom and flexibility in scheduling.

I have been able to do things with my family and for my family that I never dreamed of. It has been the best, and I am very fortunate. Both my daughter and son-in-law have joined the company, and I am able to share the expertise that I have gained over the years with them.

• Funding from Family and Friends

As we have seen in this chapter, financial support provided by family and friends can be an important source of financing for women entrepreneurs, particularly during the early stages of the firm's life cycle when it is not yet "bankable." Family and friends are part of your social capital or key networks and relationships. These are the people who know you best, trust you, and will stick by you through thick and thin. One of the advantages of financing from F&F is its flexibility. Funding can be provided in the form of debt, equity, or an outright gift. It can come in large or small amounts, and it can be short term or long term. Examples of funding from F&F might include the following:

1. A loan to help you start the firm (as in the case of Nancy Ann Flowers and Telesis)
2. An equity investment in return for partial ownership of the firm
3. A financial gift or bequest in the form of an inheritance
4. A significant other or parent who supports you financially while you are getting started
5. "Volunteer" labor or services, such as doing your books, setting up your computer system, helping to staff a retail establishment, making deliveries, and so on

Another advantage of funding from family and friends is that these individuals tend to be "patient" investors. They are typically more interested in helping you succeed than in generating either a quick or large return on their investment. In addition, if your firm goes through a rough patch, they are more likely to work with you by waiting for payment or injecting additional capital.

In spite of these advantages, however, using capital supplied by family and friends has its risks, and stories of families and friendships that have been torn apart by disagreements over money abound. In light of that, make sure your family and friend investors understand the risks and are willing to live with them. Also make sure that communications regarding the terms of the investment are clear and understood by all parties. If the investment comes in the form of a loan, agree on the amount, duration, interest rate, and timing of payments. If the investment involves giving up a percentage of equity or ownership in the firm, specify the percentage of ownership, shares of stock, voting rights, involvement or noninvolvement in day-to-day management, and the like.

Some entrepreneurs, like Patty Sue Williams, find it helpful to document the terms of these family and friend investment agreements by using the services of an attorney or investment banker. Although others may use less formal means, it can still be helpful to have a written agreement at the outset to avoid potentially damaging misunderstandings and miscommunications.

In closing, financial support provided by family and friends can be one of your most important sources of financing. The fact that the money comes from family and friends, however, is not an excuse to dispense with all formalities. Recognize the value of F&F investors and the important role they play in helping you to launch your firm. Correspondingly, treat investments by family and friends with the same sense of responsibility that you would in accepting capital from outside investors. Communicate clearly and consistently, and live up to the terms of your agreement.

Tips on Using Family and Friends as a Source of Financing

1. Clarify expectations up front. Is the investment a loan, an equity investment, or a gift?
2. Put it in writing. Work with an attorney to document the terms of the investment—for example, interest rate, repayment schedule, and collateral for loans or ownership share and voting rights for equity.
3. Treat a family or friend investment with the same respect that you would show for a "formal" investor. Make payments on time for loans, and be prepared to share future cash flows and control with equity investors.
4. Share relevant information, both good and bad, in a timely fashion.
5. Recognize the risks. Both families and friendships can break up over issues involving money.

Organizational Form and Financial Strategy

One of the decisions an entrepreneur must make fairly early in the life of her firm is the decision regarding organizational form. The three major types of organizational form are a sole proprietorship, a partnership, and a corporation, and each has implications for the types and amounts of capital that a firm can raise (Ross et al., 2008). A sole proprietorship is just what it sounds like. Although the firm may have additional employees, the entrepreneur is the sole owner. Typically this organizational form is appropriate for smaller firms that do not aspire to growth. Examples might include small retail or service types of businesses. From the standpoint of financial strategy, an advantage of organizing as a sole proprietorship is that the entrepreneur does not have to do separate tax filings for personal and corporate taxes. She simply combines earnings from the firm with her other sources of personal income on her individual tax form. These earnings are taxed at the individual rather than at the corporate tax rates. In terms of disadvantages, sole proprietorships typically have more limited sources and amounts of capital due to their relatively small size. Major sources of financing include the entrepreneur's personal sources of capital, family and friends, earnings from the firm, and personal rather than business loans. Another potential disadvantage of a sole proprietorship is the problem of unlimited liability. This essentially means that there is no dividing line between the entrepreneur and the firm. Thus, if the firm is sued, the firm owner's personal assets are also at risk. Many entrepreneurs manage this risk by purchasing liability insurance.

The second major organizational form is a partnership. In a partnership, ownership of the firm is shared by two or more individuals. An advantage of a partnership is that financial, human, and social capital can be provided by multiple owners. Simultaneously, however, earnings are shared by multiple owners. As in the case of sole proprietorships, earnings from a partnership are taxed as personal income, and partnerships share the problem of unlimited liability. Although larger partnerships exist—most notably in the legal, accounting, or financial fields—most partnerships are relatively small, with only two or three partners.

The final type of organizational form is a corporation. The corporate form of organization is appropriate for larger and growth-oriented firms. It is more costly and time consuming to establish a corporation, and publicly held corporations have extensive disclosure and reporting requirements.

Corporations also necessitate two different tax filings. Earnings are taxed at the corporate rate on the corporate tax return, while the entrepreneur's salary, dividends, and capital gains are taxed separately on the individual tax return. Thus, the same stream of earnings is taxed twice, once at the corporate level and a second time at the personal level. This is referred to as the problem of "dual taxation."

The corporate form, however, still has distinct advantages in spite of its higher costs. First, corporations provide limited liability protection, which means that the corporation rather than the individuals who work for it can be sued. Some researchers have pointed out, however, that when a firm owner provides personal assets as collateral or personal guarantees on loans, limited liability doesn't actually provide much protection. A second advantage is that corporations typically have a broader array of financing choices. These are often larger firms capable of generating more substantial earnings. In addition to bank loans made to the business rather than to the firm owner, publicly held companies also have the option of issuing stocks and bonds in public debt and equity markets.

In addition to the three major types of organizational forms, a limited liability company (LLC) is a "hybrid" that can be particularly appealing to small and entrepreneurial firms because it combines some of the benefits of a sole proprietorship or partnership with those of a corporation. In particular, an LLC offers limited liability protection, and it does not require a separate corporate tax form. By organizing as an LLC, the owners of smaller firms can access some of the benefits of the corporate form in a less labor-intensive and more cost-effective fashion. Telesis, one of the cases in this chapter, is organized as an LLC. Like an LLC, an S corporation is another hybrid form, offering smaller companies the combined benefits of limited liability and single rather than dual taxation of earnings.

In some instances, firm owners "migrate" from one type of organizational form to another as the firm moves through its life cycle. For example, a firm might start out as a sole proprietorship and eventually convert to the corporate form as it grows and requires more capital and a more sophisticated organizational form. Alternatively, however, growth-oriented firms may organize as corporations from Day 1 because they anticipate substantial size and growth as well as greater organizational complexity. When considering the various organizational forms, an entrepreneur should identify the form that is "typical" for firms such as her own, as well as her goals and motivations. She should also consider the types and amounts of capital she will need to raise and the organizational form that is most conducive and cost effective for doing so.

What Have We Learned?

In this chapter we highlighted the diversity of women-owned firms as well as the diversity of the financing strategies they use. A preview of "coming attractions" in future chapters in which we will elaborate on all of these points was presented. Above all, we learned that one size, indeed, does not fit all!

As we discussed in Chapter 1, this book is based on three complementary theories of the entrepreneurial firm: Life Cycle Theory, Resource-Based Theory, and Motivational Theory. Life Cycle Theory contends that a firm passes through different stages of development over the course of its life. Correspondingly, at each stage, different sources of financing are available, and different financial strategies are appropriate. Thus, firms in the developmental or start-up stage will rely heavily on the personal financial resources of the entrepreneur as well as funding from family and friends. Alternatively, rapid growth firms may need to draw upon external sources of capital, including bank loans and equity investments by business angels and venture capitalists. In this book we look at some examples of women-owned firms at different stages of the life cycle, as well as the financing sources and strategies they employ.

Resource-Based Theory tells us that the entrepreneur's job is to acquire and apply the resources necessary to achieve success. This is no small task! One of the most fundamental of these resources is financial capital, which can be used to start the firm, develop products and services, hire employees, acquire fixed assets, conduct research and development, and fund growth and expansion. Although other resources such as human capital and social capital are also important for entrepreneurial success, financial capital and the financial strategies of women entrepreneurs are the focal points in this book.

Motivational Theory tells us that the entrepreneur's motivations help to determine what type of business she starts, as well as her goals for that business. This, in turn, will largely determine the sources of capital that are appropriate and available to her. We saw Motivational Theory at work in the stories of both Nancy Hansen and Patty Sue Williams, and we will see it over and over in the additional entrepreneurial stories that we present in coming chapters. Nancy knew herself, and she knew her goals. This knowledge and self-awareness helped her to select the type of firm "fit" that would allow her to realize her entrepreneurial dreams. Simultaneously, she used and is using financial strategies that are consistent with her goals. In essence, her motivations have been the GPS for her entrepreneurial journey.

Throughout this book, we will see a similar pattern in terms of women's entrepreneurship. We will see a broad array of motivations and the types of firms they give rise to. Similarly, we will see extraordinary creativity on the part of women entrepreneurs in pursuing their entrepreneurial dreams. Finally, we will provide lessons learned from other women entrepreneurs—lessons that you as an entrepreneur or aspiring entrepreneur can also apply.

What Does All This Mean for Me?

As we saw in this chapter, different financing sources and strategies are appropriate at different stages of a firm's life cycle. Thus, if you are considering launching a new firm, it is important for you to recognize that you will be the primary provider of financing during the early stages of the firm's life cycle. You will need to be prepared to use your personal savings, credit cards, or a home equity loan. During those early days, you may also be able to draw upon the financial support of family and friends, and the effective use of bootstrapping techniques can help you to minimize the amount of external capital that has to be raised. All of these strategies are important because you will probably not be able to attract external funding until your business idea is formulated, you have a product or service to sell, and you have developed your revenue model. That process can take several months to several years. Those early years can be tough, and you need to be prepared. Early on in the process of establishing your firm, you need to determine the extent to which you are willing to make sacrifices, put your own financial resources at risk, and deal with the possibility of failure, since many new firms do fail. For many entrepreneurs, however, failure is not the end of the line. Rather, it is a part of their learning process and contributes valuable experience that can set the stage for launching a successful firm.

We also saw that successful entrepreneurship is a function of being able to secure the resources—including financial resources—needed to launch, develop, and grow your firm. We discussed how the type of firm you start, as well as the financial resources required, will be determined by your motivations and goals. What does this mean for you? It means that an important first step in your entrepreneurial journey is to do a self-assessment that will help you to identify your primary motivations and goals. What measures of success are most important to you? Is it independence and creativity as in Nancy Hansen's case? Is it the chance to pursue an opportunity or unmet need in the marketplace as in Patty Sue Williams's example? Is it financial gain? Is it growth and market share? Is it flexibility to balance the demands of work and family? Is it the opportunity to address some social or environmental concern?

Your motivations and goals will set the stage for the type of firm you start. Correspondingly, your motivations and firm type will determine your resource requirements, including financial resources. Once you have identified your motivations and goals and the type of firm that will allow you to achieve them, you then need to conduct a "resource inventory." Your resource inventory will help you to identify the types of resources you already have. For example, in terms of financial resources, you may already having savings, assets such as a house that can serve as collateral on a loan, a working significant other who is willing to support you while you get started, or friends and family who are willing to invest in your venture.

Your next step is to identify the resources you need but do not already have. These are the resources that you as an entrepreneur need to acquire. Additional financial resources could include a bank loan or line of credit, external equity investors, a government-sponsored loan or grant, or earnings that are sufficient to eliminate the need for other financial resources. Once you have identified the gap between the financial resources you already have and those that you will need, you can start to develop your financial strategies and action plan. Everyone's plan will be different because we all have different motivations and goals, different types of firms, and different levels of resources going into the process. Nevertheless, we can find patterns and similarities that will help us learn from the experiences of others.

Public Policy Implications

Because one size does not fit all, many public policy implications are available that can help promote the launch, development, and success of women-owned firms. First, an important first step in the entrepreneurial process is self-assessment and goal setting. Aspiring women entrepreneurs can benefit from workshops and seminars that will help them go through this process in order to identify their individual motivations and goals and the types of businesses that will allow them to achieve those goals. It does not surprise us that so many entrepreneurial ventures fail, since many entrepreneurs do not invest time in this critical first step. Thus, they end up starting firms that are not a good fit in terms of their real priorities.

A second public policy consideration pertains to the diversity of women's motivations and businesses. In light of that diversity, we also need a diverse array of financing sources. Small or home-based firms may benefit from microloan programs, whereas larger firms will need more substantial sources of external capital such as bank loans or equity from angel investors or venture capitalists. In the wake of the recent financial crisis, it is very difficult for many firms to get loans. This is particularly true for smaller and newer firms. Further, as we will discuss in future chapters, it has traditionally been very difficult for women entrepreneurs to penetrate angel or venture capital networks that could provide substantial amounts of financial capital for high-tech and growth-oriented firms. An important public policy measure would be to ensure that a full spectrum of financial providers and products is available to women entrepreneurs.

A third public policy option would be to determine the role and importance of entrepreneurship in general, and women's entrepreneurship in particular, within the larger context of economic development at the local, state, and national levels. If, in fact, entrepreneurship is a key element of job creation and economic growth, it is in the interest of state and local governments to structure their tax and regulatory laws, policies, and delivery systems in such a way that it will be encouraged. Similarly, at the national level, laws pertaining to taxation, research and development, and education have the potential to either encourage or discourage entrepreneurship and innovation. In other words, our local, state, and national policies should match our priorities.

One approach to public policy at the local, state, and national level would be to search for "best practices." In other words, look at those states and communities that have high levels of entrepreneurship and high levels of women's entrepreneurship in particular. What are they doing? What is their infrastructure for fostering entrepreneurship? What is their tax and regulatory profile? What types of financial providers and programs are available? By looking at communities that are doing it right, we can gain a better understanding of policies, programs, and providers that would have a positive impact on a larger scale.

NEW KID ON THE BLOCK

The Nascent Firm

At one time or another, all firms are "nascent" firms. Nascent simply means a business that is just getting started. Women entrepreneurs may start new businesses for a variety of reasons: to take advantage of an opportunity in the marketplace, to escape the confines of a corporate environment, or to provide the flexibility needed to balance work and family. In other words, women entrepreneurs have many different types of motivations for starting their firms, just like men do.

When we refer to nascent firms, we are typically referring to firms in their first year of existence. This is the period during which the entrepreneur transforms her business idea into action, creates an organization, begins to develop and sell products and services, and generates both revenues and expenses. This time is exhilarating, challenging, and, often, stressful! It is a time when the entrepreneur has the opportunity to let all her creative juices flow to create a business that is the embodiment of her ideas, talents, and hard work. Every newly developed product or service is a milestone, and every new customer is a victory. In fact, many of us have seen a framed dollar bill hanging on the wall in a newly opened business: that entrepreneur's first dollar in revenues!

Nascent entrepreneurs are important because they are recognized as a potential source of innovation, jobs, and economic growth. As such, both researchers and policy makers have sought to identify the factors that contribute to entrepreneurship in general and growth-oriented entrepreneurship in particular. Davidsson and Henrekson (2002) explain as follows:

> There are strong reasons to believe that productive entrepreneurship is an essential explanatory factor of the economic performance of a country, and hence that cross-country differences in the degree of productive entrepreneurial activity are likely candidates for explaining part of observed cross-country differences in economic performance.

Most entrepreneurial ventures start out and remain relatively small. In contrast, however, growth-oriented firms are those firms that achieve significant size and, in doing so, produce significant numbers of jobs. Because of their importance to the overall economy, particularly in this environment of high unemployment, growth-oriented firms will receive special attention in Chapter 7.

Who Are the Nascent Entrepreneurs?

The Panel Study of Entrepreneurial Dynamics (PSED) was undertaken specifically to learn more about the characteristics of nascent firms in the United States (Reynolds et al., 2004). More than 64,000 individuals were contacted and screened over an 18-month period beginning in July 1998 to determine the number of people who were engaged in the process of starting new businesses. Findings revealed that 6.1 percent of the total sample were involved in starting either a standalone business or a new business within an existing business. Further interviews and questionnaires revealed that one-third of these nascent entrepreneurs were women. Table 4.1 provides a breakdown of the level of nascent entrepreneurship by gender, race/ethnicity, and age. It reveals, first of all, that women of all ages and race/ethnicities had lower levels of participation in nascent entrepreneurship than men. Further, it reveals that the highest level of nascent entrepreneurship for women for all races and ethnicities occurred in the 25- to 34-year-old age range, followed by the 35- to 44-year-old age range for white and black women entrepreneurs, and the 18- to 24-year-old age range for Hispanic women entrepreneurs.

Subsequent research using the PSED data found that 33 percent of nascent entrepreneurs actually made the transition to operating firms after one year (Parker and Belghitar, 2006). Firms were more likely to make the transition if they had established credit with suppliers and if they had begun to receive some money from operations. These findings demonstrate the importance of financial capital, even during the earliest stages of the firm, particularly in

TABLE 4.1 Prevalence of nascent entrepreneurs in the United States

	Women				Men			
	Mean	*SE*	*Low 95%-confidence interval*	*High 95%-confidence interval*	*Mean*	*SE*	*Low 95%-confidence interval*	*High 95%-confidence interval*
ALL: 18–64 YEARS OLD								
White	5.10	0.20	4.71	5.49	8.60	0.20	8.21	8.99
Black	8.30	0.50	7.32	9.28	13.60	0.70	12.23	14.97
Hispanic	5.10	0.50	4.12	6.08	10.30	0.70	8.93	11.67
WHITE								
18–24 years old	3.70	0.40	2.92	4.48	8.50	0.50	7.52	9.48
25–34 years old	6.30	0.40	5.52	7.08	10.90	0.50	9.92	11.88
35–44 years old	6.00	0.30	5.41	6.59	9.10	0.40	8.32	9.88
45–54 years old	5.40	0.30	4.81	5.99	8.10	0.40	7.32	8.88
55–64 years old	2.20	0.30	1.61	2.79	5.10	0.40	4.32	5.88
BLACK								
18–24 years old	5.60	1.00	3.64	7.56	12.90	1.70	9.57	16.23
25–34 years old	10.10	1.10	7.94	12.26	15.60	1.40	12.86	18.34
35–44 years old	9.70	1.10	7.54	11.86	16.20	1.50	13.26	19.14
45–54 years old	9.40	1.40	6.66	12.14	12.10	1.60	8.96	15.24
55–64 years old	2.90	1.00	0.94	4.86	5.50	1.50	2.56	8.44
HISPANIC								
18–24 years old	5.10	1.00	3.14	7.06	10.10	1.40	7.36	12.84
25–34 years old	7.50	1.20	5.15	9.85	12.20	1.40	9.46	14.94
35–44 years old	3.60	0.90	1.84	5.36	10.40	1.50	7.46	13.34
45–54 years old	4.20	1.30	1.65	6.75	10.00	2.10	5.88	14.12
55–64 years old	1.40	1.10	0.76	3.56	2.50	1.50	0.44	5.44

Source: Used by permission by Springer Science + Business Media (license 2678920527041). Reynolds et al. (2004).

Note: Any comparison between women and men where the confidence intervals do not overlap is statistically significant at the 0.5 level.

TABLE 4.2 Survival rates of 2004 start-ups

Follow-on year	*Women-owned firms (%)*	*Men-owned firms (%)*
2005	89.4	92.4
2006	74.1	79.5
2007	64.7	68.3
2008	61.7	62.8
2009	55.1	56.8

Source: Kauffman Firm Survey Microdata.

the form of trade credit and earnings from the business. Additional studies have revealed that greater financial resources significantly decrease the likelihood of discontinuance in nascent firms (Liao et al., 2004) and significantly increase the likelihood of making a first sale (Brush et al., 2008). In terms of the outcomes for women-owned nascent firms, although women were less likely to be nascent entrepreneurs, their firms were no more likely to terminate than men's if they did get started (Diochon et al., 2005). An examination of Kauffman Firm Survey data on new U.S. firms founded in 2004 reveals that over half of new firms survived through 2009, the fifth follow-up year (Table 4.2). Consistent with the findings of research using the PSED data, women-owned firms were only slightly less likely to survive than men-owned firms in each of the follow-up years. It is important to remember, however, that firms discontinue for a variety of reasons, both voluntary and involuntary. As an example, voluntary closure could be the result of an entrepreneur's decision to sell the firm or, alternatively, to pursue other activities. In contrast, firm failure in the form of bankruptcy or liquidation is an example of involuntary closure.

The Attractions of Entrepreneurship

From the standpoint of nascent entrepreneurship, we now find ourselves in the midst of a very exciting and promising time for new firms. The economic upheaval that we have experienced as a result of the recent financial crisis will create opportunities for new firms and new industries. Some of the most promising sectors going forward include "green" and sustainable industries, education, health care, information technology, security and defense, and international trade, just to name a few. Many women entrepreneurs are already tapping into these vital and growing sectors.

Prior research distinguishes between "opportunity-based" entrepreneurs and "necessity-based" entrepreneurs (Block and Sandner, 2007; Reynolds et al., 2002). Opportunity-based entrepreneurs are those who recognize an opportunity in the marketplace and set out to pursue it. Many of the women entrepreneurs we describe in this book, including Debbie Godowsky (Cookies Direct), Kate Meyers (Brown & Meyers), and Patty Sue Williams (Telesis), are opportunity-based entrepreneurs. In contrast, necessity-based entrepreneurs are those who do not necessarily have other alternatives for employment. In our current environment of high unemployment, we are likely to see a growing number of necessity-based entrepreneurs. These are individuals who lost their jobs, often through no fault of their own, and cannot find another. Entrepreneurship in the form of consulting, contract work, or work within various sectors of the service economy often provides a way to pay the bills for these displaced workers.

Necessity-based entrepreneurship is less prevalent in developed economies like the United States, compared with developing nations where it often provides a means for women to sustain themselves and their families. We discuss the importance of necessity-based entrepreneurship much more fully in Chapter 10, which addresses global entrepreneurship.

Starting a new firm has many advantages. First of all, you are not inheriting someone else's vision and strategy, as would be the case if you acquired an existing firm. Similarly, you are not cleaning up someone else's messes. Alternatively, by starting a new firm, you give life to your own vision, ideas, and strategies. You develop products and services that are consistent with *your* goals and values. Further, you hire people with the characteristics you want who will be loyal to you and share in your vision for the firm. Thus, the firm is a reflection of you and your motivations.

Starting a new firm also provides you with an opportunity to launch products and services that are new to the marketplace, thus becoming a market leader. If you are first to market with a new product or service, you have a "window of opportunity" before the competition jumps in. This is a period of time during which you can add customers, build market share, and solidify your position. In marketing terms, this is called the "first mover" advantage, and it can be a significant factor in helping a new firm get established and survive. For many firms, revenues from sales are one of the most important sources of capital. Thus, a firm that can gain significant market share in its early years is in a better position to generate financing from this important source.

Pitfalls and Perils

In spite of all the excitement, the first two years are a critical time for new entrepreneurs because the firm is not yet fully established and there is a high risk of failure. According to data from the U.S. Census Bureau, 31 percent of new employer establishments that began in 2000 closed within the first two years, while 49 percent closed within the first five years. Firms born in 1990 had very similar survival rates. Survival rates were also similar across states and major industries.*

New firms face a variety of challenges. Often the founding entrepreneur is also "nascent" and does not have a lot of experience in starting or operating a firm. New entrepreneurs make mistakes in a variety of areas, including products, markets, people, and financing sources.

A number of studies attest to the role of human capital in helping to launch and sustain fledgling firms. One of the best ways to avoid being exploited as a new entrepreneur is to educate yourself as much as possible before you actually start your firm. Prior research attests to the positive relationship between educational level and entrepreneurship (Delmar and Davidsson, 2000; Reynolds, 1997). This is particularly important in many of the emerging fields within the technology and bioscience sectors. Previous researchers have also discovered that experience in both the business as well as the industry is an important predictor of success (Cooper et al., 1994; Delmar and Davidson, 2000; Diochon et al., 2008). In terms of general management skills, it is important to develop capabilities in the area of financial management in order to sustain a firm once it has been launched (Diochon et al., 2008).

From the perspective of social capital, it is helpful to have a team of trusted advisors, particularly individuals who have experience in various aspects of the business. Networking is essential in assembling such a team and in developing a support group of business colleagues who can provide advice, guidance, and encouragement. For example, when Radha Jalan of Electro-Chem (see Chapter 8) experienced difficulties with a group of outside investors who wanted to take over her firm, her friends and advisors rallied around her and advised her to fight back and maintain her leadership role in the firm (Amatucci and Coleman, 2007). Support of this type is critical during difficult times.

---

* U.S. Department of Commerce, Bureau of the Census, Business Dynamics Statistics.

Another challenge for entrepreneurs founding new firms is that many such firms are based on new products, services, or technologies. Thus, because no market exists, one has to be created. A large part of the entrepreneur's task is to educate potential customers on the benefits of her product or service and to spread the word of its success through satisfied users. We can see an example of this in the case of Zipcar, an entrepreneurial firm based on the concept of car sharing. Case author Myra Hart (2002) explains:

> Zipcar's marketing plan relied on several low-budget tactics. Chase and Danielson expected that approximately 30 percent to 40 percent of their marketing impact would be driven by word-of-mouth, another 25 percent by free media coverage generated through public relations (PR), and the rest through their own "grassroots" guerilla marketing efforts.

The concept of car sharing versus car owning was relatively new to the U.S. market, although it was well established in Europe. Entrepreneur Robin Chase had to educate those who might use her service—environmentally conscious urban dwellers—and then relied on them to spread the word. She was also astute in securing media attention and coverage precisely because Zipcar was such a new concept in the United States.

• Tips on Avoiding Pitfalls and Perils

1. Develop financial acumen. In particular, learn to manage your cash flows.
2. Establish the systems and controls required to manage key aspects of your firm, including cash, receivables, and inventories.
3. Recognize gaps in your knowledge and skill set, and develop strategies to address these gaps through education, training, or developing a trusted team of employees and advisors.
4. Network strategically to develop your knowledge, skills, and key contacts.

One of the most difficult challenges for entrepreneurs in nascent firms is building an organizational infrastructure to manage future growth. One of the most important yet most difficult tasks for any organizational leader is picking the right people and delegating responsibility. It is often particularly difficult for a new entrepreneur to give up control. She had been doing everything herself in the beginning, and now she has to stand by and watch other people make the inevitable mistakes. It's hard to know when to intervene and when to stand back and let others figure it out for themselves.

Women entrepreneurs also tell us that they tend to be very trusting of other people—perhaps too trusting. When hiring managers or employees, or when considering partners or investors, it is important to check them out thoroughly. Don't just take their word for it, no matter how good you feel about them. Check their references, credentials, and track records. It takes some time up front, but much less time than trying to get rid of someone who becomes a problem down the road.

Many new firms fail because they do not have the necessary systems and controls in place. By "systems and controls," we mean financial management and reporting systems and systems for managing cash, receivables, and inventories. All three of these are areas where new firms often get into trouble. Firms don't go out of business because they don't have any customers. They go out of business because they don't have any cash. Thus, it is particularly important to manage your cash flows frequently and carefully. If you don't collect your receivables in a timely fashion, you don't get the cash. If you carry excessive levels of inventory, you use up too much cash. It's all about managing cash and making sure you have enough. Systems and controls will help you understand when and how much cash is coming in and, conversely, when and how much cash is going out. This knowledge is critical to the survival of new firms. If you anticipate a cash shortfall in the coming months, that's your cue to start lining up sources of financing.

How does a new entrepreneur go about setting up systems and controls? One of the best ways to get started is to identify and start working with an accountant. Accountants are trained in financial management, and a good accountant can provide invaluable support to the "new kid on the block." Too often entrepreneurs seek out an accountant after their firm has gotten into financial difficulties. The time to establish a relationship is early on, before you have signed away your life on a long-term lease, misplaced half of your inventory, or forgotten about collecting your receivables!

An accountant can also be particularly helpful to nascent women entrepreneurs who may lack confidence in their own financial abilities. He or she can help prepare financial statements and other documents required to apply for a loan and can even accompany the entrepreneur when she goes to the bank to seek funding. The fact that the firm has financial statements prepared by an accountant may increase a bank's willingness to advance funds. From the standpoint of acquiring equity, accountants are typically well networked in the business and investment communities. Thus, they are well positioned to identify potential angel investors who may have an interest in investing in new and growing firms.

Financing Strategies for Nascent Firms

Speaking of financing, how *do* nascent firms get started? What sources of financing do they rely on? As we have noted in earlier chapters within the context of Resource-Based Theory, financial resources are often a key to the survival of new firms (Cooper et al., 1994). One of the particular challenges of new firms, however, is the problem of asymmetric information (Ang, 1992). "Asymmetric information" refers to the fact that insiders have more information than outsiders. Thus, it is difficult for outsiders, including external providers of finance, to evaluate the prospects of the firm. The problem of asymmetric information is particularly acute for new firms, precisely because they are new. They do not have a track record, and often they are not yet profitable. Further, if the new firm is based on the introduction of a new product, service, or technology, it is difficult to evaluate the extent to which it will be successful. Prior research suggests that the problem of asymmetric information often causes new firms to rely more heavily on internal rather than external sources of financing. Those firms that are able to attract external financing are typically larger and more growth-oriented, or they have tangible assets that can be used as collateral for loans (Cassar, 2004).

We examine the first three years of the Kauffman Firm Survey to evaluate the effect of asymmetric information, as well as the differences in financing between women and men nascent entrepreneurs. As mentioned earlier, the KFS is a longitudinal survey of new businesses in the United States. The KFS has detailed information on the firm, including industry, physical location, employment, profits, intellectual property, and financial capital (equity and debt) used at start-up and over time. Information on up to ten owners includes age, gender, race, ethnicity, education, work experience, and previous start-up experience. The details these data provide allow us to compare the financial strategies and use of both debt and equity for new women- and men-owned firms over time. A public use dataset is available for download from the

Kauffman Foundation's website. If you would like to take advantage of this valuable source of data on new firms, you can go to www.kauffman.org/kfs.

Alternatively, if you are not thrilled with the idea of manipulating data, we have already done some of that for you! Tables 4.3 and 4.4 show the financing sources, by gender, for new firms in their first year of operation (2004) and in two subsequent years (2005 and 2006).

Table 4.3 sheds light on the financing sources and amounts for new firms. It reveals that women used dramatically lower amounts of total capital, debt, and equity to start their firms than men did. Mean amounts of start-up capital in the baseline year (2004) were about $71,000 for women compared to $134,000 for men. The differences are even more dramatic when we look at external sources of capital. Men used more outside debt to establish their firms than women ($56,191 vs. $36,057). Men were also able to raise larger amounts of both owner and insider debt. Similarly, men raised dramatically higher levels

TABLE 4.3 Kauffman Firm Survey: Start-up capital (2004) and new financial injections (2005–2006)

	2004 ($)		*2005 ($)*		*2006 ($)*	
	Female	*Male*	*Female*	*Male*	*Female*	*Male*
Total financial capital	71,484	134,139	62,120	111,197	46,624	121,842
Total debt	44,725	69,375	44,379	57,225	36,270	83,504
Owner debt	3,897	5,412	5,222	4,225	3,178	4,311
Insider debt	4,771	7,772	3,198	6,138	2,183	6,050
Outsider debt	36,057	56,191	35,959	46,863	30,908	73,144
Total equity	26,759	64,764	17,741	53,971	10,354	38,338
Owner equity	23,948	36,697	9,693	19,585	8,424	14,726
Insider equity	1,876	2,088	437	1,880	587	824
Outsider equity	935	25,980	7,612	32,507	1,342	22,788
LEVERAGE RATIOS (%)						
Debt/equity	167.1	107.1	250.1	106.0	350.3	217.8
Debt/total financial capital	62.6	51.7	71.4	51.5	77.8	68.5
Insider financing/total financial capital	9.3	7.4	5.9	7.2	5.9	5.6
Outsider financing/ total financial capital	51.7	61.3	70.1	71.4	69.2	78.7
Owner financing/total financial capital	39.0	31.4	24.0	21.4	24.9	15.6

Source: Kauffman Firm Survey Microdata.

of external equity than women ($25,980 vs. $935), as well as higher levels of owner and insider equity.

The fact that women small business owners start their firms with much smaller amounts of capital may have implications for their ability to hire employees, develop new products and services, grow, or even survive. One of the things that you as a new entrepreneur have to evaluate carefully is how much capital you really need to launch your business. It is important to raise enough money at the outset because, as we have said before, companies don't go out of business because they don't have customers; they go out of business because they run out of cash!

Table 4.3 shows that the pattern persists for the years 2005 and 2006. In 2005 women raised roughly half of the amount of incremental financing that men did ($62,120 vs. $111,197), while in 2006 they raised just over one-third ($46,624 vs. $121,842). Again, there is a large gap between women and men, particularly when we consider the categories of outsider debt and external equity. To summarize, for the first three years of operation, women-owned firms raised an average of approximately $180,000, compared with more than $367,000 for firms owned by men. Similarly women raised a total of $103,000 of outsider debt and $10,000 of external equity, compared to $176,000 in outsider debt and $81,000 of external equity for men. In terms of the impact of asymmetric information, we can see from Table 4.3 that both women and men used higher ratios of owner and insider financing to total financial capital in the start-up year than in subsequent years. We would anticipate this to be the case as the firm becomes established and develops a track record of performance.

These findings are consistent with prior research that attests to the difficulties faced by smaller and newer firms in their attempts to secure external sources of capital (Lee and Denslow, 2004). As just noted, consistent with the theory of asymmetric information, KFS data for the first year of operation indicate that new firms rely primarily on internal sources of debt and equity to get started. What exactly does that mean? It means your personal savings, money from family and friends, and personal loans such as a home equity loan and credit cards. This is even more the case for new women-owned firms. Thus, if you decide to "take the plunge" into entrepreneurship, you will need to be prepared to either put up or raise internal sources of financing. In all likelihood, external sources will not be available to you until the firm is more fully developed and has achieved some milestones in terms of product development or sales.

Table 4.3 also suggests differences in the financing sources and strategies of women- and men-owned firms. Specifically, women start their firms with much smaller amounts of financial capital than men, and they are more likely to rely on internal rather than external sources of capital. Beyond those differences, only a small percentage of either women or men used external capital in the form of business loans, lines of credit, angel investments, or venture capital. Is this true because of issues of demand ("I don't need it.") or of supply (They won't give it to me.")? To find the answer, we talked to a sample of women entrepreneurs to get their perspectives. Not surprisingly we found that their financing sources and amounts were often tied to the goals and objectives they had for the firm. In some instances, our entrepreneurs wanted small, manageable, lifestyle businesses. Those falling into that category relied primarily on personal and internal sources of financing. Examples include both Debbie Godowsky (Cookies Direct) and Melanie Downey (Wilava). Both of these entrepreneurs established home-based firms with goals of relatively modest growth.

Alternatively, women entrepreneurs such as Sue Bouchard (Pioneer Telephone) and Patty Sue Williams (Telesis) who started growth-oriented firms actively pursued external sources of capital. In some instances they were successful in securing it, and in others they felt that they encountered barriers. As successful entrepreneurs, however, they found ways to circumvent these roadblocks in order to achieve their goals. The point is that your motivations for starting the firm and your goals will largely determine the sources and amounts of financing that are appropriate for and accessible to you as an individual entrepreneur.

• Angel and Venture Capital

Our discussion of external sources of financing thus far has touched upon the dramatic differences between women and men firm entrepreneurs in securing and using sources of external equity. Two important sources of external equity, particularly for growing firms, are angel funding and venture capital investments. Angel investors are individual investors who invest their own money into business ventures. These are typically high–net worth individuals who seek attractive investment opportunities. Angel investors can also include individuals who have a particular interest in or an affinity for specific industries—for example, entertainment, communications, or biotech. Traditionally the angel investor market has been highly fragmented, and entrepreneurs have found angel investors by using some variation of the pick and peck approach. More recently, however, angel investors have been organizing into networks (www.angelinvestorforum.com). These networks facilitate the exchange of information, and they allow groups of angel investors to make larger investments than would be feasible for individuals. This is an important innovation because traditionally angel investors have made smaller investments than venture capital firms.

Whereas angel investors invest their own money, venture capitalists invest someone else's money. A venture capital fund is a professionally managed pool of funds that is invested in potentially high-growth business ventures. High–net worth investors or organizations, such as college endowment funds or pension funds, invest in VC funds, which are managed by a professional manager or management team. The team selects the firms in which to invest, monitors their progress, and eventually "harvests value" for those companies that succeed, either through an initial public offering or through selling the firm to another company. If a VC firm has a portfolio of 20 different companies, it is very possible that only one or two will be highly successful. However, those one or two highly successful firms can more than compensate for the losses experienced from the other 18.

Venture capital investing is a risky business. Since a high proportion of portfolio companies fail, venture capitalists look for a high return from those that succeed. Within the context of a portfolio, one successful Google can compensate for a lot of smaller failures. In light of that, VCs seek out firms with the potential for rapid growth. Rapid growth firms can go from being very small to being very large within a relatively short span of time. At that point, they become candidates for an initial public offering (IPO) or acquisition by a larger firm, thereby providing a return to the entrepreneur and her VC investors.

Venture capital firms provide value to portfolio companies in a variety of ways. The most obvious is that they provide not only large amounts of equity capital but an ongoing source of funding as well. The typical VC investment is at least $1 million. When the firm invests, however, it also establishes targets or benchmarks. As the portfolio company achieves those targets, it will receive additional "tranches" of investment. Over time, a VC firm may invest $10 million, $20 million, or even hundreds of millions of dollars in an individual firm. By investing in stages, a VC firms limits its losses; portfolio firms that do not achieve their targets do not receive later rounds of financing. Further, investing in stages helps to minimize the agency problem, since the entrepreneur retains a larger chunk of ownership for a longer period of time. Thus, she remains a major shareholder and is motivated to see the firm succeed. Alternatively, owners who lose too much of their ownership share too soon may lose interest in the firm and move on to greener pastures.

In addition to financial capital, a venture capital firm also supplies both human and social capital. VC firms typically specialize by industry. By doing so, their professionals are able to build a substantial base of knowledge and expertise that can be used to benefit new firms. As a part of this relationship, the VC firm will assess the strengths and capabilities of a portfolio company's management team. If additional expertise is required, the VC firm will take steps to bring additional people on board. Throughout the portfolio company's development, the VC firm monitors its progress closely to provide guidance and direction as required. One of the added benefits of specializing by industry is that VC firms are able to develop an extensive network of contacts, professionals, advisors, and additional financing sources. This network provides portfolio firms with a ready-made social capital framework.

Differences in Capital Requirements by Industry

Capital requirements vary considerably by industry. To determine if different patterns in financing by gender hold within given industry sectors, we examined three industry groupings: high-tech industries, financial-capital-intensive industries, and human-capital-intensive industries. Our definition of high-tech industries is based on two sources. First, Chapple and colleagues (2004) include a set of occupations that are science- and engineering-intensive, as well as industries whose shares of employment in those occupations were three times the national average. Second, the National Science Foundation's Survey of Industrial Research and Development classified firms as high-tech if they exceeded the U.S. average for both research and development expenditures per employee and for the proportion of full-time-equivalent R&D scientists and engineers in the industry workforce (Paytas and Berglund, 2004).

We defined financial-capital-intensive industries (FK Intensive) using Annual Capital Expenditure Survey (ACES) data, which examine average firm fixed private capital for 11 broad industry groups. Those emerging as financial-capital-intensive or well above the all-industry average regarding capital intensity included manufacturing, wholesale, professional and related services, and finance/insurance/real estate (FIRE). Finally, we defined human-capital-

TABLE 4.4 Start-up capital by industry subgroup in 2004

	High-tech ($)		*HK intensive ($)*		*FK intensive ($)*	
	Female	*Male*	*Female*	*Male*	*Female*	*Male*
Owner equity	20,967	31,857	20,293	32,310	23,636	43,986
Insider equity	1,993	2,482	1,954	1,565	970	1,666
Outsider equity	2,654	74,004	817	34,553	1,175	36,263
Owner debt	5,558	6,871	2,236	5,400	2,889	5,690
Insider debt	2,699	4,292	3,530	7,554	7,829	8,202
Outsider debt	31,317	36,981	43,807	49,332	47,957	62,889
Total financial capital	65,187	156,486	72,638	130,715	84,455	158,697

Source: Kauffman Firm Survey Microdata.

intensive firms (HK Intensive) using the 2000 census of population PUMS* data to determine educational attainment by industry. Those industries emerging as human-capital-intensive or well above the all-industry average regarding owner educational attainment included professional and related services, business services, FIRE, and entertainment/recreation services. Table 4.4 shows the levels of start-up capital (2004) by gender for these three industry subgroups.

Table 4.4 reveals that women-owned firms raised approximately half of the amount of total financial capital in the start-up year for each of the three industry subgroups. In each instance, women owners were more heavily dependent on owner equity and outsider debt than men owners were. Further, men raised substantially more external equity for each of the three industry subgroups than women. These results confirm our findings in Table 4.3 and reinforce the fact that the financing sources and patterns of women and men entrepreneurs are different.

Principles in Action: DailyWorth.com

Amanda Steinberg started DailyWorth.com (www.DailyWorth.com) in order to give women insights into building their net worth. Raised by a single mom, Amanda grew up watching her mother struggle to make ends meet. That experience helped her to understand how important it is for women to be able to support themselves and manage their financial affairs. Later, when Amanda

---

* PUMs stands for Public Use Micro-sample. This is a 5 percent sample of the decennial census.

and her husband bought their first home, they found themselves struggling to make mortgage payments. Although they had a high household income, they somehow managed to overmortgage themselves without realizing the impact that would have on their lives.

After scrutinizing my patterns in the areas of budgeting, spending, saving, and investing, I made the conscious choice to value my net worth and to hyper-educate myself in all areas of personal finance. DailyWorth.com is the outcome of this resolution. (Biddle, 2010)

DailyWorth.com has become the go-to source on personal finance for women and has more than 100,000 subscribers. The firm's core service is a daily email to subscribers covering some topic in the area of personal finance. Amanda also runs Soapbxx, a web consultancy and contributes to Forbes-Woman.com. Recently, she has been highlighted in *Cosmopolitan* magazine, the *New York Times*, *Forbes*, and *USA Today.*

The first time we spoke to Amanda, she was in the midst of trying to raise $1.5 million from VCs. She had raised about $250,000 of initial capital from friends and family, and she was taking in about $15,000 in revenues per month. She realized that having her sister, her uncle, and her uncle's friend invest was a huge advantage in launching her venture. Nevertheless, she was frustrated in her search for venture capital backing.

I haven't been able to get a term sheet after five months of constant pitching and ninth-round meetings with some VCs. . . . I'm the last person to cry "woman," really. I just have to wonder if what I am going through is because I'm a mother and a woman. Yes, the economy is impacting capital without question. I just see companies like mine being funded in other circumstances. The money is there, and money is moving.

When we spoke with Amanda again several weeks later, however, she was celebrating after pitching to several angel investors and quickly getting some bites. She realized that most of the VCs she had been talking to had billions of dollars in their funds, and her deal just wasn't big enough to attract their interest. Her goal of a $50 million exit in the next five to seven years seemed like a lot of money to her, but she realized it really wasn't a lot of money for many venture capital firms. The angel investors she approached were more receptive, and she now has $1.5 million committed from two angel investors. She thinks some of the VCs might also be more receptive at this point.

VCs have no incentive to invest early, and they can string you along forever until they might lose the deal. Angels can move more quickly.

Now that Amanda has secured financing, she is hiring a CEO for Soapbxx and moving to DailyWorth full time to grow her newest venture. She is already looking ahead and thinking about other ways to create value through business development. She is also committed to exploring new ways to help women create wealth.

Postscript on DailyWorth

After our initial interview with Amanda in late 2010, she continued to work on financing and eventually succeeded in making inroads into the venture capital market. Techcrunch.com had the following announcement on March 2, 2011:

> DailyWorth, the personal finance daily email and community for women, has raised $850,000 in funding led by Robin Hood Ventures with Eric Schmidt's TomorrowVentures, Howard Lindzon's Social Leverage, 500 Start-ups, Venture51, Investors' Circle, Joanne Wilson, David Cohen, Scott Becker, and Carol Chow participating in the round.

Founded in 2009 by Amanda Steinberg, DailyWorth is a daily email newsletter that includes information on financial literacy and money management skewed toward a female audience. DailyWorth's subjects range from how to organize your finances to tax tips to saving advice. And DailyWorth has an impressive editorial staff to create content. M. P. Dunleavey, previously a personal finance columnist with the *New York Times* and currently a contributor with *Money* magazine, is leading DailyWorth's editorial team.

With 55,000 subscribers, the newsletter currently makes money via advertising and already has sponsorships in place with a number of financial institutions, including ING and H&R Block. And DailyWorth plans to hold sponsored educational events as an additional revenue channel. The new funding will be used to expand audience reach with customized email newsletters, develop the start-up's website, add video content, and host sponsored events.

DailyWorth is similar in many ways to LearnVest, a personal finance community for women. But DailyWorth is committed to the email newsletter model (which is making a comeback). And there's definitely room for many personal finance sites oriented toward women.*

What Have We Learned?

We have seen in this chapter that starting a new firm is an exciting, exhilarating, and somewhat stressful process. There are so many things to think about in those early days! It may help us to look at starting a firm within the context of the Resource-Based Theory of the firm. This theory tells us that the task of the entrepreneur is to develop, assemble, and mobilize resources in order to achieve success. What kinds of resources are we talking about? Well, obviously, since this is a book about financial strategies, financial resources come to mind. Financial resources include things like savings or earning that can be devoted to the firm; family and friends who are willing to invest as in Amanda Steinberg's case; and relationships with lending institutions in the event that a loan may be required. Frequently, this will be a loan secured by the personal assets of the entrepreneur, such as a home equity line of credit. Many entrepreneurs also rely on personal credit cards during the early stages of the business. Although the interest rate is not particularly attractive, credit cards are readily available and act as a revolving line of credit.

Nascent firms like DailyWorth.com have a difficult time attracting external sources of capital for a variety of reasons. First, these firms are typically unprofitable. Even though the firm may have sales, expenses usually exceed revenues. This makes them an unlikely candidate for bank loans that are not secured by the personal assets of the entrepreneur. Second, nascent firms may be based on new, and as yet untested, products or services. Thus, external providers of both debt and equity may be reluctant to provide funding until they are sure the new concept "catches on." Finally, new firms have a high rate of discontinuance. As noted previously, research using the Panel Study of Entrepreneurial Dynamics found that after one year, only 33 percent of firms had advanced to entrepreneurship, 20 percent had discontinued, and 47 percent were still in the nascent stage (Parker and Belghitar, 2006). In other words, only one out of every three start-up firms actually advanced beyond the start-up stage after one year!

---

* http://techcrunch.com/2011/03/02/dailyworth-raises-850k-to-become-the-daily-candy-for-personal-finance/

In light of the uncertainty surrounding the prospects of start-up companies, new entrepreneurs must be prepared to generate internal and personal sources of funding during the early stages of the firm. That means your own savings, money from family and friends, personal loans (including credit cards), and earnings from the business. Prior research highlights the importance of earnings from the firm as a source of financing during the early stages (Parker and Belghitar, 2006). The sooner an entrepreneur can begin to generate earnings, the sooner she will have an additional source of capital to draw upon. Further, the fact that the firm is generating earnings will make it more attractive to external providers of debt such as banks and equity from angel investors or venture capitalists.

Financial resources alone, however, do not guarantee success. Prior research also reveals that an entrepreneur can benefit from both human capital and social capital. Human capital includes education and relevant experience that will help to prepare her for the process of entrepreneurship. Studies reveal that having an advanced degree or other specialized knowledge (Kim et al., 2006; Parker and Belghitar, 2006), managerial experience (Kim et al., 2006; Liao et al., 2004), and prior start-up experience (Davidsson and Honig, 2003) were all important in the start-up process. In other words, you may want to prepare yourself for the process of entrepreneurship by taking a specific major in college, doing a graduate degree in a specialized field, or taking courses to acquire specialized knowledge about your chosen field. Similarly, you may want to work in the industry or work in another start-up before you launch your own firm. These are all types of human capital that can help you prepare and increase your chances for success.

Previous research has also revealed the importance of social capital (Davidsson and Honig, 2003; Parker and Belghitar, 2006). Social capital refers to the networks that you are a part of that can provide you with access to resources. Examples of social capital include membership in business networks and positive relationships with banks that can provide loans and with suppliers who can provide trade credit. In other words, don't wait until you need a loan to start developing a relationship with a bank. And don't wait until you are short of cash some month and can't cover your accounts payable to start talking with your suppliers. If you are starting a rapid growth firm, you may also want to connect with angel and venture capital networks that can provide access to larger amounts of capital. Most states have angel investor and venture capital associations. Start going to their monthly networking events and lunches to meet people and educate them about your firm and the products and services you offer.

What Does All This Mean for Me?

So what is our advice to you as an aspiring entrepreneur? There are so many things to think about during the early days of a firm that it's difficult to boil them down into a few key considerations. Nevertheless, we will give it a try.

1. Educate yourself about the dynamics of your business and its industry. In other words, is it a business that will start to generate revenues quickly, such as catering, which can be done out of your home, or is it a business where revenues may take years to materialize, such as developing a new drug? The longer it takes your firm to start generating cash, the more external capital you will need.
2. Understand that your tasks as a new entrepreneur are to assemble, develop, and mobilize the resources you need to make your firm successful. These include financial, human, and social capital. Take an inventory of what you already have in each of these areas and match it to a corresponding inventory of what you think you will need. By identifying the gaps, you can develop a road map for the additional resources that you need to acquire.
3. Depending on the capital and growth requirements of the firm, be prepared to invest a substantial amount of your own money. This can be in the form of savings, earnings from a full-time job, personal credit, or money from family and friends. During the earliest days of the firm, you will probably not be able to attract external sources of capital, so you will have to fund start-up activities out of your own pocket. This is your "skin in the game," and it's something that external providers of capital look at carefully.
4. Learn to love bootstrapping! Bootstrapping refers to minimizing expenses in order to minimize the need to raise external capital, and it is particularly important during the early stages of the firm. If you can work out of your home, get people to volunteer time and talent, and stretch out your payables without alienating your suppliers, you can reduce the amount of external funding you have to raise. These are just a few of the bootstrapping strategies that new firms use, but there are many more!
5. Assess your human capital attributes to determine if you have the right education and experience to succeed in your business. If you identify

gaps, consider strengthening your human capital by taking some courses or perhaps starting the firm as part of a team. Evidence shows that firms started by teams have better outcomes because different team members can bring unique skills and resources to the table (Davidsson and Honig, 2003).

6. Network! Network! Network! We have met many women entrepreneurs who become consumed by the activities associated with their businesses and do not take the time to get out and connect with key groups and individuals. We cannot stress enough how important networking is to entrepreneurial success. No matter how good you are and how hard you work, no one person has all the attributes and resources needed for entrepreneurial success. As a former First Lady titled her book, "It takes a village" (Clinton, 1996). The same is true for entrepreneurship. At the same time, be strategic in your networking activities. Identify the individuals and groups who can provide access to key resources, and find ways to connect with them. Further, once you connect, *stay* connected. Don't drop off the radar screen because you are too busy. Make networking a systematic and sustained part of your business operations.

Public Policy Implications

As we have said before, new firms are a major source of new jobs, new products, new services, and new technologies. As such, they are major contributors to the economy in a variety of ways. From a more micro perspective, entrepreneurship provides women with choices and a path to economic empowerment. It gives women a way to support themselves and their families and to thrive economically. In light of these benefits, it is important to create an environment that encourages and sustains entrepreneurship—especially women's entrepreneurship—since that is the topic of this book. How do we do that? If we return to our Resource-Based Theory of the firm, we can do that by making sure that women have opportunities and encouragement to access the types of financial, human, and social capital they need to succeed. From the standpoint of human capital, we can ensure that women have access to a full range of educational opportunities, college majors, and fields in order to acquire specialized knowledge. We can also take steps to ensure that women reach the senior ranks of corporations, where they will able to obtain both depth and breadth of managerial experience. Finally, it is important for women to gain access to networks that can lead them to key resources, whether they be talent, advice and mentoring, or financial capital.

From a public policy perspective, additional insights regarding nascent entrepreneurship can be gleaned from findings using the Global Entrepreneurship Monitor (GEM). The GEM is a longitudinal study of nascent entrepreneurship in multiple countries, some developed and some developing. Research using this data has documented the relationship between entrepreneurship and economic growth as measured by gross domestic product (GDP) per capita (Acs et al., 2005).

Figure 4.1 illustrates the relationship between the number of entrepreneurs per 100 adults and GDP as a U-shaped curve. It demonstrates that entrepreneurship levels are higher in developing countries with low levels of GDP. These are "necessity-based" entrepreneurs, or individuals who start their own firms because there are few other avenues for employment or support. Correspondingly, high-GDP countries such as the United States have high levels of entrepreneurship. These are "opportunity-based" entrepreneurs who are attracted by unmet needs in the marketplace and the potential for substantial growth and earnings.

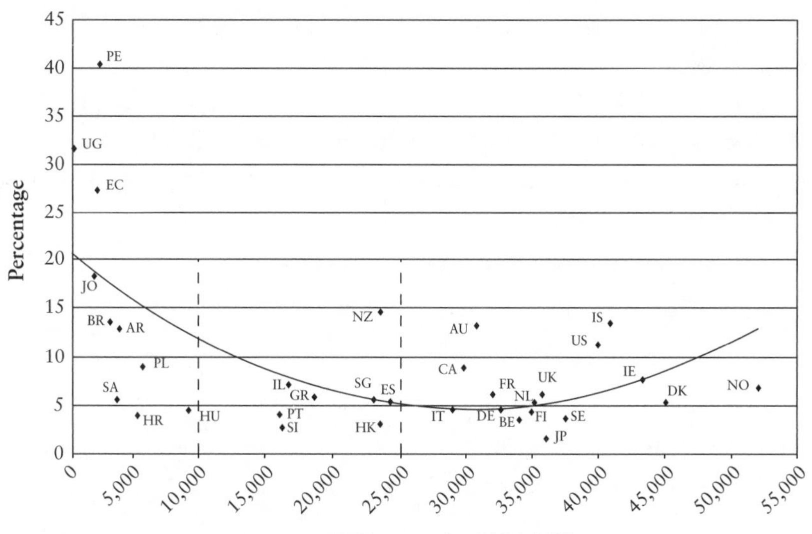

FIGURE 4.1 National income and fitted parabolic trend in 2004
Source: Used by permission of Acs et al. (2005).

Both types of entrepreneurship are important. Necessity-based entrepreneurship provides an employment and income alternative to individuals who may not have other choices. In many developing countries, women fall into this category. Alternatively, opportunity-based entrepreneurship results in new products, new services, and new technologies. Many opportunity-based entrepreneurs start growth-oriented firms that provide large numbers of jobs and a substantial impact on economic growth (Wong et al., 2005). As we will see in Chapters 7 and 8, the number of women who are pursuing opportunity-based entrepreneurship in the United States is increasing thanks to both educational and employment gains as well as improved networks for support.

Consistent with the PSED data that focus on nascent entrepreneurs in the United States, the GEM data also point out that, whatever the country, men are twice as likely to become nascent entrepreneurs as women (Acs et al., 2005). The gap between women and men is smaller in countries where necessity-based entrepreneurship predominates, suggesting that women in low-income countries turn to entrepreneurship as a means of supporting their families. Similarly, the gap between women and men is lower in countries where opportunity-based entrepreneurship is high. These are countries where income and educational levels are also high, so women have more opportunities to acquire both financial and human capital.

One important study drawing upon the GEM data (Wennekers et al., 2005) distinguished between economic policies that would benefit developing countries versus developed countries. In the case of economically advanced countries, such as the United States, they concluded that the most promising approach to public policy regarding nascent entrepreneurship would include the following:

1. Fostering investment in research and development
2. Improving the incentives for self-employment
3. Stimulating entrepreneurship education
4. Promoting commercial exploitation of scientific findings through transparent intellectual property rights
5. Having a well-developed market for venture capital

We would add to these policy recommendations from a recent *GEM Executive Report* (Acs et al., 2005) that include the need to strengthen technology transfer; make early-stage funding available; support entrepreneurial activity at the state, corporate, and university levels; and have universities play a larger role in research and development, commercialization, and scientific education. This report also recommends that we need to create a "mindset of creativity and innovation" in order to stimulate and encourage entrepreneurial activity at all levels.

Some of these policy recommendations are particularly relevant for nascent women entrepreneurs. First, improvements in scientific education, particularly those programs that seek to attract and engage girls and young women, will provide women with opportunities in growth-oriented fields such as bioscience and technology. Second, improvements in entrepreneurial education have the potential to engage more women in the entrepreneurial process while equipping them with the skills they will need to succeed. Finally, increasing the availability of early-stage funding and having a well-developed and accessible venture capital market will benefit all entrepreneurs, but it will benefit women entrepreneurs disproportionately. Women, on average, have lower levels of income and accumulated wealth than men. Thus, they have lower amounts of personal capital that can be devoted to a business start-up. In this chapter, we saw that women raise much less capital from external sources than from internal sources. Sometimes this is because of lower levels of demand, but in other cases it is because of problems with supply, specifically barriers and obstacles in the financial markets. Prior research has documented the difficulties that women entrepreneurs have in penetrating the venture capital market, which tends to be closely knit and heavily male dominated.

In summation, the national and worldwide gap between the number of women and men nascent entrepreneurs suggests tremendous opportunity for women. Today, women in the United States are better educated than ever, and more women are actually graduating from college than men. Simultaneously, the current economic and financial turbulence will create new entrepreneurial opportunities going forward. From the standpoint of financing strategies, one of our challenges, as the economy rights itself, is to ensure that we have financial institutions and capital available to the next generation of nascent entrepreneurs.

THERE'S NO PLACE LIKE HOME

The Risks and Rewards of a Home-Based Business

The authors have a particular fondness for this chapter because it gives us the opportunity to focus on an underresearched and underappreciated segment of entrepreneurship: the home-based business. A home-based business is one that operates out of the business owner's residence as opposed to renting space or facilities at another location. We believe that home-based entrepreneurship offers special benefits to many women entrepreneurs, particularly those who juggle competing responsibilities and those who face capital constraints.

What do we mean by that? Well, as we will reiterate throughout this book, women's motivations and goals determine the types of businesses they start. In turn, the type of business you start determines the types of capital that are available and appropriate for your needs. Prior research indicates that operating a home-based business allows women to address at least three different yet equally important types of goals: balancing the demands of work and family, starting a business with less funds, and doing something they genuinely love to do.

Many women with children in the home need to deal with the competing demands of work and family (Kirkwood and Tootell, 2008). Although men today are much more involved in child rearing and household tasks, women still shoulder the major responsibilities for child care, housework, grocery shopping, carpools, entertaining, and the like. Further, for those women who work outside the home, the cost of child care, particularly for multiple children, can be very high. Home-based entrepreneurship can provide these women with a source of income and professional fulfillment, as well as a way to juggle child care and work. A study of women entrepreneurs in New York State found that those women who established home-based firms were more likely to cite the need to balance work and family than women who established non-home-based firms (Loscocco and Smith-Hunter, 2004). Similarly, a study of Australian home-based business owners revealed that work–family balance and lifestyle flexibility were the primary motivations for women with children (Walker et al., 2008).

After holding managerial positions in several major advertising agencies, Jude Workman founded her home-based business, MediaWorks, in 1994 when her son was born. MediaWorks, located in West Hartford, Connecticut, assists a broad range of clients with their advertising and media buying needs. Jude's primary motivations when she started her firm were a desire for independence combined with a need for greater flexibility in scheduling.

In my industry there was the expectation that you would constantly be available for client meetings and events at all hours, including nights and weekends. That's very difficult when you have a baby. At that time in my life, it was very important to me to have a more flexible schedule. Today, my son is 15, and I work 40 hours a week, but I still like the flexibility.

Women entrepreneurs are typically more capital constrained than their male counterparts. They are less likely to have come from the senior ranks of corporations where they would have enjoyed higher salaries, opportunities to accumulate personal wealth, and multiple business contacts. The *2009 Catalyst Census of Fortune 500 Women Executive Officers and Top Earners* (Catalyst, 2009) revealed that only 13.5 percent of executive officers were women and only 6.3 percent of top earners were women. Catalyst also noted that as of January 2010, only 29 of the Fortune 1000 firms had women chief executive officers. Women, on average, occupied lower corporate ranks with lower salaries and thus fewer opportunities to accumulate personal wealth than men. This can serve as a major constraint on their ability to start and finance new firms.

For women who are capital constrained, starting a home-based business represents a great opportunity to bootstrap. By working out of the home and often using volunteer and free labor and services from other family members, they are able to minimize their expenses while they build their business and start generating revenues. The knight in Chaucer's *Canterbury Tales* advises us to make virtue out of necessity.* Well, that's what these women entrepreneurs do in a very creative way!

Melanie Scheibenpflug owns Connecticut Computer Assistants (www.consultcca.com), which provides computer support and training for businesses. She found that 90 percent of her clients wanted CCA to come to them as opposed to sending employees to the CCA training center/office. Realizing that the firm's office was an unnecessary expense, Melanie recently closed the office and began serving clients from her home. For a firm like this, the office is where the talent is, so Melanie, an expert in her field, acts as "mobile unit."

Many women turn to entrepreneurship as a lifestyle choice. Although financial gain is not unimportant, it is not their primary goal (Still and Walker, 2006; Walker and Webster, 2004). Many of them say, "I want to be my own boss," "I want to do something I really love," or "I need a flexible schedule." For those of us who may have experienced our own share of corporate burnout at one point or another, these goals sound pretty appealing. Women who operate lifestyle businesses often choose to work out of their home because the home is a reflection of their lifestyle. They operate smaller, often one-person firms to avoid the complexities of managing a large organization, and they have minimal needs for space and equipment. The technological revolution has been a boon to these entrepreneurs because they can now work at any time and from any place. One of our entrepreneurial friends, Marilyn Steinmetz of Mutual Service Associates (Marilyn.Steinmetz@lpl.com), is a very successful financial planner. When she originally established her own firm, she worked out of her home, spending part of the year in Connecticut and part in Florida.

Thanks to technology, I can stay connected with my clients and serve them from any location. I have flexibility in terms of both time and place. I love this business, and I love the people I work with!

Even though Marilyn now shares an office in a neighboring town with another financial planner, she continues to use her home as a base.

I still see a good part of my client base in my home. Many do not want to come to Avon, and many more want to see me in the evenings or after work. I have a full office in my home, so I can work from there. With a laptop, I can really work from anywhere.

---

* The exact phrase from Chaucer's Knight's Tale is "And so it is wisdom itself, it seems to me, To make a virtue of simple necessity. . . ."

In many instances, home-based entrepreneurship does not get the attention or respect that it deserves. In light of that, we are using this chapter as a forum to speak out on behalf of home-based entrepreneurship, which, in fact, is smart entrepreneurship for many women because it allows them to achieve the goals that are important to them. It also provides women entrepreneurs with an opportunity to leverage the resources they have access to very effectively.

Another reason home-based businesses deserve our respect is that there are so many of them! Home-based businesses often provide products and services for their communities, thereby contributing to both economic development and quality of life (Walker and Webster, 2004). The U.S. Census Bureau's *2002 Survey of Business Owners* (U.S. Census, 2002) provided data on 16.7 million businesses, of which roughly half were home-based. More recently, *Entrepreneur Magazine* placed the number of income-generating home-based firms at 13.8 million (http://www.entrepreneur.com/sbe/homebased).

Table 5.1 uses data from the U.S. Census to break down home-based firms by gender. It reveals that 49.4 percent of all firms were home-based in 2002. For women-owned firms, however, 56.1 percent were home-based, compared with 47.1 percent of men-owned firms. Thus, women entrepreneurs are more likely to operate a firm out of their home than men. Table 5.1 also reveals that the smaller the firm in terms of total revenues, the greater the likelihood that it will be home-based. For those firms with revenues of less than $5,000 annually, roughly 60 percent were operated out of the home. Interestingly enough, however, almost one-quarter of firms having revenues in the range of $250,000 to $499,999 were also home-based. This reinforces our point that

TABLE 5.1 Comparison of home-based firms by annual revenues and gender

Revenues ($)	*All firms (%)*	*Women-owned (%)*	*Men-owned (%)*
All firms	49.4	56.1	47.1
Less than 5,000	64.7	67.7	61.1
5,000–9,999	62.5	65.0	59.8
10,000–24,999	58.7	59.6	57.6
25,000–49,999	54.5	52.6	55.4
50,000–99,999	49.0	45.0	50.9
100,000–249,999	37.4	32.5	39.1
250,000–499,999	23.4	20.1	24.2
500,000–999,999	14.4	14.1	14.3
1 million or more	5.8	7.2	5.8

Source: U.S. Census. *Survey of Business Owners, 2002.*

in many instances operating a home-based business is a lifestyle choice rather than simply a matter of financial necessity.

In addition to the obvious "psychic" benefits of starting a home-based business, there are financial benefits as well. Most home-based businesses have minimal capital requirements. They do not require a separate office building, vehicles, employees, furniture, large inventories, and so forth. What *do* you need to start a home-based firm? You need a computer and a printer, business cards and a letterhead, an email address, and, ideally, a website. If you add up the costs associated with these, you can see that it doesn't need to be a huge sum of money. For some home-based firms, specialized types of equipment or tools, inventories, licensing requirements, and insurance may be required, but nevertheless, the costs are still much less than they would be if the firm were operated outside of the home. In fact, when we ask most home-based entrepreneurs how they financed their business, the answer we get most frequently is "Oh, I didn't need any money to start." Most do not recognize that by using household resources and space, they are using bootstrapping techniques—one of the most important and widely used of all financing strategies!

Another consideration for entrepreneurs of any type is the issue of "opportunity costs," which are the potential benefits (financial and others) that one might forego by choosing entrepreneurship over paid employment. In other words, are you giving up a salary of, say, $50,000 in order to earn $30,000 as an entrepreneur? In an environment of low unemployment when jobs are plentiful, the question of the opportunity costs associated with entrepreneurship becomes more pressing. In the current environment of economic uncertainty and high unemployment, however, it is less of an issue because some entrepreneurs, and particularly home-based entrepreneurs, may not have attractive employment alternatives.

Further, as some of our case studies illustrate, when we subtract the cost of day care from paid employment, the financial gap between employment and entrepreneurship narrows considerably. Fifty weeks of day care at $300 per week comes to $15,000 per year, so a $50,000 salary suddenly looks more like $35,000. Suddenly that gap isn't so large after all!

• Tips on Starting a Home-Based Business

1. Evaluate your goals. What is most important to you? Is it a flexible schedule, balancing work and family, earnings, stability, career advancement?

2. Evaluate the relative tradeoffs of paid employment versus home-based employment. Will home-based employment meet your financial and other needs?
3. Set boundaries. Have a separate office or work space in the home. Separate "work time" from "family time."
4. Don't isolate. This is easy to do as a home-based entrepreneur. Select key organizations and events, and network consistently and strategically.

In spite of the many benefits and attractions of operating a home-based business, there are some risks. Typically the home-based entrepreneur is "sharing" resources that are also used by other members of the family, such as a recreation room, a vehicle, or a computer. Conflicts may arise about how much of the resource should be available to the business versus how much should be available to the family (Fitzgerald and Winter, 2001). For example, if you use the den for your office, but the den is also where the wide-screen TV is, you will probably have some conflicts during Super Bowl season or the Final Four. The same is true for time. If the entrepreneur works out of her home, other family members may not recognize that she cannot be available 24/7 to meet their needs. She may face constant interruptions and demands that prevent her from focusing on the business.

This brings us to one of our most important recommendations for home-based entrepreneurs: Create some boundaries regarding time and space. Obviously, if the business is to succeed, you need to be able to devote time to it. This doesn't mean that you have to spend every hour of every day working, but it does mean that you need blocks of time to concentrate. Prior research reveals that home-based entrepreneurs devote fewer hours per week to the business than non-home-based entrepreneurs (Walker et al., 2008). This is not surprising in light of the goals of home-based entrepreneurs, but it does mean that the hours they devote to the business must be "quality" hours. In other words, you have to manage your time wisely so that when you are working you can accomplish the things you need to do. Thus, a home-based entrepreneur with children may choose to work during the hours that her children are in school or after they have gone to bed at night. Alternatively, she may use a day care provider just as she would if she worked in an office.

Similarly, any business, small or large, needs an air of professionalism, and this is particularly true of home-based businesses. Along with the business cards and website, if your business involves face-to-face meetings or telephone conversations, you need a quiet and professional space to interact with your customers. Your clients may get annoyed when they call your "business" and hear children arguing and dogs barking in the background (and sometimes in the foreground). Home-based entrepreneurs can create a separate space by allocating a room, attic, basement, or garage to the business. They also need to discuss boundaries for times when they are "working." Although these may not be observed all the time, it's a step in the right direction.

One of the major risks for home-based entrepreneurs is the problem of isolation. Typically a home-based entrepreneur is the only employee in her firm. Because she works out of her home, the people she sees most frequently are other family members rather than professional associates. Many women entrepreneurs have told us, "I just don't have the time!" Although it can be difficult, it is extremely important to establish networks that include mentors, professional advisors, and other key contacts—something that's hard to do if you never leave your house. Although the capital requirements for many home-based firms are minimal, you still need customers to generate revenues, so you need visibility. You also need access to key markets, suppliers, and buyers. In light of this challenge, it is particularly important for home-based entrepreneurs to devote attention to developing their networks and getting out of the "office." They can do so by joining the local Chamber of Commerce, professional and trade associations, and organizations that promote entrepreneurship. When Marilyn Steinmetz, our financial planner, established her firm, she became active in her professional association, the Institute of Certified Financial Planners. Over the years she has held offices in that organization at both the local and national levels, thereby bringing her into contact with other professionals throughout the country. Another strategy that Marilyn used when she started out was to teach adult education classes on financial planning and accept speaking engagements. These activities got her in front of potential clients and helped establish her as an expert and authority in the area of financial planning.

During the early years, my business started out slowly, but by the fifth year it began to grow exponentially. For four years I planted the seeds by establishing myself and working on my networks and relationships. In the fifth year those seeds started sprouting! Today all my new business comes through word of mouth. Existing clients refer new clients. Even after 25 years in this business, I am still growing!

Networking is one of the strategies that Jude Workman (MediaWorks) used very effectively. As a "sole practitioner," Jude does not necessarily have the expertise or capacity to do some assignments on her own. To address that challenge, she developed a network of other advertising and media professionals who could help her out with the bigger assignments. They, in turn, referred clients to Judy and shared assignments with her. This strategy has not only allowed Jude to take on bigger and more complex assignments, but it has also enabled her to keep her costs down because she pays for additional expertise only when she needs it. In talking about her professional network, Jude observes:

We're competitors, but we also help each other out. That way everyone does better, and we can provide superior service to our clients.

One of the types of groups we learned about recently from home-based entrepreneur, author, and professional coach Jane Pollak (www.janepollak.com) is a Mastermind Group. This is a group of six to eight women entrepreneurs who meet once a month to discuss their firms. They don't talk about their children, the great sale at Macy's, or their family vacation to the Grand Canyon; they talk about *business.* At each meeting, the participants share successes and key challenges. They also set goals for the next session, thus providing an element of continuity as well as accountability both to oneself and to the group. The main purpose of Mastermind Groups is to provide support, advice, and education to women entrepreneurs. So as you can see, there are a lot of different ways to develop your networks, but it's your responsibility to get out and do it. You will find that networks are a key resource for your firm.

• Forming a Mastermind Group

The idea for the Mastermind Group was originally developed by Napoleon Hill (2010) in the 1930s. In his book *Think and Grow Rich*, Hill described this theory as "the coordination of knowledge and effort of two or more people, who work toward a definite purpose, in the spirit of harmony." Hill further observed that "no two minds ever come together without thereby creating a third, invisible intangible force, which may be likened to a third mind."

In a Mastermind Group, the agenda belongs to the group, and each person's participation is key. Members give one another feedback, brainstorm new possibilities, and impose a level of accountability that helps women entrepreneurs stay focused (Greenstreet, 2004).

When creating a Mastermind Group, you should identify other participants who have a similar interest, such as starting or operating their own firm. You should also select members who have a passion to achieve their goals and are prepared to make changes and take action based on feedback from the group. Finally, you want members who can be supportive and provide constructive feedback to other members of the group.

Typically a Mastermind Group meets once a month, and the group should be small enough so that all members can share their goals and progress and receive feedback from the group. Thus, a group of five or six members is probably the ideal. Guidelines for starting a Mastermind Group or joining an existing group can be found in *How to Start a For-Profit Mastermind Group* on Karyn Greenstreet's website (www.thesuccessalliance.com).

Financing Strategies of Home-Based Businesses

Let's turn our attention to the financing strategies of home-based firms. As mentioned before, many home-based businesses require minimal amounts of capital to start—$10,000 or less. Typically the entrepreneur provides this funding herself by using either her personal savings or, in some instances, credit cards. Most home-based entrepreneurs use little, if any, business (versus personal) debt or equity (Still and Walker, 2006). This is often a matter of personal choice for the entrepreneur because she does not want the risks associated with debt or the obligations associated with equity. She just wants to keep it simple.

Working out of the home allows the woman entrepreneur to use a variety of bootstrapping techniques to keep down costs, and like Jude Workman at MediaWorks, she will probably contract out work to others when the need arises rather than hiring employees. Marilyn Steinmetz started her financial planning practice with about $2,000. Her source of financing was her husband, who supported her and her family while she was establishing her firm.

Once the firm is "up and running," revenues from the sales of goods and services become the primary source of financing. In light of that, it is important to make sure that those revenues actually materialize. Even though the business is small, it is important to have the necessary systems, controls, and advisors to ensure success. Our media entrepreneur Jude Workman was delighted to secure her first client back in 1994 when she founded her firm. Unfortunately, she never got paid. She learned, the hard way, that she needed to have a signed contract and letter of agreement in hand before she started the work. A handshake and a verbal agreement are not sufficient. Jude also learned that her business depended on cash flow, so she needed to bill her clients on an ongoing basis rather than waiting until the end of the assignment. She offered the following advice:

Don't be afraid to ask for your money. Bill for your work at least monthly—or even biweekly, if you can. Don't let them talk you into waiting for six months to get paid. When you're a small, new firm, they know you don't know very much, and they will try to take advantage of you. Stick to your guns.

Jude also learned that the best customer is the one you already have. She relies heavily on repeat assignments and referrals for new business. To develop those types of longer-term relationships, she has to price her work reasonably and provide superior value.

I want accounts, not projects. With a project, they'll pay you, but you may never hear from them again. With an account, they recognize the value you provide, and they want to maintain that relationship. That means more business for me.

Today, Marilyn Steinmetz's financing comes entirely from revenues from the business. To accommodate the growth of her firm, she has moved out of her home office and now shares an office and office support with another professional.

My expenses are obviously higher now that I have the office, and I spend a ton of money on research and advisory support to improve the quality of information I provide to my clients. I have never had a loan, however, and don't need external financing now. I am able to pay for everything out of revenues.

• Earnings as a Source of Financing

Throughout this book, we will see that one of the major sources of financing for the firm is earnings. That has certainly been the case with Jude Workman of MediaWorks and Marilyn Steinmetz of Mutual Service Associates. Where do earnings come from? Let's take a look at an income statement (Figure 5.1) for the Heavenly Chocolate Company.

Sales	$10,000
Cost of goods sold	5,500
Advertising and marketing expense	1,000
General and administrative expense	500
Depreciation	1,000
Earnings before interest and taxes	2,000
Interest expense	300
Earnings before taxes	1,700
Taxes	560
Net income	$1,140

FIGURE 5.1 Heavenly Chocolate Company income statement, 2010 ($ thousands)

Whereas the balance sheet in Chapter 2 represented a snapshot in time of assets, liabilities, and equity, the income statement summarizes performance over a period of time—in this instance the 12-month period ending December 31, 2010. The two major parts of an income statement are revenues and expenses. Revenues represent what you earn from the sale of your product or service. Expenses are the costs associated with producing and selling those products and services. Net income is what is left over after you subtract expenses from revenues and pay your taxes.

In large, publicly held firms, part of the net income goes out to shareholders in the form of dividends, while the remainder is reinvested in the firm in the form of retained earnings, which appear on the balance sheet. Most entrepreneurial firms are privately held, however, and as such they do not pay dividends, although owners may withdraw funds from the firm for personal use. Alternatively, many entrepreneurs, including those interviewed for this book, reinvest their earnings into the development or growth of their firm. They may invest in research and development to develop a new product or technology, invest in new facilities to increase production or penetrate new geographic territories, or invest in human resources (people) to create an organization or infrastructure to support firm growth.

The women entrepreneurs we interviewed shared a number of strategies for maximizing or accelerating earnings. Here are some of them:

1. Get paid up front. That way you have the cash in hand to work with. This is the strategy that Debbie Godowsky used when she first started Cookies Direct. She asked parents to pay an annual "subscription fee" in order to have cookies shipped to their college student each month.

2. Speed up your collections of accounts receivables. Jude Workman at MediaWorks highly recommends this strategy. A sale doesn't do you any good until the cash is in your hand. Believe it or not, many entrepreneurs are so excited about selling their product or service that they forget to actually collect the money. Set up a system to monitor your receivables, and make sure you collect them in a timely fashion.

3. Bootstrap like a fiend. As we will see throughout this book, many of our entrepreneurs use creative strategies to minimize or eliminate expenses. Kate Meyers of Brown & Meyers started out in a postage stamp–sized office in order to keep expenses down. In time, as the firm became established, she bought a building that would provide room for later growth. Similarly, Melanie Downey started and continues to operate her firm out of her home.

4. Make as many of your expenses as possible variable rather than fixed. Variable expenses are expenses that can be adjusted up or down depending on whether your revenues increase of decrease. Fixed expenses are just what they sound like: They remain constant regardless of where your revenues are (or aren't). If you can make more of your expenses variable rather than fixed, you have more flexibility to adjust to earnings fluctuations. Kate Meyers has mastered this technique by using contract employees to do medical and legal transcriptions.

5. Find ways to minimize salary expenses, particularly during the early stages of the firm. For many companies, the biggest expenses are salaries and benefits. Obviously the firm needs to find a way to bring in the necessary talent and human resources, but high salaries and overly generous benefits can be a major drain on young companies. Many entrepreneurs work without a salary until the firm is "up and running." Marilyn Steinmetz did this when she first started her business. Her husband, who had a full-time job, supported her until her firm

became established. In other instances, entrepreneurs give key employees shares of ownership rather than high salaries. In this way, these key players are able to share in both the risks and the rewards of the new firm.

6. Get yourself an accountant. A study of Australian home-based women entrepreneurs revealed that 81 percent found their accountants to be their most helpful source of professional advice (Still and Walker, 2006). Another study found that firms that used the services of an accountant were significantly more likely to survive and grow than firms that did not (Watson, forthcoming). This same study suggests that an accountant is particularly important for women entrepreneurs, who often have less time for networking due to their need to balance work and family. You can see in Heavenly Chocolate's income statement that taxes take a major bite out of its earnings. In light of that, it is in your interest to find ways to minimize your tax burden. Although profitable firms do have to pay taxes, you don't want to pay any more than you need to. An accountant who has experience in advising small and entrepreneurial firms can be a key resource in helping you to identify strategies that are appropriate for your firm.

These are just a few of the strategies for maximizing and accelerating earnings that we will see in upcoming chapters. The important thing to remember is that for many women entrepreneurs, earnings from the firm are a major source of financing. Therefore, you need to find ways to generate sales, minimize expenses, and bring in the cash as quickly as possible.

Table 5.2 provides data on home-based and non-home-based firms from the Kauffman Firm Survey. It reveals that, on average, home-based firms owned by women were established with roughly one-third of the amount of capital used by non-home-based firms founded by women ($37,037 vs. $107,965). Our interviews suggest that many home-based firms actually start with considerably less! The Kauffman Firm Survey also revealed that women-owned home-based firms were more reliant on the owner's personal sources of financing (40.7 vs. 30.9 percent) and less reliant on both external debt and equity than women-owned firms that were not home-based. For both, however, the dominant sources of financing were owner equity (savings) and outside debt (loans).

Table 5.2 also shows that women-owned home-based firms were established with smaller amounts of capital, on average, than men-owned home-based firms ($37,037 vs. $48,678). In terms of sources of capital, firms

TABLE 5.2 Sources and amounts of start-up capital by home-based status

	Home-based		Not home-based	
	Female	*Male*	*Female*	*Male*
Owner equity	$15,070	$18,806	$ 33,351	$ 53,834
Insider equity	$ 438	$ 832	$ 3,398	$ 3,298
Outsider equity	$ 148	$ 4,273	$ 1,768	$ 46,780
Owner debt	$ 2,373	$ 2,346	$ 5,511	$ 8,360
Insider debt	$ 1,747	$ 2,467	$ 7,974	$ 12,882
Outsider debt	$17,260	$19,954	$ 55,964	$ 90,979
Total financial capital	$37,037	$48,678	$107,965	$216,132
Owner equity	40.7%	38.6%	30.9%	24.9%
Insider equity	1.2%	1.7%	3.1%	1.5%
Outsider equity	0.4%	8.8%	3.6%	21.6%
Owner debt	6.4%	4.0%	5.1%	3.9%
Insider debt	4.7%	5.1%	7.4%	6.0%
Outsider debt	46.6%	41.0%	51.8%	42.1%
Total financial capital	100.0%	100.0%	100.0%	100.0%

Source: Kauffman Firm Survey Microdata.

owned by men were able to raise larger amounts of outsider equity (8.8 vs. 0.4 percent), allowing them to rely less heavily on owner equity and outside debt during the start-up year.

Table 5.3 provides data on the amounts of capital raised by home-based and non-home-based firms in the years following start-up (2005–2008). It shows that home-based firms (both women-owned and men-owned) continued to raise smaller amounts of new capital than firms that were not home-based. Interestingly enough, however, Table 5.3 also reveals that after the start-up year, women- and men-owned home-based firms raised roughly the same amount of new capital each year. They continued to rely on different sources, however, with men raising larger amounts of outsider equity and women contributing larger amounts of owner equity.

These findings from the Kauffman Firm Survey data suggest that after the start-up year, women-owned home-based firms were not necessarily disadvantaged relative to men in terms of the amounts of capital they raised. Both women- and men-owned home-based firms raised considerably less than non-home-based firms, possibly reflecting a lower level of demand. As just noted, home-based firms tend to be smaller and have more modest growth aspirations. Thus, it stands to reason that they would use smaller amounts of capital, regardless of gender.

TABLE 5.3 New financial injections by home-based status, 2005–2008

	Home-based ($)		*Not home-based ($)*	
	Female	*Male*	*Female*	*Male*
2005				
Owner equity	7,089	7,591	12,353	30,883
Insider equity	620	396	250	3,169
Outsider equity	1,106	3,735	14,259	59,959
Owner debt	5,349	2,967	5,092	5,368
Insider debt	3,279	1,692	3,116	10,382
Outsider debt	20,541	26,972	51,710	65,902
Total financial capital	37,982	43,352	86,779	175,663
2006				
Owner equity	7,879	5,507	8,995	23,459
Insider equity	432	297	750	1,326
Outsider equity	1,701	4,076	967	40,574
Owner debt	2,104	3,157	4,303	5,415
Insider debt	920	1,326	3,507	10,541
Outsider debt	29,299	25,473	32,594	118,497
Total financial capital	42,335	39,835	51,116	199,812
2007				
Owner equity	10,226	6,665	7,451	14,822
Insider equity	180	182	1,360	3,222
Outsider equity	235	8,923	3,421	15,574
Owner debt	6,372	2,760	4,939	5,160
Insider debt	86	978	2,260	7,532
Outsider debt	28,868	27,104	37,043	100,726
Total financial capital	45,967	46,612	56,474	147,036
2008				
Owner equity	6,839	5,657	7,352	19,679
Insider equity	92	148	743	1,038
Outsider equity	1,102	4,166	922	10,779
Owner debt	2,286	4,201	7,789	5,413
Insider debt	3,007	4,697	2,548	4,694
Outsider debt	21,947	18,903	49,245	88,606
Total financial capital	35,274	37,772	68,600	130,210

Source: Kauffman Firm Survey Microdata.

Nevertheless, women-owned home-based firms may have been disadvantaged relative to men in terms of the sources of capital they used. Women-owned firms relied heavily on owner-provided equity—that is, their own savings. They also appeared to have good access, on average, to outsider debt when compared to men-owned firms. Women, however, used much smaller amounts of outsider equity. This suggests that women-owned home-based firms, in particular, have less access to networks and contacts that could lead them to outsider equity investors. Alternatively, it may suggest that women are more concerned with maintaining control over their firms than men and are more reluctant to take on outside investors (Watson et al., 2009).

Principles in Action: Wilava

When Melanie Downey gave birth to her first child, her priorities changed. At that time, Melanie had a "to die for" career as director of public relations and B2B marketing for Monster.com. In that capacity, she was instrumental in the growth and success of a company that is one of the largest online employment websites in the world. Both Melanie's daughter, Ava, and son, William, had severe allergies almost from birth. Their symptoms ranged from hives to severe eczema, and even to episodes of anaphylaxis, which can be fatal.

Melanie began researching allergies and skin disorders, and she discovered that many of the chemicals and additives in our food, cosmetics, and baby products consist of carcinogens, hormone disruptors, and skin irritants. Faced with a very personal need and equipped with an entrepreneurial spirit, Melanie decided to attack this problem by creating homemade soaps, lotions, and other products for her children. As word spread through family members, neighbors, and friends, she found herself getting orders from more and more people. In response to this unmet need and demand, her company, Wilava (http://www.wilava.com), named for her children, was founded in April 2009 (*Observer,* Spring 2010).

I make all the products myself in a dedicated room in my house, and 95 percent of my business is done through my website at wilava.com.

Initially, Wilava was established with approximately $3,000 from Melanie's personal savings, and as the business has grown, financing has come from profits. Melanie has not needed or sought external investors as yet. She continues to minimize expenses by hiring contract workers to help fill orders during periods of high demand.

Since I am a sole proprietor, everything falls on my shoulders. Because of my marketing background, I have a lot of connections, and sometimes I go overboard on marketing my products. I am also the production person, however, so I have to keep up with producing and shipping products. Last Christmas I found that I was working about 22 hours a day to try to fill orders. I brought on some short-term contract workers at that time because I am not ready to hire full-time yet.

When asked about the advantages of working from home, Melanie responded:

You have flexibility, not only in terms of days and hours but in terms of the direction of the business and your rate of growth. I could probably grow the business more rapidly, and if I had external investors or partners, they would expect that. This rate of growth works for me and my family right now, however, so I am happy with that.

Melanie's advice to aspiring entrepreneurs is to thoroughly research the industry they are considering *before* they take the jump into entrepreneurship. She actually spent two years planning for her business before starting it. It is also important to identify your target audience and keep them in mind at all times. They are your focal point, and they are where your major source of financing—revenues—will come from. Although Melanie has been advised that she could charge more for her products, her objective is to have her products appeal to a broad range of individuals who can benefit from them. She also wants those individuals to become repeat customers rather than occasional users. She wants her customers to share her passion for her products *and* their results.

Melanie also advises new entrepreneurs to have a long-term vision and a plan:

Have a written plan! Write things down! It will help to guide you and make sure that you don't overlook important aspects of the business. At the same time, be flexible, and revise the plan as often as you need to.

What Have We Learned?

We saw in this chapter that home-based businesses are the dominant type of entrepreneurial venture for women. In fact, home-based firms represent over 50 percent of all women-owned firms. We also saw that just as "one size does not fit all" in general, it does not fit home-based firms in particular. Women-owned home-based firms run the gamut in terms of industries and earnings. As Table 5.1 revealed, 7.2 percent of women-owned firms with revenues in excess of $1 million are home-based. In most instances, the stereotype that women start home-based businesses to do cute little craftsy things on the side just doesn't hold. Although some women entrepreneurs may, in fact, be doing cute little craftsy things, in most instances they are doing them because they want to generate an income that will support or help to support their families. Thus, home-based entrepreneurs have a strong economic motivation; the business is not just a hobby to fill their time.

We discussed how operating a home-based firm can help to reduce some of the financial risks associated with entrepreneurship. By operating the business out of the home, the entrepreneur eliminates the need to purchase or rent space elsewhere, thereby cutting down considerably on fixed costs. Similarly, other personal resources such as space, furniture, computers, and phones can also be used for the business in order to keep a lid on expenses. As any undergraduate finance major knows, there are two ways to increase company profits: increase revenues and decrease expenses. Operating a home-based business allows entrepreneurs to do the latter by using a variety of smart bootstrapping techniques.

Finally, we saw that operating a home-based business can provide women with a way to balance the demands of work and family. Many home-based entrepreneurs value the flexibility associated with working out of the home. This allows them to juggle family demands and child care while also devoting time to the business and scheduling around the needs of various constituencies. Families are stressful, and running a business is stressful, but many women entrepreneurs feel that the stress level is lower if they can at least do both in the same place!

What Does All This Mean for Me?

The majority of home-based businesses are relatively small, so their capital requirements are modest. In most instances, the home-based entrepreneurs we talked to started the business with their own savings and then financed it with a combination of revenues and bank loans, typically guaranteed by personal assets. The good news is that you often don't need a lot of money to start a home-based business, but the not-so-good news is that you do need *some*. Therefore, it is important to have savings or friends and family who will invest in you. You may also want to have the option of raising debt through personal loans, a home equity loan, or credit cards. In other words, you want to have good credit in order to be able to raise debt if you need it. Think of that as your safety net!

Another implication of having a home-based business is that you need to allocate space in your home. Although some people claim they run the business from the kitchen table or out of their car, that's probably not ideal. It is better to have a separate room where you can have an office or workroom, equipment, some degree of quiet, and, if necessary, a professional environment where you can meet with clients or customers. Although not a direct cost, use of space in the home does represent an "opportunity cost" because it is space that cannot be used for other purposes. If the home office needs to be equipped with a desk, computer, printer, and phone, those all represent additional costs as well, since you may not want your three-year-old fooling around with the printer or your teenage daughter using up all the minutes on your family calling plan.

One thing that home-based entrepreneurs have to guard against is the danger of professional isolation. It is easy when you are working out of your home to just stay there. You find yourself making excuses to avoid professional events or networking opportunities. "I couldn't get a sitter." "It would have meant driving into the city during rush hour." "My book club is coming that night." There are a billion different excuses. The point is, however, that as a home-based entrepreneur, networking and establishing connections are even more important for you. Activities of this type will lead you to customers who, in turn, provide revenues, your most important source of capital. Your networks can also lead you to other sources of capital or provide insights on ways to improve your skills as an entrepreneur. Get out! Network systematically, and learn to view it as an investment in your business and yourself.

Another takeaway that we gleaned from our conversations with home-based entrepreneurs is that you are the revenue generator. Therefore, it is important for you to stay healthy. There are many benefits to working from home, but there are challenges as well. You need to find a way to balance business and family demands that works for you. Maybe you do most of your work when the kids are in school or in bed at night. Maybe you get somebody in to clean the house so you don't go nuts trying to keep the bathroom immaculate. Maybe you schedule specific blocks of "work time" and "family time" that are sacred, no matter what. The bottom line is, do what it takes to make it work for *you*. Along the same lines, "small" and "home-based" do not equate to getting sloppy in your business practices. According to Melanie Scheibenpflug of Connecticut Computer Assistants, you have to be "super organized" to manage both a family and a business.

There will be times when you go 24/7, but you also need to know when to give yourself a break or you'll go crazy!

Public Policy Implications

Our discussion of home-based businesses gives rise to some fairly obvious public policy measures. We have noted the large number of women-owned home-based firms, and we have also discussed that most are driven by an economic motive: the need or desire to generate earnings that will benefit the entrepreneur or her family. In this sense, home-based entrepreneurship contributes to the greater economic good by enhancing the ability of households and businesses to purchase goods and services. In light of that, it makes sense, from a public policy perspective, to support the establishment and well-being of home-based firms.

We also noted that many home-based firms have minimal capital requirements—often less than $10,000. One measure that could benefit home-based entrepreneurs would be microloans to help firms launch. Microloans are just what they sound like: small loans typically provided by government or nongovernment agencies. Another source for microloans is Prosper.com, a web-based peer-to-peer lending marketplace. These loans can subsequently be repaid out of operating earnings once the firm is up and running.

• Prosper.com

The Prosper Loans Marketplace (www.prosper.com) is a web-based peer-to-peer lending marketplace that brings together borrowers and lenders (Bruett, 2007). The borrower determines the amount she wants to borrow within a range of $1,000 to $25,000 and the maximum interest rate she is willing to pay. Lenders then bid on the loan using an online auction platform. Lenders may bid on an entire loan, or they may bid on smaller pieces of multiple loans to spread their risk. Prosper provides lenders with credit information on the borrower, as well as a space for borrowers to tell their story and describe their needs. This "personalizes" the lending process for potential lenders. Once the auction concludes, Prosper handles the funding and servicing of the loan on behalf of the matched borrowers and lenders. To date, Prosper has helped small borrowers raise over $100 million.

A second public policy measure would be incentives to encourage more individuals to establish home-based businesses. As just noted, this may be a particularly attractive alternative in the current environment of high unemployment. In its *Index of Entrepreneurial Activity*, the Kauffman Foundation found that from 2007 to 2010, as employer business creation trended down, the rate of entrepreneurial activity trended up (Fairlie, 2011). They interpreted these opposing trends as a sign that more individuals are turning to necessity-based entrepreneurship in a still challenging job market. Measures to encourage home-based entrepreneurs could include an expansion of the list of deductible items for home-based firms, as well as tax rate changes or exemptions for home-based business owners. These measures could represent comparatively low-cost ways of getting people back to work and enabling them to begin generating income.

A third public policy measure that would benefit home-based entrepreneurs would be further development of community-based training or educational programs that help new home-based entrepreneurs learn the basics of running a business. Financial topics could include financial record keeping and reporting, strategies for managing cash flows, and information on low-cost and no-cost sources of assistance. Such programs could be sponsored through area Chambers of Commerce, adult education programs, or local chapters of SCORE (Service Corps of Retired Executives).

In light of the importance of financial literacy for entrepreneurs and their need to learn how to prepare and manage financial statements, a fourth public policy measure would be to provide some type of subsidy or funding to pay for their first two or three sessions with an accountant. As we said, an accountant can serve as a key member of the entrepreneur's management team by providing training, expertise, and contacts. This is particularly important for women entrepreneurs who lack either skills or confidence in the area of financial management.

A final public policy implication is the importance of finding ways to engage home-based entrepreneurs with the larger community through networking. We discussed the risk of isolation for entrepreneurs who work out of their homes, particularly those who also balance the demands of work and family. It is important for these entrepreneurs to engage in a larger sense in order to make valuable contacts, identify new customers, and add to their knowledge and skills. In our highly networked age, some of this can be done electronically through sites such as Facebook or LinkedIn. Wikis and blogs by and for entrepreneurs are also available.

We are old-fashioned enough, however, to believe there is no substitute for face-to-face contact. The same organizations just mentioned could schedule networking and informational events specifically to target home-based entrepreneurs and their needs. Ideally these would be offered at a variety of times to accommodate different schedules—not just "after hours" when small children need to be fed. Alternatively, child care could be available to ensure that home-based entrepreneurs can attend. Home-based entrepreneurs are an important component of their local communities—as citizens, as taxpayers, as consumers of local services, and as providers of goods and services. As such, it is in communities' interests to help these entrepreneurs find ways to launch and prosper. Remember: A rising tide lifts all boats.

ALL IN THE FAMILY

One for All and All for One

Alexander Tolstoy said, "Happy families are all alike."* The same, however, cannot be said of family-owned businesses. They run the full gamut of size, industry, products, services, and markets. By definition, a family-owned firm is one that is owned and operated by two or more members of the same family, sometimes a husband and wife or a parent and child. We often have a tendency to underestimate the importance of family-owned firms and lump them together with other small, low-growth firms. In fact, however, family-owned firms include some of the largest firms in this country. These firms include household names like Walmart, Ford Motors, L.L. Bean, Estee Lauder, and Anheuser-Busch. In fact, over 30 percent of the firms in the Standard & Poor's 500 are family-owned (Anderson and Reeb, 2003). Other family-owned firms are small and locally based, providing products and services to their communities. They include restaurants, nurseries, car dealerships, and a vast array of service and retail establishments. Beyond their economic contributions, family business owners are often deeply involved in their communities. They provide services on Chambers of Commerce, school boards, and other organizations, and sponsor softball teams, soccer leagues, fund-raisers, and the like.

In a sense, family-owned businesses represent the web and fabric of their communities; their firms and civic activities are interwoven into the well-

---

* The full quote, which is the first line in Tolstoy's classic *Anna Karenina*, is "Happy families are all alike; every unhappy family is unhappy in its own way."

being of their neighborhoods. Not surprisingly, given their numbers, family-owned firms also provide economic and career opportunities for women as well. One study estimates that 34 percent of all family-owned firms expect the next CEO to be a woman, and 52 percent of family-owned firms hire at least one female family member full time (*American Family Business Survey*, 2003).

We also find family-owned firms fascinating and worthy of attention because their motivations are even more complex and varied than is the case for entrepreneurial firms in general. That's just another reason why we felt it was important to include them in this book. Like many of the entrepreneurs in this book, family-based entrepreneurs often want independence and the opportunity to do something they love. Not surprisingly, they may also typically strive for some level of economic success in terms of size, revenues, and profits. Beyond that, however, family-owned firms have an entire range of motivations that do not necessarily come into play for other types of entrepreneurial ventures, and these motivations shape their financial strategies.

One important motivation for family-owned firms, by definition, is the desire to work with other members of the family. Whereas most families may see one another for only a few hours a day, family businesses provide an opportunity for family members to spend more time together and to share in mutual successes. Thus, the family business represents shared goals and a shared commitment. Family-based entrepreneurs also have a common history as well as a common understanding; they know the unwritten rules that form a basis for the firm. In other words, it's not necessary to spell out the firm's basic values for managers and employees. They are the values you grew up with or the values you taught your children. This unique feature of family-based firms creates a level of trust and commitment that goes beyond what one might encounter in a "typical" firm. It is one of the most important advantages of a family-owned firm.

A second motivation for family-owned firms is somewhat more economically based and less values based. It is to provide employment and a certain quality of life for the entrepreneur and for other members of her family. This is also a unique characteristic of family-owned firms because it means the entrepreneur must not only create and sustain a job for herself but do it for others as well. In fact, this goal may be more important than other more financially oriented goals, leading family-based firms to employ multiple generations and multiple members of the family and extended family. Having a family-based business can shield family members from economic ups and downs that could result in layoffs and downsizing. It can also provide employment for family members such as grandparents and teens who might experience difficulty in today's highly competitive job market.

A third important motivation for family-owned firms is to create a legacy for current and future generations (Kelly et al., 2000). Whereas some individuals seek to leave a legacy of wealth, family entrepreneurs often seek to leave a legacy of ongoing entrepreneurial opportunity by providing jobs and income for future generations. In this sense, family-based entrepreneurs have a long-term vision, and they are less likely to be preoccupied with short-term results and profits. Family-owned firms also have important links with their communities and often have a desire to leave a legacy of "good works" that will carry the family's good name into future generations.

• Tips on Running a Family Business

1. Someone has to be in charge. Decide who will hold key roles such as president, chief financial officer, and chairman of the board.
2. Have written job descriptions for different roles with clearly articulated performance expectations.
3. Have a written business plan. This can serve as a "road map" for the firm that helps to define current and future priorities.
4. Create opportunities for nonfamily managers and employees who can provide needed skills.
5. Deal with nonperforming employees—both family and nonfamily—fairly and promptly.
6. Develop and communicate a succession plan so different family members know and can prepare for their roles going forward.

Several researchers contend that the unique characteristics of family-owned businesses create opportunities for competitive advantage and superior performance (Anderson and Reeb, 2003; Habbershon and Williams, 1999). One of the primary advantages of family-owned firms is a higher level of trust and commitment. This creates a deeper loyalty combined with a willingness to work toward shared goals. Another advantage of family-based businesses is that they are often more flexible than non-family-based firms. This is particularly important for women entrepreneurs who need to balance the demands of home and family. A family-based business has a greater understanding of and appreciation for the needs of the family as well as for those of the business. Family members are more willing to pitch in and help one another out in a variety of ways because of their shared goals and commitment to the well-being of the firm and to one another.

A number of researchers have pointed out that family-based firms do not have to invest the time and energy in "corporate governance" that non-family-based firms do (Randoy and Goel, 2003). Corporate governance means incorporating systems and controls to ensure that the firm's paid managers act in the best interests of the shareholders rather than "ripping off" the firm for their own purposes. Common examples of corporate governance include having frequent meetings of a Board of Directors that is composed of independent outsiders, requiring audited financial statements and requirements for disclosure and transparency, and developing an internal system of checks and balances to prevent and detect fraud and mismanagement. When the managers and the owners are the same people, however, the need for such controls is less pressing. Stated simply, it is less likely that family members will have to spend time and energy watching other managers and employees to make sure they act in the best interests of the firm. One study (Anderson and Reeb, 2003) found that the beneficial impacts of family ownership on performance extend beyond firms in which the family member is both owner and manager to include those firms where family members may not manage the firm on a day-to-day basis but continue to have an ownership interest. The involvement of these family members as shareholders and as members of the Board of Directors mitigates "managerial opportunism" and provides a valuable role in firm oversight.

Perhaps one of the greatest advantages of a family-based business is the lifestyle it provides to members of the family. They have the opportunity to integrate their business life with their family life in a way that is very satisfying to them. The values that form the basis of their family are the same values that form the basis of their firms. This consistency helps to alleviate many of the work/home conflicts and frustrations experienced by individuals who work for others. In addition, family-based entrepreneurs often assume leadership roles in their communities. This provides a level of recognition and appreciation, as well as the opportunity to shape the direction, programs, and policies of their community. In their article "Work-Family Conflict: A Study of

American and Australian Family Businesses," Smyrnios and colleagues (2003) said the following:

> A substantial portion of family business owners report experiencing a range of positive feelings in relation to their business. Owners regard their enterprises as challenging, valuable, and providing them with a sense of accomplishment.

In keeping with this commitment to the larger community, family-based entrepreneurs are very concerned about the reputation of the firm and its relations with suppliers, customers, financing sources, and other stakeholders. The motivation to create and maintain a positive reputation for current and future generations makes it less likely that managers will act imprudently.

Principles in Action: Pioneer Telephone

When Sue Bouchard and her husband Peter established their company Pioneer Telephone (www.PioneerTelephone.com) in 1989, they knew they wanted to be able to realize multiple goals. First, they wanted to combine work and family, and in order to do so, they knew they needed careers that would allow for flexibility in scheduling. They were also fascinated by the telecommunications industry and anticipated changes and developments in that field that would pave the way for entrepreneurial opportunities. Another consideration was the longer-term viability of the industry they selected. The Bouchards believed that telecom would be relatively recession-proof because people would always need phone service. Thus, their firm, if successful, would provide a sufficient income to help them raise and educate their family.

Initially, Sue and Peter established Pioneer Telephone, based in South Portland, Maine, as a pay phone company. At the time, both had full-time jobs, Sue in banking and Peter in sales, so they worked on the business at night and on weekends out of their home. They financed the launch of their firm with approximately $2,500 from cash advances on credit cards. As the business grew, Sue and Peter left their jobs to work for the firm full-time. According to Sue:

I knew I was taking a big step and a big risk in leaving a well-paying full-time job to start a new firm, but it's the best thing I ever did.

Over time, Pioneer evolved into a long-distance phone company. In that capacity, the Bouchards purchase service from a variety of long-distance carriers and then match the needs of their customers to the most cost-effective plan for service. Pioneer's customer base includes a mix of both residential and business customers, and today they have customers in every state.

In operating their firm, Sue and Peter realized that they had different skills and interests. Peter's background in sales equipped him to deal with the sales and marketing side of the business. Sue's background in banking allowed her to develop and manage the finance and human resources side of the firm. One of the things they had to learn as an entrepreneurial couple was to stay out of each other's "space." Peter became the expert in his areas of responsibility and Sue in hers; they learned not to interfere or second-guess each other. In describing the blend of work and family, Sue stated:

My children grew up in the business. When I came to work in my office, they had their "office" next door with their toys and books. As they got older and started school, I would work the hours that they were in school and then be with them after school. That might mean I also worked from 9 to midnight as well, but having my own firm gave me the flexibility to do that.

The Bouchards' emphasis on importance of family has shaped the culture of their firm. Sue views her employees as an extension of her family. Each day when she comes in, she takes the time to say hello to each employee. Raffles, company outings, and a newsletter help to keep employees informed and connected to the firm and one another. According to Sue:

The human side of the business is so important. It's all about relationships and how you treat people. You have to know when to be tough, but you also have to show compassion when the circumstances require it.

Over the years, the Bouchards have relied on a variety of informal and formal financing sources. Initially, all of their profits went back into the business to help finance its start-up and growth. They knew that they were not "bankable" at that point because the company was too new and did not have a track record of profitability.

As the firm became larger and more profitable, Sue established a relationship with a local branch of a large, national bank. She started out by taking small loans to build a track record of repayment and good credit. This evolved into securing larger loans, a line of credit, a commercial mortgage for their building, and leasing. Sue stresses the importance of developing a banking relationship over time:

It is really important to get to know your banker and to get her to know you. That doesn't happen overnight. I really worked on developing that relationship, so when I needed credit, I would be able to get it. Today, I could probably pick up the phone and be approved for a major loan within 48 hours. That's because they know me, they know my business, and I have a history with them.

In recent years Pioneer Telephone made two company acquisitions, both financed with private placements of debt. Sue explained that when these opportunities emerged, Pioneer had to act quickly, and it was more expeditious to arrange private debt than to pursue other sources of financing. Subsequent to the acquisitions, however, Pioneer refinanced the private debt with loans from its bank at a lower interest rate.

The Bouchards have not used any external sources of equity to finance their firm, and that has been a deliberate choice. They want to retain ownership and keep the company private in order to maintain the kind of culture and reputation for service they have developed over the years.

Today, Pioneer Telephone generates approximately $20 million in revenues and has almost 400,000 customers nationwide. Pioneer has 34 full-time employees and an additional 50 sales agents who work on commission. It was selected as one of the "Best Places to Work in Maine" for three consecutive years. Pioneer is also continuing its tradition of innovation in order to adapt to a changing marketplace. The Bouchards are currently rolling out local phone service, starting with a test in several states.

Sue emphasizes the importance of networks and contacts in developing and growing the firm. She participates in industry trade shows, business roundtables and forums, and, more recently, a network of women entrepreneurs called the Echelon Circles. The purpose of this group is to allow women entrepreneurs to share methods and business practices, as well as to give and receive advice from their peers.

In discussing the benefits of having her own firm, Sue notes that she and Peter have achieved both financial independence and job security. She stresses the importance of flexibility in scheduling, even today, since her children, now teenagers, are still at home. Another reward of entrepreneurship has been watching the company and its employees grow, develop their skills and careers, and, in some instances, move on to new opportunities themselves. For the Bouchards, the firm has become a reflection of their priorities and values. In a recent interview, Sue reflected:

They always say that women can't have it all: career, marriage, and a family. I want other women to know that they can have it all, and starting your own firm like we did is a way to do it. Once we started down this road, I never looked back and I have never regretted it!

Prior researchers have also noted performance and financial advantages in family-based firms. Family members often supply a large portion of start-up capital. They may also provide additional injections of new capital, while also reinvesting a substantial portion of earnings. Some have referred to family-provided capital as "patient capital" because it is long term in nature and does not necessarily expect or demand an immediate return (Habbershon and Williams, 1999). Consistent with this level of "patience," family-based entrepreneurs are more willing to invest in capital projects or research and development because one of their primary motivations is to create a strong and thriving firm for future generations. Thus, they are less concerned with short-term performance and results (McConaughy and Phillips, 1999).

In spite of their many benefits and attractions, operating a family-owned business has its risks. The most significant of these is the lack of diversification for the entrepreneur and for other members of the family. In other words, multiple family members depend on the firm for their livelihood, and multiple family members may have the bulk of their wealth tied up in the business. Because of this, family-owned firms may tend to be more risk averse in their financial strategies and in their growth aspirations. Similarly, they may prefer moderate rather than rapid growth in order to maintain control. In keeping with a higher level of risk aversion, they prefer internal rather than external sources of capital to avoid the risks associated with excessive levels of debt that can lead to bankruptcy.

Another risk associated with family-owned firms is the need or desire to employ family members who may not have the necessary skill set for their designated roles. As just noted, one of the major motivations for family entrepreneurs is to provide jobs for other family members. This can sometimes lead to managerial weaknesses and difficulties in attracting outside talent. If outsiders perceive that all the best jobs go to family members and that there are no avenues for their own advancement in the firm, they may be reluctant to sign on. Correspondingly, it is very difficult for family entrepreneurs to "fire" or demote a family member due to unsatisfactory performance on the job. It's tough enough firing someone in a nonfamily business, so you can probably imagine what it's like to fire your favorite nephew. It could make for some difficult Thanksgiving dinners!

There is also the risk of succession for family-owned firms. Statistics published by the Family Firm Institute (www.ffi.org) indicated that only 30 percent of family firms survive into the second generation, and only 12 percent survive into the third. Often family entrepreneurs start a firm with the intention of leaving a legacy to their children and grandchildren. Their goal is not necessarily to enjoy substantial levels of wealth in their lifetimes but rather to create and sustain a firm that can then be passed on. What happens, however, if no one in the younger generation wants to run the business? Alternatively, what happens if someone does want to run the business but has very different goals from those of the founding entrepreneur? These issues create challenges that may necessitate selling, liquidating, or repositioning the firm, all of which have dramatic consequences for both the entrepreneur and family members.

Linked with the issue of succession is the issue of control. Founding entrepreneurs often have a difficult time delegating responsibility and passing the reins of control to their daughters and sons. They have worked so hard to launch and build up the firm, and they are familiar with its operations down to the smallest detail. It's hard to let the next generation of management make its own set of decisions and mistakes. A big part of succession planning for family-based firms involves helping the founding entrepreneur determine when and how to share authority, control, and decision making.

Finally, another risk for family-based entrepreneurs, and a serious one, is that if the business gets into trouble, the family may, too. Emotions and expectations run high in family-based firms, and disappointments in the firm can lead to strains in the family as well. Unfortunately, there is no shortage of unhappy stories about family-based firms that have resulted in divorce or siblings who no longer speak to each other. It happens. Experts say that one of the best ways to avoid these types of disappointments is to have a business plan *and* a succession plan and to communicate expectations and the condition of the firm on a regular basis.

Financing Strategies of Family-Owned Firms

As is the case for our other types of entrepreneurs, the motivations for family-based entrepreneurs have an impact on the types of financial strategies they use. These motivations include the desire to employ multiple family members and, often, to leave a healthy firm as a legacy to subsequent generations. Both of these motivations lead family-based entrepreneurs to embrace relatively conservative financing strategies. The last thing a family-based entrepreneur wants to do is to increase the riskiness of the firm by taking on excessive levels of debt (Mishra and McConaughy, 1999). Similarly, family-based entrepreneurs do not want to share control with outside equity investors who might change the direction of the firm or replace family members with outsider employees or managers. This strong desire for control prompts family-based entrepreneurs to rely more heavily on debt and on internally rather than externally generated sources of equity (Wu et al., 2007). Stated simply, family-based entrepreneurs in general prefer to borrow or to invest more of their own money rather than opening the firm up to additional outside equity investors who would also have a role in ownership and control (Mishra and McConaughy, 1999).

To avoid the need for sharing control with external providers of equity, family-based entrepreneurs rely heavily on bootstrapping techniques and internally generated funds. Bootstrapping techniques take a variety of forms, including extra hours (at low cost or no cost) put in by family members. Similarly, family members may be more flexible in their willingness to perform tasks that do not strictly fall under their job description. For example, if someone needs to wait on customers for a few hours, it gets done. If someone needs to work on a holiday, they make themselves available. On a recent trip to have a car serviced, the owner of a very large and successful family-owned car dealership was actually driving the shuttle van that day. In other words, you do what it takes to get the job done!

A second major source of internal financing for family-based firms is reinvested earnings. Because family-based entrepreneurs often wish to leave a legacy, they are less concerned with current wealth than with building something for the future. Thus, they are willing to accept relatively modest salaries and other forms of current income in order to invest a large chunk of earnings back into the firm. Consistent with this desire, family firms also tend to avoid the "trappings" of power, such as lavish spending accounts, fancy offices, and other types of expenses that would eat into earnings available for reinvestment.

By reinvesting earnings, family-based entrepreneurs are able to address two other motivations: the desire to minimize risk and the desire to maintain control. If they provide the bulk of financing for the firm from internal sources, they do not need to rely on external debt that could increase the risk of failure or external equity that could dilute ownership and control. In their article "Financial Structure of the Family Business," Lopez-Gracia and Sanchez-Andujar (2007) state the following:

> These findings . . . reaffirm that family firms mainly base their financial policies on internally generated resources, passing up growth if necessary, as their first financing objective is not to lose control of the business.

A third major source of financing for family-owned firms is debt, often secured through relationships with local banks. Although debt does create obligations to firm outsiders, debt holders, unlike equity holders, are not "owners." When you pay off the loan, the debt holder goes away. From the perspective of acquiring external debt, the web of relationships and contacts provided by various family members can serve as a competitive advantage. Some researchers contend, however, that women family business owners still rely more heavily on noninstitutional lenders such as family and friends rather than banks to finance their firms (Haynes et al., 2000). Another study found that family-owned firms with high involvement by women family members used significantly more internal equity to finance their firms than firms with low involvement by women family members (Sonfield and Lussier, 2004). Taken together, the results of these two studies suggest that women owners are more risk averse than men and more inclined to use financing from internal or personal sources. Thus, it appears that women owners are more concerned than men owners about putting either the firm or the family at risk by using external debt that could increase the likelihood of bankruptcy.

The Kauffman Firm Survey began to ask about family ownership in 2008, so no data are available on family-owned firms that did not survive until 2008. However, there are still some things we can learn, given the striking differences in new capital injections by gender for these surviving firms (Table 6.1). By definition, we restrict family-owned businesses to firms that have two or more owners. About 28 percent of surviving businesses owned by women had more than one owner, compared with about 32 percent of businesses owned by men. Of multi-owner firms, 42 percent of those owned by women were considered family-owned, compared with 36 percent of those owned by men. Thus, women-owned firms were more likely to be family-owned than men-owned firms.

TABLE 6.1 New financial injections by family business status, 2008

	Female	*Male*
Multi-owner firms (%)	28	32
Family-owned	42	36
Team-family-owned ($)		
Owner equity	17,420	29,608
Insider equity	2,355	1,022
Outsider equity	—	3,014
Owner debt	10,424	5,316
Insider debt	2,787	3,943
Outsider debt	21,078	97,090
Total financial capital	54,064	139,993
Team-not family-owned ($)		
Owner equity	4,520	20,439
Insider equity	80	2,084
Outsider equity	6,081	35,157
Owner debt	5,391	7,435
Insider debt	1,284	13,761
Outsider debt	111,797	106,210
Total financial capital	129,153	185,086

Source: Kauffman Firm Survey Microdata, 2008.

As we saw in previous chapters, Table 6.1 shows that women-owned firms had much smaller levels of new financial injections compared to men. The differences were smaller, however, between the multi-owner firms that were not family-owned than between those that were. In fact, multi-owner firms that were family-owned and had a female primary owner invested about $54,000 in new financial capital in 2008, compared with $140,000 for those that had a primary owner who was male. Thus, male family business owners invested almost three times as much additional financial capital in 2008 as female owners. For multi-owner firms that were not family-owned, those with a female primary owner had new financial capital injections of nearly $130,000, compared with $185,000 for those with a male primary owner. This represents a substantially smaller gap between new investments by women and men owners than was the case for family-owned firms.

What Have We Learned?

We saw in this chapter that a substantial percentage of firms in the United States are, in fact, family-owned. These firms include not only thousands of small and entrepreneurial firms but many large and established firms that are household names. We also saw that one of the advantages of family-owned firms is that their family members have a special "chemistry" in the form of shared trust and understanding. They are united not only by economic goals such as growth and profits but also by more personal goals such as the ability to spend time with family members, opportunities to employ family members, and a desire to pass on a legacy to subsequent generations. Further, family-owned firms play an important economic and civic role in their local communities. They provide employment, pay taxes to maintain municipal services, support local organizations and causes, and often take roles as civic leaders.

We noted that family-owned firms have fairly unique financial characteristics and strategies. Because family-based entrepreneurs often try to build a firm that will last into future generations, they are less likely to focus on short-term profits and performance. Similarly, they often prefer moderate rather than rapid growth to minimize risks. In terms of sources of capital, family members are a major source of both start-up and follow-on capital. Family-based entrepreneurs also reinvest a substantial portion of earnings into the business, consistent with their longer-term vision for the firm. Bootstrapping is an important financial strategy for family-owned firms because family members are willing to "pitch in" and help other members of the family.

Another consideration for family-owned firms is the importance of maintaining ownership and control. This motivation leads family-based entrepreneurs to avoid external sources of equity in particular. Family-based entrepreneurs do not want to share control with "outsiders" who could have an impact on the direction or culture of the firm. We saw this clearly in our interview with Sue Bouchard at Pioneer Telephone. She and her husband were able to grow their firm fairly dramatically, but they found ways to do so without bringing in additional equity investors.

In reviewing the data on family-owned firms from the Kauffman Firm Survey, we saw that a higher percentage of women characterize their firms as "family-owned" than men do (42 vs. 36 percent). We also learned that women family-owned entrepreneurs invested substantially lower amounts of capital in their firms than men family-owned entrepreneurs and than women non-family entrepreneurs. In particular, women family-owned entrepreneurs relied heavily on owner equity as a source of financing. Correspondingly, they used almost no external equity and lower amounts of external debt than non-family-based entrepreneurs. This finding is consistent with a preference for small to moderate size and growth combined with a desire to minimize risk and maintain control.

What Does All This Mean for Me?

The phrase that resonates for us is Sue Bouchard's comment *"I want women to know that they can have it all. . . ."* Sue is a powerful example of a very successful entrepreneur who found a way to combine entrepreneurship and family in a way that is rewarding for her personally as well as financially. Sue and Peter identified the goals that were important to them at the outset, and they found ways to make it work. In this sense, your takeaway from this chapter is that family-based entrepreneurship can provide many benefits in the form of personal growth, the ability to combine work and family, financial success, and civic leadership. It represents an opportunity to work with people you trust and love toward a set of shared goals and vision for both the firm and the family.

At the same time, we cannot ignore some of the risks associated with family-based entrepreneurship. Family entrepreneurs are highly undiversified in their financial holdings. They have not only invested capital in the firm, but they are also dependent on it for their income and the income of other family members. A second risk is the danger of relying too heavily on family members and not bringing in outside managers and employees with talents and skills that are needed. Finally, it is not uncommon for family emotions and rivalries to spill over into the business. When that happens, it can be highly detrimental for both the family and the firm.

From the standpoint of financial strategy, we have seen that family-based entrepreneurs are often motivated by a desire to minimize risk and maintain control. This is particularly true for women-owned family firms who rely much more heavily on insider rather than external sources of financing. If one of your goals is to avoid sharing control with outside equity holders, you, like the Bouchards, will have to be very creative in finding ways to secure needed financial resources. As we saw in the case of Pioneer Telephone, the Bouchards started out with credit card debt and bootstrapping the new firm from home while they maintained their full-time jobs. As the firm grew, they established a strong relationship with a bank, leading to both short- and long-term loans. Finally, when attractive acquisition opportunities emerged, they used private placements of debt that were subsequently refinanced at a lower interest rate. Last, but not least, they have consistently reinvested earnings to finance the growth of the firm. As with other entrepreneurs we have encountered in this book, Sue Bouchard has been able to leverage her human capital in the form of education and a background in the banking industry, as well as her social capital in the form of relationship banking and using industry contacts to secure financial capital. She and Peter have also relied on the reputation, reliability, and performance of their firm to develop and strengthen key relationships that have opened the door to financial capital. To summarize, one of your takeaways from their story is that relationships matter, reliability matters, and performance matters.

Public Policy Implications

As we saw in this chapter, family-owned firms are vitally important to the U.S. economy, not only because of their number but also because of their contributions to the gross domestic product and employment. Nevertheless, the majority of family-owned firms do not survive into the next generation, let alone longer. In light of that, one public policy initiative would be to explore strategies for increasing the survival rate of family-owned firms. This could include training programs on how to develop a succession plan and how to find and develop talented nonfamily members in the event that no second-generation family members want or are qualified to lead the firm. In conjunction with this, family firm owners would benefit from learning how to fairly share company ownership, control, and returns between family members and outsiders who are brought into key leadership positions.

Since so many family-owned firms exist today, tax policies—and, more specifically, both individual and corporate income tax rates and estate taxes—obviously have an impact. High income tax rates discourage entrepreneurial activity because entrepreneurs are allowed to retain less of the wealth they create. The "tax the rich" debates raging in many states and at the national level have the potential to negatively affect the owners of many smaller family firms, since these firms often include firm earnings with personal earnings when filing their taxes (*Wall Street Journal,* March 26–27, 2011). Correspondingly, high estate taxes make it less likely that family-owned firms will be passed on to subsequent generations. If the firm ends with the death of the founding entrepreneur, jobs and future tax revenues will end with it. In light of that, it makes sense to find ways to sustain and strengthen family-owned firms.

From the standpoint of women entrepreneurs, family-based entrepreneurship can be a way to achieve financial success, create a culture consistent with the values of the entrepreneur, and balance the dual roles of work and family, as shown by entrepreneur Sue Bouchard. Family-based entrepreneurs are more likely to understand the importance of family and to incorporate this understanding into the culture of their firms. Similarly, family entrepreneurs are more willing to help one another out in order to fulfill both business and family responsibilities. This flexibility and family support may be particularly important for women entrepreneurs with children. In our current highly competitive environment, many firms are focusing on productivity improvements to increase earnings. From an employee's perspective, this typically means more work, more hours, and less flexibility. Family-based entrepreneurship may offer an alternative path for women entrepreneurs seeking a way to balance financial and family needs and goals.

THE RACE IS TO THE SWIFT

Financing High-Growth Firms

As we saw in previous chapters, women traditionally start relatively small, low-growth firms in the service and retail sectors. Often these firms are based in the home, which allows the entrepreneur to balance the demands of work and family. More recently, however, we have seen an increasing number of women establishing growth-oriented firms, often in previously male-dominated fields. Unlike home-based businesses, these firms place a higher priority on growth in revenues, profits, and market share. In keeping with these different motivations, their founders employ dramatically different financing strategies.

High-growth firms are a very small percentage of all firms, regardless of whether they are male- or female-owned. Like new firms in general, growth-oriented firms typically start small, but they grow at a rapid pace, often increasing sales by well over 100 percent annually during the early years of their existence. "Explosive" growth places tremendous pressure on the entrepreneur's ability to secure funding, manage cash flows, and implement necessary systems and controls. She can quickly exhaust internal sources of capital in the form of personal savings, loans, and credit cards, and find it necessary to turn to external sources of equity, which is often in the form of angel or venture capital funding. We introduced angel and venture capital financing in Chapter 4 and provided an example in the Daily Worth minicase. In the next two chapters, we will revisit the role of angel and venture capital as a source of financing for growth-oriented and technology-based firms in particular.

The Venture Capital Industry: Some Female Perspectives

The last ten years have been fairly dismal for the venture capital industry overall (U.S. Small Business Administration Office of Advocacy, 2011). On average, VC firms have generated disappointing results during this time frame. Funds have closed down and exited the industry, and many of the surviving funds cannot raise follow-on funding in this environment. Due to poor results and a higher level of risk aversion in the current economic environment, less money is going into venture capital funds, so there is less funding available to invest. The number of venture capitalists and the number of VC funds have both declined dramatically over the last decade.

In this relatively challenging environment, it is much more difficult to break into the industry, regardless of gender. Further, there are fewer promotions from the lower ranks of VC professionals. Historically, firms promoted because they needed more capacity at the top in order to be able to provide partners to sit on boards of the firm's portfolio companies. In the current environment, however, the rate of exits by portfolio firms has slowed dramatically. There are fewer IPOs, more firms are closing down, and fewer and smaller deals are being made. Few of the founding partners in VC firms are women, and the percentage of women in the VC industry has actually declined. Given that fewer partners are needed, fewer of the newer associates are moving up, and this is mainly where the relatively small number of women in VC firms can be found.

Several researchers have addressed the issue of "homophily" in funding patterns for both entrepreneurs and providers of financing. One study found that entrepreneurs were more likely to seek financing from angel investors of the same sex (Becker-Blease and Sohl, 2007). Since relatively few angel investors are women, this represents a problem for women entrepreneurs. A second study found that women angel investors were marginally more likely to invest in women-owned firms (Harrison and Mason, 2007). Again, this study also noted that this is a potential problem for women entrepreneurs given the small number and lack of visibility of women angel investors. In their study of growth-oriented women-owned firms, the researchers associated with the Diana Project found that women constitute less than 10 percent of the decision makers in venture capital firms (Brush et al., 2004). Correspondingly, women entrepreneurs receive only a tiny percentage of venture capital financing

(Brush et al., 2002). Taken together, the findings of the studies suggest that in order to increase the flow of equity capital into women-owned firms, the number of women who can serve as investors and decision makers in angel networks and venture capital firms must also increase. Let's take a few moments to get the perspective of women who do invest as venture capitalists, as well as the perspective on one woman entrepreneur who has sought venture capital.

Principles in Action: Conversations with Three Venture Capital Investors

Elaine Jones, Pfizer Inc.

Elaine Jones is a venture capitalist and executive director at Pfizer Venture Investments (www.Pfizer.com). When asked about the lack of women in the biosciences industry, she hypothesized that it was due to a lack of knowledge of opportunities in that sector, as well as uncertainty regarding the best way to explore such opportunities. Elaine was trained as a scientist and began her career as an industrial researcher. It was only after she had to choose between her position relocating to another state or changing jobs that she ended up on the business side of science and was exposed to other sectors within the industry. For her, this business development experience was the key to understanding how to successfully invest in business ventures. In her tenure with Pfizer, and at EuclidSR Partners prior to that, she has seen a shift in the types of businesses women are founding, as well as their motivations for founding their ventures.

Ten years ago, very few women business owners were looking for significant external capital. They were founding consulting businesses because the existing jobs wouldn't accommodate the flexibility they were looking for. Last year when we surveyed 35 women who had raised at least $2 million of financing, these women almost exclusively said they were pursuing an entrepreneurial endeavor because they came across a compelling idea. These women were not afraid to try and fail.

In her work with Pfizer Inc., Elaine noted that there are no women CEOs in Pfizer's current venture portfolio of 16 firms. There are, however, a good number of firms that have women as part of the senior management team (CFO, clinical director, etc.). While Pfizer has considered firms with women CEOs, the reasons for not funding them had to do with technical or intellectual property issues or the lack of a compelling market opportunity. In other words, the gender of the CEO was not a factor in the funding decision. Elaine noted that many firms, regardless of CEO gender, are turned down for funding. In 2009, Pfizer looked at approximately 250 deals, reviewed about 20 of them in depth, and funded only 2 of them. In 2010, they looked at more than 250 deals, investigated 15 more fully, and made only 4 deals.

Alison Kiley, Alta Partners

Alison Kiley is a venture capitalist and partner with Alta Partners (www.altapartners.com). She has been with Alta Partners since 2001, so she has witnessed the ups and downs of the venture capital industry firsthand. Currently, Alison has four biotech and medical device companies in her investment portfolio. None of her portfolio firms have a woman CEO, or even had a woman in senior management until 2011. As an investor, she sits on the boards of these firms. Of the board members of the four firms, only one is a woman. Like Elaine, Alison stressed that the lack of women leaders and senior managers was not by design. In fact, Alison just participated in a CEO search for one of her portfolio companies. During the search, which was conducted by an executive search firm, only one of the 50 candidates presented or considered was female, and that candidate wasn't a viable candidate because she was unable to relocate. This example reflects a more systematic issue in that women are not meeting the specifications of the search criteria for these types of positions. Why is this the case? Alison suggests that some women in the pipeline leading to more senior positions opted out to pursue motherhood and family. She noted that it can be difficult for women to compete against men with stay-at-home wives when they do not have that same level of support and assistance at home themselves.

Upon further reflection, Alison was surprised when she realized how few dual-career families were "traditional" families in her field. She said that most of the women she knew in the field were married to men who were semiretired, investing, or in scaled-back careers. In terms of family, most of the women she knows who have children are married with stepchildren or adopted children. In the cases of two hard-charging parents, she says, the woman typically steps back from pursuing her career. She could name only two female colleagues with children who were still married and part of a "traditional nuclear family."

The picture for women is considerably brighter when we consider all of the portfolio companies for Alta Partners. Alison was kind enough to pull information on the senior management teams of all 68 of Alta's portfolio companies, which are typically later-stage investments. Seven of those firms had a female CEO, and 24 of the other firms had at least one woman on their senior management team. Four firms out of the 24 had more than one female on their senior management team.

As a female venture capitalist, Alison noted that Alta is one of the few VC firms that has more than one female VC partner (Alta has two). Although many of the larger VC firms have a woman partner, many of the smaller firms do not. She says that persistence and especially performance are the keys to advancement in the VC industry. Having a mentor that will champion you is also helpful, especially in the early stages of your career. In comparing her background to other female VCs, Alison noted that most came through the ranks from the science side (M.D., Ph.D.) rather than through the finance route as she did.

Alison meets regularly with female VC partners in the San Francisco Bay area to talk about issues in their field. During a discussion regarding family issues, one of the women, who was stepping back to spend more time with her family, said, "I know our group of women will be so disappointed." Clearly, there is still a shared sense that women are the exception rather than the rule in the VC field. Alison finds that she has a lot more flexibility in her career now because she has established herself. At this point in her career, deals come to her rather than her having to fight for them. She is also able do more by phone and travel less while still fulfilling her responsibilities with her portfolio companies. As the mother of two young children, Alison appreciates being able to spend time with her kids. Before having children, she often worked close to a hundred hours a week. Now that she has established her reputation and credentials, she no longer feels the needs to maintain such an arduous schedule.

Cindy Padnos, Illuminate Ventures

While Elaine and Alison did not have any firms with women CEOs in their own investment portfolios, 60 percent of Cindy Padnos's portfolio have at least one female cofounder. Cindy is the founding managing director of Illuminate Ventures (www.illuminate.com), an early-stage VC firm with a current fund performing in the top 10 percent as compared to other VC funds of the same vintage. Prior to founding Illuminate, Cindy was a director of Outlook Ventures, where she was one of three investment professionals responsible for committing the firm's $140 million fund. Immediately before joining Outlook, Cindy's long-standing relationships within the VC ecosystem allowed her to "apprentice" in the industry as a venture consultant, working with several top-tier venture capital firms and their portfolios. Cindy has been on both sides of the investing table. As a female founder and CEO of Vivant, she launched an innovative venture-backed SaaS (Software as a Service) company that she successfully led to its acquisition by a publicly traded company (EVLV). Now, as a venture capitalist, Cindy focuses on the cloud computing space. She is particularly interested in start-ups with a diverse management team because she has seen hard data demonstrating that these types of teams are more innovative and deliver superior performance.

Recently, Cindy completed a white paper on high-performing women-owned ventures as part of her desire to better understand the funding gap in equity financing between female and male entrepreneurs (Padnos, 2010). In it she notes that although women still receive a smaller percentage of venture capital funding, things are improving. Cindy stresses that an increasing number of women are receiving advanced degrees in business and technology-related fields. This prepares them for the tasks of launching and managing growth-oriented firms. Further, a growing number of high-growth firms have women as a part of their senior management teams, including at the time of IPO, thereby providing critical management skills for future entrepreneurs. Finally, Cindy observes that as more women gain experience in starting and managing entrepreneurial ventures, and as more of them achieve the financial rewards that come with entrepreneurial success, the number of women who are willing and able to invest in other women-owned firms as angel investors will also increase. In essence, women-owned firms represent an untapped investment opportunity for venture capital firms. She explains in her white paper:

> The current discontinuity that exists between the growing numbers of women entrepreneurs and actual investment levels creates a unique investment opportunity. Our research suggests that investors who are well positioned to tap into this emerging sector and who apply innovative strategies designed to fit capital-efficient outcomes will be well positioned to deliver advantaged investment returns.

In keeping with Cindy Padnos's observations regarding the increasing number of growth-oriented women entrepreneurs, the authors of the Diana Project surveyed participants in the Springboard Forums (www.springboardenterprises.org) and found that the vast majority anticipated significant and rapid growth for their firms (Brush et al., 2001a). A second study conducted by the Diana Project research team confirmed that a substantial pool of women entrepreneurs are pursuing growth strategies for their firms (Gatewood et al., 2009). Penny Herscher, CEO of FirstRain, is one such entrepreneur.

Principles in Action: Penny Herscher

Penny Herscher knows how to raise venture capital. As CEO of Simplex Solutions, an electronic design automation company, she raised more than $23 million between 1996 and 1998. Then, as CEO of FirstRain (www.firstrain.com), the leading provider of intelligence from the Business Web, she raised more than $40 million from 2006 to 2010.

In searching for venture capital, Penny has had her share of patronizing meetings with male VCs who had no real intention or interest in funding her ideas. But she notes that many VCs really don't care what gender you are. She says, "They care who you are as a person, and they care about your experience, and your ideas, and your ability to build a team."

When asked about the dearth of women leading VC-backed firms, she noted that you're more likely to get VC financing if you are in a technical field (she comes from a technical background), and few women are coming up through the ranks in technology-related firms. Penny also notes that she has met a lot of women entrepreneurs who "don't play the game like men, don't take themselves seriously enough; they're emotional. To get funded as a woman, you just have to have executive presence." Taking yourself seriously is one of the keys to successfully attracting venture capital. Operational experience is another. Women need to get experience in operations, and companies need to develop talented women in this area. What's the third key to successfully selling your idea to venture capitalists? It's having a *good* idea!

While Penny is not a huge fan of incubators targeted at women, she says they can be helpful because incubators provide women with the opportunity to see other successful women. Unfortunately, these types of programs can perpetuate segregation. Penny doesn't feel that women have been excluded from male-dominated networks but rather that women have excluded themselves because they lack confidence. This lack of confidence may come from many sources, but Penny observes that our society projects a pervasive negative image regarding women—whether it be through the lack of female leads in films, objectification of women in the media, or teachers devoting more time to boys' education, especially in science and math. These are all actions that perpetuate gender stereotypes and limit the ability of women to level the playing field. Ultimately, such subtle, and even less subtle, forms of discrimination affect our ability as a country to launch innovative firms and to create jobs. To tackle this early on, Penny says, "We need to provide education for girls to deal with and overcome the prejudice they are going to face."

Financing Challenges for Growth-Oriented Entrepreneurs

As Penny Herscher's example illustrates, a growth-oriented entrepreneur has to be particularly resourceful. Not only does she have to identify appropriate sources of financing for various stages of firm growth, but she has to be persistent in doing so. Failure to assemble the needed financial resources can lead to failure of the firm or loss of opportunity to a more nimble competitor. Penny's experience also suggests that most investors are less concerned with the entrepreneur's gender than with the quality of the business model and the entrepreneur's and management team's ability to launch and grow a successful company that will provide investment returns.

Bootstrapping as a Strategy for Survival and Growth

Growth-oriented entrepreneurs typically start out using a combination of personal financial resources, F&F (family and friends), and bootstrapping. Bootstrapping is particularly important because high-growth firms consume resources rapidly but are not in a position to generate profits early on. Similarly, growth-oriented firms may have to "prove themselves" by achieving certain benchmarks in terms of sales, product development, or regulatory approvals before they are candidates for external equity financing. The Diana Project team noted the role of bootstrapping in a study of growth-oriented women entrepreneurs who sought equity financing (Brush et al., 2006). They identified a number of different bootstrapping techniques:

1. Bootstrapping product development: Using customers and suppliers to finance research and development and operations, such as prepaid expenses, royalties, or special deals on access to product hardware.

2. Bootstrapping business development: Using the owner's cash to sustain the business, such as personal savings, working from home, or personal credit cards.
3. Bootstrapping to minimize the need for capital: Limiting cash flow and expenses, such as borrowing equipment, employing used equipment, using temporary employees, or trade credit.
4. Bootstrapping to meet the need for capital: Raising cash and money to meet short term needs, such as working without or delaying the owner's salary, delaying payment to suppliers, or loans from friends and relatives.

These researchers found that bootstrapping strategies differed according to the stage of firm growth. In other words, firms in the earliest stages of development used different strategies than firms in the rapid growth stage. Nevertheless, the Diana Project team found that women-owned firms used bootstrapping strategies at all growth stages and that the importance of bootstrapping actually increased after the firms received equity financing. A recent study cautions, however, that growth-oriented firms should not become overly reliant on bootstrapping (Patel et al., 2011). Typically bootstrapping strategies raise capital in relatively small increments. This helps, but growth-oriented firms also need to develop sources of capital that can provide capital in large increments. This same study points out that bootstrapping can be very time consuming and that this time might be better devoted to key activities that support firm growth. Taken together, these research findings suggest that bootstrapping is an important financing strategy for firms at all stages of growth. Nevertheless, growth-oriented firms, in particular, need to balance their focus on bootstrapping with their need to raise large amounts of external capital.

Biting the Bullet on Debt

Debt or borrowed money can also be used to help growth-oriented entrepreneurs get started. Debt providers such as banks are risk-averse lenders, however, so typically loans are secured by the personal assets of the entrepreneur. What does this mean for you? It means that the bank may give you a loan, but it will probably want to use your home as collateral. In this sense, the amount of debt you can raise is limited by the amount of equity you have in your home. You also run the risk of losing your home if the business fails or if you cannot service the debt. Although many entrepreneurs are willing to accept this risk in order to pursue their entrepreneurial dream, it is not a risk to be taken lightly.

When the firm has reached the point of generating revenues and profits, the debt picture becomes more promising. At that point, lenders can assess the firm's ability to service debt from cash flows, and they may be more willing to lend and to lend larger amounts. If the business has assets such as buildings or facilities, equipment, inventories, or receivables, these can also be used as collateral on larger loans.

Bridge loans are another alternative for entrepreneurs seeking equity financing. A bridge loan is just what it sounds like: a loan to get you from point A to point B. Typically entrepreneurs use a bridge loan to help them "bridge" a gap in funding until they receive equity financing. Obviously, to obtain a bridge loan you must be fairly certain that follow-on funding will materialize.

In the wake of the recent financial crisis we must caution women entrepreneurs and aspiring women entrepreneurs that the lending environment continues to be challenging, although commercial banks began to ease lending conditions in mid-2010 (U.S. Small Business Administration Office of Advocacy, 2011). The U.S. banking system is still struggling, and one article in the *Wall Street Journal* noted that in 2009 loans outstanding dropped to the lowest level since 1942 (*Wall Street Journal*, February 24, 2010). There has been some recovery since that time, but loan volume remains below prerecession levels.

In this type of adverse lending environment, entrepreneurs have to be even more creative and resourceful in pursuing sources of debt. In addition to commercial banks, finance companies, asset-backed lending companies, factoring companies, and leasing firms may be viable options. This is also a good time to investigate loans provided or guaranteed by the state or federal government. In fact, there may actually be more of these types of loans available at the current time as Congress and state legislatures attempt to repair the economy and stimulate particular types of industries. It will take some time to research these types of loans and go through the application and approval process, but in a hostile lending environment, government programs can help to fill a need. A good place to start is your state's Department of Economic Development's website. That should provide you with information or links to various types of loan programs. Another valuable resource is your district office of the U.S. Small Business Administration (SBA). The SBA operates a loan guarantee program and is a valuable source of information on other funding alternatives for small and growing firms.

The three main lending programs of the SBA are the 7(a) loan program, the CDC/504 program, and the microloan program. The 7(a) loan program includes financial help for businesses, including loans to businesses that handle exports to foreign countries and businesses that operate in rural areas. These loans can be used to establish a new business or to assist in the acquisition, operation, or expansion of an existing business. The CDC/504 loan program is a long-term financing tool that is designed to encourage economic development within a community. It provides small businesses with long-term, fixed-rate financing to acquire major fixed assets for expansion or modernization. Finally, the microloan program provides small, short-term loans to small business concerns and certain types of not-for-profit child care centers. The SBA makes funds available to specially designated intermediary lenders, which are nonprofit community-based organizations with experience in lending as well as management and technical assistance. These intermediaries make loans to eligible borrowers. The maximum loan amount is $50,000, but the average microloan is about $13,000.

After the economic crisis, the SBA took several steps to ease access to finance through SBA programs. First, the SBA temporarily raised guarantees and eliminated fees for borrowers of its 7(a) loans. Additionally, the SBA temporarily eliminated fees for borrowers and third-party lenders on its 504 Certified Development Company loans. The guarantee on some types of 7(A) SBA-backed loans to small businesses will be temporarily increased to 90 percent. Another provision created the America's Recovery Capital (ARC) loan program, which makes deferred-payment loans of up to $35,000 to small businesses that need help making payments on an existing qualifying loan for up to six months. Small businesses repay the loan beginning one year after full disbursement of the loan. The goal of the program is to assist small businesses that are struggling to make payments on an existing loan in the current economic climate. Funds from the loan will help small businesses retain employees, pay rent, and keep their businesses open until revenues improve. The SBA also expanded its microloan program. The Recovery Act provides $50 million in new SBA microloans. Finally, the SBA is expanding Surety Bond Program limits, creating a new Section 504 refinancing program, expanding the Small Business Investment Company (SBIC) Program, and increasing the secondary market for first mortgages associated Section 504 Certified Development Company loans.

However, as shown in Table 7.1, even with these changes, the levels of lending over the 2008–2010 period were dramatically lower than in previous years. And even though 2010 levels increased over 2009 levels, women continued to receive just 18 percent of 7(a) loans, 16 percent of 504 loans, and less than 14 percent of the total amount loaned for these programs. Clearly there is room for more active participation by women.

Raising Equity

The Hunt Is On! The Launch of the Diana Project

In 2001 a group of experienced entrepreneurship scholars established the Diana Project (Brush et al., 2001). The purpose of that project was to gain a better understanding of the dynamics of growth-oriented women entrepreneurs, as well as their financing strategies. Diana, the mythological goddess of the hunt, is an apt symbol for these aggressive and dynamic firms that have taken women into new entrepreneurial territory.

The Diana Project researchers challenged the "myths" that women do not want to establish high-growth businesses, that they only start firms in industries that are unattractive to equity providers, and that they do not have the necessary resources in the form of human, financial, and social capital to embark on a path of growth-oriented entrepreneurship. To combat these stereotypes, the Diana Project scholars studied the experience of Springboard forum participants. They found that over 80 percent of the Springboard entrepreneurs wanted to grow their ventures as rapidly as possible. They also found that over half of the applicants estimated the size of their target markets to be more than $15 billion and international in scope. In terms of industry sector, over half of the Springboard firms that were funded were in the areas of computer hardware, software, or services—fields that have traditionally been dominated by men.

As a testament to the importance of human capital, 49 percent of Springboard applicants had graduate degrees. Their management teams had an average of 39 years of industry experience per venture, while over 40 percent of the applicants had team members with previous start-up experience. The Diana Project researchers also found that the Springboard entrepreneurs had diverse and well-developed networks and devoted substantial amounts of time to networking activities to increase their level of social capital.

TABLE 7.1 Small Business Administration business loan approvals

	2006		2007		2008		2009		2010	
	Number of lines	*Amount (1,000s)*	*Number of lines*	*Amount (1,000s)*	*Number of lines*	*Amount (1,000s)*	*Number of lines*	*Amount (1,000s)*	*Number of lines*	*Amount (1,000s)*
7a										
All firms	97,291	$14,524,100	99,606	$14,292,141	69,434	$12,671,136	44,222	$9,286,218	52,938	$12,630,559
Women-owned	21,812	$ 2,655,354	22,743	$ 2,613,815	16,112	$ 2,247,468	8,652	$1,410,302	9,629	$ 1,740,989
504										
All firms	9,943	$ 5,729,695	10,669	$ 6,313,826	8,883	$ 5,289,790	6,608	$3,834,263	7,833	$ 4,433,308
Women-owned	1,563	$ 787,102	1,757	$ 957,783	1,494	$ 836,217	1,061	$ 528,592	1,228	$ 603,854
WOMEN AS A %										
7a	22.4	18.3	22.8	18.3	23.2	17.7	19.6	15.2	18.2	13.8
504	15.7	13.7	16.5	15.2	16.8	15.8	16.1	13.8	15.7	13.6

Source: Small Business Administration, Office of Advocacy.

In the area of financial capital, the Springboard entrepreneurs relied on a diverse array of financing sources, including personal funds, funds from family and friends, credit cards, loans (business and personal), retained earnings, and external equity from angel investors, venture capital firms, or other entities. Contrary to the belief that women are unwilling to share control with outside equity investors, the Diana Project scholars actually found that women entrepreneurs' demand for external equity far exceeded the capacity of the Springboard forums. During the first year alone, over 800 women entrepreneurs applied to participate, while only 100 were selected to present.

The Importance of Social Capital

Due to some of the constraints associated with raising debt, particularly in the current economic environment, growth-oriented entrepreneurs typically turn to external equity as a major source of financing. Equity investors such as business angels and venture capitalists are more willing to accept the risks associated with early-stage entrepreneurship, and they are able to provide larger amounts of capital to firms that meet their criteria for investment. But the maxim of "many are called, but few are chosen" still applies. To date, over 4,000 women entrepreneurs have applied to present at the Springboard forums. Only 400 of these have actually been chosen to present, and not all of these received funding.

The nature of the entrepreneur's relationship with equity holders differs from her relationship with debt holders. Debt providers such as commercial banks are lenders. They expect to be paid back, typically with interest, but they are not owners of the firm. In contrast, equity holders have an ownership share in the company. They provide "permanent capital." In other words, one does not pay them off and make them go away. As owners, they anticipate sharing in future returns from an initial public offering or sale of the firm to another company. They also expect to have a voice in management and decision making. The larger their equity share, the louder that voice will be. In a sense, choosing an equity partner is like choosing a significant other. You have to choose carefully because that person will be around for a long time.

Research done by the Diana Project team revealed that women entrepreneurs have historically obtained only a small percentage of total venture capital investment—less than 5 percent in 2000 (Brush et al., 2001). This is true in spite of the fact that many women entrepreneurs have the requisite levels of human capital in the form of education and prior experience and are starting growth-oriented firms in the "right" kinds of industries, such as technology and bioscience.

Alternatively, the Diana Project researchers concluded that women's difficulties in raising equity capital come from deficiencies in social capital rather than deficiencies in human capital or industry selection (Brush et al., 2002). In an extensive study of venture capital firms and their employees in the United States, the Diana Project team found that few women venture capitalists held decision-making roles. In fact, they found that the venture capital industry is heavily male dominated and acts as a closed network that often excludes high-potential women entrepreneurs. The team concluded that given the small number of women venture capitalists, it is less likely that the networks of women entrepreneurs will overlap with those of VCs. In light of their findings, the Diana Project team highlighted the need for more women in decision-making roles in VC firms, as well as more women with the financial and experiential wherewithal to serve as venture capital investors (Brush et al., 2004).

So what does all this mean for you as a woman entrepreneur seeking equity financing? First, understand that equity financing typically comes with strings attached. Equity holders are co-owners with you, and they will expect a proportional share of future returns as well as a voice in important decisions affecting the firm. Angel investors tend to make smaller investments and thus play a smaller role in firm decision making. Venture capitalists, on the other hand, make substantial investments, and they expect to be closely involved with the firm on an ongoing basis.

Second, network, network, network! The findings of the Diana Project team clearly illustrate the importance of social capital in the form of networks and key contacts in securing equity financing. Identify sources of equity that are appropriate for your firm early on, and begin networking to gain access to them. Equally important, be strategic in your networking activities. Networking takes a lot of time and energy, and one study actually found that if too much time is devoted to networking, it can detract from the performance of the firm (Watson, 2007). In other words, use your networking time wisely!

Third, carefully assess what your equity partners will bring to the table. An added value of equity investors, particularly venture capitalists, is that they provide not only financial capital but human capital in the form of expertise and social capital in the form of networks as well. If you accept funding from a venture capitalist, you will be "married" to them for a long time.

Make sure this is a relationship that adds value to your firm beyond the more obvious attraction of the funding they can provide. Also, make sure the firm has values and long-term goals for your firm that are compatible with your own. There are too many horror stories about entrepreneurs who jump into the first financial relationship that presents itself, only to find that the new investor has very different goals and objectives for the firm than the founding entrepreneur. Typically, these stories do not have a happy ending, so look before you leap!

Ask for Enough, and Learn How to Negotiate!

Entrepreneurs—and especially entrepreneurs who start high-growth firms—often underestimate the capital demands of their firm. Rapid growth chews up a lot of cash—much more than you might anticipate! Prior research suggests that women entrepreneurs may be more conservative in their estimates of the amount of capital required than men. Previous studies have found that women raise dramatically smaller amounts of financial capital than men (Alsos et al., 2006; Boden and Nucci, 2000; Coleman and Robb, 2009). Further, in-depth interviews with women entrepreneurs revealed that they wished they had sought financing sooner and had raised more money (Amatucci and Sohl, 2004).

Failure to raise sufficient capital can threaten the survival of the firm. Insufficient capital can also restrict the firm's ability to hire key employees, conduct needed research and development, develop new products and services, and grow market share. Another risk of not asking for enough capital is the risk of diluting the entrepreneur's ownership share. Every time you ask for equity, you have to give up a piece of ownership. If you don't ask for enough up front, you will have to keep going back to the well, and each time you do so, your share of ownership gets smaller. The lesson in all this is that revenues never materialize as quickly as you think they will, and expenses always materialize in a bigger way than you think they will. Do not underestimate your firm's demands for capital. Raise enough so you have the flexibility to develop, grow, and take full advantage of your opportunities.

This brings us to another subject: learning to negotiate with equity providers such as angel investors and venture capitalists. The objective of angels and venture capitalists is to maximize the returns to their investors. Obviously they want you and your firm to do well, because that's where their returns will come from. They are not, however, in the business of looking out for *your* interests. That's your job.

As just noted, equity providers typically take a share of ownership when they provide capital. Their return comes when the firm goes public or is sold to another firm. It is therefore in their interests to extract as large a share of equity in return for their investment as possible. Conversely, it is in your interest to maintain as much of an ownership share as possible. Negotiations around the issue of firm valuation and the allocation of equity shares are intense! Do not go into them unprepared. A big part of the entrepreneurial process for you as a growth-oriented entrepreneur is learning to identify and acquire appropriate sources of capital. It is also important for you to learn how to negotiate with equity providers in order to protect your interests. These are some of the things that growth-oriented women entrepreneurs learn as a part of their participation in the Springboard forums. If you are not part of the Springboard forums, other groups are available that will work with you to help prepare for negotiating with equity providers. Other examples of groups that focus on training and networking for growth-oriented women entrepreneurs include Astia, based in California, and the Echelon Circles, based in Maine. Actually, one of the best ways to prepare is to talk to other women entrepreneurs who have successfully raised equity and learn from their experience. Seek out and use mentors!

Amatucci and Swartz (2010) conducted a recent study of women who negotiated for equity capital. They found that the women entrepreneurs they interviewed used a variety of strategies to prepare. These included speaking with other entrepreneurs who had negotiated for equity capital (75 percent), using the Internet to gather data (40 percent), and attending venture fairs to learn about the process (40 percent). These entrepreneurs also had several recommendations for effective negotiation strategies, including the following:

1. Start early! Identifying an appropriate source of equity capital can be time consuming, so give yourself plenty of time.
2. Have a defined agenda, and know what you want. Also, know what you want to accomplish at each meeting with equity providers. Determine in advance what your overarching priorities are, as well as the things that could be deal breakers.
3. Seek a win-win situation; look for middle ground. This will be a long-term partnership, so each of you has to walk away with some of what you want.
4. Back up your negotiations with data and financial analysis. This is your best defense against aggressive negotiation tactics. If you know your stuff and can articulate it, it will be harder for them to wear you down.

5. Be prepared to walk away from a deal. No deal is better than a bad deal. For a variety of reasons, some equity partners may just not be a good match for you and your firm.

Principles in Action: W3 Partners

In light of the lingering aftereffects of the recent financial crisis, most people would look at the real estate market today and say, "I'm not touching that!" Not so for partners Diane Olmstead and Susan Sagy, who, with a third partner, founded their commercial real estate investment firm, W3 Partners (www.w3partnersllc.com), in June 2009. W3 stands for "three women," or as Diane likes to say, "Wit, wisdom, and will!" Instead of lemons, they saw the lemonade of opportunity. As Susan explained:

The real estate market runs in cycles . . . a big down usually followed by a big up. We are near the bottom of the down cycle now, and we want to position our firm to take advantage of the next up cycle. In the past, we have worked for other companies, and we have seen them get the big profits from an up cycle. This time we want to take advantage of those profits by having our own firm.

Diane and Susan feel that current industry conditions are well aligned to supporting their firm's strategy. Banks are foreclosing on commercial loans, and little property is changing hands due to lack of financing and uncertainty about values. Many existing owners are burdened by overleveraged properties accompanied by declining performance and liquidity. Ultimately, there will be an ownership shift from individual owners to banks and other financial institutions, many of which do not have the onsite real estate skills required to manage or reposition properties. That's where W3 Partners comes in. Diane and Susan have positioned W3 Partners to act as a joint venture operating partner capable of supplying both fresh capital and real estate expertise. Their firm is in a position to buy loans and properties or recapitalize the assets of existing owners. In other words, W3 Partners targets two major unmet needs in the commercial real estate market today: capital and expertise.

In terms of resources, both Diane and Susan have extensive amounts of both human and social capital. Diane has over 25 years of experience in corporate finance, raising capital, and acquisitions. She has originated and closed over $2 billion in loans, property acquisitions, and joint ventures and has been responsible for the workout and restructuring of $1.3 billion in real estate assets. Similarly, Susan has over 25 years of experience in all aspects of real estate development and investment. She has developed, redeveloped, or repositioned 3.8 million square feet of office, industrial, and mixed-use projects.

In addition to their track record as real estate professionals, Diane and Susan also have deep and long-standing relationships with property owners, lenders, brokers, and investors. Those relationships provide them with superior access to deal flow through the major markets in the western United States. Diane is a member of the Policy Advisory Board of the Fisher Center for Real Estate and Urban Development at U.C. Berkeley, and Susan is active in the Urban Land Institute and has served as a member of the Executive Committee of the San Francisco District Council since 1997.

Armed with these many talents, Diane and Susan had to develop a financial strategy for launching their firm and financing its activities. Establishing a firm of this type requires substantial amounts of capital to purchase and develop sites, as well as to fund the operations of the firm. In light of that, the founders developed a multipronged financial strategy:

1. W3 Partners is in the process of raising capital for a $200 million fund that will invest in office and office/research and development properties located in the western United States (California, Oregon, and Washington State). The fund is expected to provide net returns of 13 to 15 percent to investors based on a five- to seven-year holding period. This fund will provide capital to allow W3 Partners to purchase, develop, and redevelop properties.

2. W3 Partners has entered into a joint venture agreement with another company that wishes to be active in the commercial real estate market but does not have the in-house expertise. W3 Partner's portion of the joint venture will be to provide that expertise. Their JV partner company will provide approximately $100 million to participate in the fund and buy properties. Part of their funding will also go toward W3 Partners' operating expenses.

3. Currently, W3 Partners has five employees besides Diane and Susan, all of whom are experienced real estate or finance professionals. These employees are working for free until deals start to come in. The employees also own a part of the fund and will participate in those returns.

4. On a personal level, Diane and Susan put in approximately $30,000 of their own capital. They are also working without salaries in order to establish the firm.

Both Susan and Diane stress the importance of networks and contacts in this business. In fact, their networks and relationships are the underpinning for each of the preceding financial strategies:

The three partners all knew each other before, and we have worked together. We know the quality of each other's work, and in this business, reputation is key. Our employees also joined up with us and are willing to work for nothing at this point because of our track record of success. They know that, down the road, they will participate in the success of this new firm. We even used Facebook to make contact with our JV partner. It was someone we had worked with before, and we saw that she was doing something new, so we got in touch. That has led to a relationship that will be highly beneficial to both sides. We are constantly networking, looking for investors, opportunities, and talent.

Diane and Susan's story and the story of their firm illustrate our two theories, Motivational Theory and Resource-Based Theory, in action. Diane and Susan were motivated to take advantage of what they perceived to be an opportunity in the commercial real estate market. Similarly, they were motivated to establish a growth-oriented firm that would provide substantial returns to them and their investors. To achieve these goals, they set about putting their resources in the areas of human and social capital to work in order to establish their firm and raise the substantial amounts of capital required. As is often the case for growth-oriented firms, most of that capital will be raised from external sources. Nevertheless, Diane and Susan have invested their own financial capital, they have foregone salaries during the start-up phase, and they have also invested their considerable talents and energies into this venture.

Resources for Women Raising Equity Capital

In light of the growing number of women seeking to launch high-growth firms, a number of organizations have emerged to help them develop their human capital through training and development, their social capital by providing access to key networks, and their financial capital by linking them with investors and providers of capital. Several of the better-known and more successful of these include Springboard Enterprises, Astia, and Women 2.0.

Springboard Enterprises

To address the need for equity financing for growth-oriented women entrepreneurs, Springboard Enterprises (www.springboardenterprises.org) was established in 1999 in cooperation with a consortium of leading women's business advocates and organizations. Venture-catalyst Springboard Enterprises is the premier platform where entrepreneurs, investors, and industry experts meet to build high-growth women-led businesses. Springboard educates, sources, coaches, showcases, and supports high-growth companies seeking equity capital for expansion. The first series of Springboard forums were held in 2000 with the purpose of providing opportunities for growth-oriented women entrepreneurs to present their businesses to leading investors, financiers, and business development professionals. During its first two years, the Springboard forums attracted 1,700 applications, showcased 175 women-owned firms, and attracted approximately 1,000 investors. Since January 2000, Springboard has helped more than 425 women-led companies raise $5 billion in equity financing, including several initial public offerings and many high-value mergers and acquisitions. Eighty percent of Springboard companies are still in business and have created more than 10,000 jobs. Springboard provides a platform for media visibility and access to active investors and sector experts. The importance of networks to encourage and promote the development of growth-oriented women-owned firms cannot be underestimated. A recent study conducted for the Kauffman Foundation (Cohoon et al., 2010) found the following:

> Mentoring is clearly very important to women, as are the encouragement and financial support of business partners, experience, and well-developed professional networks. An effort focused on those proven success factors for women entrepreneurs could enhance efforts to recruit more of them and help make those who take the plunge more successful.

Astia

Astia (www.astia.org) is a global nonprofit organization that provides innovative programs that ensure companies gain access to capital, achieve and sustain high growth, and develop the executive leadership of the founding team. Their programs are implemented by more than 700 members of the Astia Advisor Network, which includes more than 100 former and current CEOs and more than 125 investors. Astia's "Doing It Right" program is an intensive six-day workshop followed by two months of personal coaching by field experts combined with opportunities to network with angels, venture capitalists, and other entrepreneurs.

Women 2.0

Women 2.0 (www.women2.org) is a social venture for future founders of technology start-ups. It provides an incubator for ideas (preincubator), which consists of a five-week program for engineers, designers, business, and marketing individuals to begin to develop high-growth technology ventures. Twenty participants work together in teams for five days a week to produce five viable products over the five-week period. Teams work on a problem hypothesis, with the intent of applying to incubators such as Astia, TechStars, Springboard, or YCombinator after the idea is validated and a basic prototype has been created. The team can choose to launch and grow their start-up(s) after the program independently. Women 2.0 also hosts an annual business plan competition that culminates in a Pitch Night, where finalists present their best pitches to a judging panel of VCs and executives for funding.

What Have We Learned?

In this chapter we saw that a growing number of women are pursuing the path of high-growth entrepreneurship. Growth-oriented firms typically consume large amounts of capital, so the entrepreneur needs to raise funds from both internal and external sources. One of the major differences between growth-oriented firms and smaller, lifestyle firms is their reliance on external equity. Entrepreneurs generally finance lifestyle firms with personal and internally generated sources of equity. In contrast, growth-oriented entrepreneurs require substantial amounts of external equity financing from angel investors or venture capitalists.

As we noted in this chapter, external equity comes with strings attached. Equity providers share in the ownership of the firm and expect to have a voice in its management. They also anticipate sharing in future cash flows from an IPO or sale to another company. Unlike debt holders, you cannot make equity holders "go away," so it is important to choose wisely.

In addition to capital, equity providers can provide a number of benefits to the firm. These include industry-specific expertise and access to key employees, as well as industry contacts and contacts with additional providers of capital. Traditionally, women entrepreneurs have had limited access to networks of equity providers. More recently, however, organizations such as Springboard Enterprises and Astia have developed programs to help growth-oriented women entrepreneurs identify and secure sources of equity capital. Although the angel and venture capital networks are still heavily male-dominated, women VC professionals, investors, and entrepreneurs are beginning to make inroads. Consistent with the theme of this book, the rising tide of successful growth-oriented women entrepreneurs will lift the boats of those who follow.

Another takeaway of this chapter is that growth-oriented women entrepreneurs have to be extraordinarily resourceful in their search for capital. Successful entrepreneurs take advantage of bootstrapping techniques, funding from family and friends, loans, external equity, and strategic partnerships. The growth rate of your firm may compel a large chunk of your time to be devoted to the search for capital.

This chapter highlights the importance of networks and effective networking strategies. It's not enough to know a lot of people; you have to know the right kind of people and cultivate them over time. The Diana Project team found that venture capital networks, in particular, are less accessible to women entrepreneurs, so it will take additional time to identify and get close to key players who can help you further your goals for your firm. As with negotiating strategies, networking is a skill to be learned and practiced.

What Does All This Mean for Me?

Growth-oriented entrepreneurship provides opportunities for substantial personal and financial rewards. The owners of high-growth firms are often leaders in their field as well as leaders in their local, state, and national economies. In this sense, growth-oriented entrepreneurs have the opportunity to provide "high impact" as well as high growth. Because they operate on a larger stage, growth-oriented entrepreneurs often serve as role models and as spokeswomen on issues that are important to them and many others. In light of their larger revenues and profits, high-growth firms can also provide entrepreneurs with high levels of earnings and wealth. Depending on their personal priorities, many growth-oriented entrepreneurs devote a substantial portion of that wealth to improving the lot of others by giving to universities, medical research, environmental or social causes, or those in need in the United States and abroad.

As this chapter pointed out, however, growth-oriented entrepreneurship does not come without risks, not the least of which is the ability to secure financing to support high growth. As a growth-oriented entrepreneur, you will face many challenges. Part of your journey will be to develop the strategies and tools that will help you overcome them:

1. Understand that growth-oriented entrepreneurship is an arduous path. Have a long-term vision for your firm so the potholes along the way don't divert you.
2. Talk to other successful growth-oriented entrepreneurs so you can learn from their experience. Don't be shy! Successful entrepreneurs often welcome the opportunity to talk about how they got to where they are, and they are willing to mentor those who are embarking on the same journey. Find these individuals, and use them as mentors and role models.
3. As noted in this chapter, high-growth firms consume tremendous amounts of capital in their early years. Recognize that you will have to raise far more capital, much of it external, than you may have anticipated. Although effective use of bootstrapping techniques may help you to hold down costs, thereby minimizing your need for external sources, at some point in the firm's growth you will have to take the plunge. Accept the fact that you will have to spend a significant amount of your time seeking out and developing sources of capital. Also, don't skimp! Prior research indicates that women raise much less capital to fund their firms than men do. Failure to raise sufficient capital in the early stages of a high-growth firm increases the risk of failure as well as the likelihood that some competitor will pass you by.
4. A large portion of the capital used to finance high-growth firms comes in the form of external equity—that is, funding from angel investors or venture capitalists. These investors will want to share in the ownership of the firm and in its future cash flows. Depending on the size of their investment, they may also expect to participate in the firm's management by sitting on the Board of Directors or having a voice in the selection of key managers. In other words, you are not the Lone Ranger anymore! Many entrepreneurs are concerned about sharing ownership and control with outsiders. Prior research suggests, however, that growth-oriented entrepreneurs are willing to trade off those concerns in return for the capital that will allow them to achieve their longer-term goals (Hustedde and Pulver, 1992). These are the tradeoffs!

5. Network strategically. One of the most important "jobs" of an entrepreneur is to acquire the resources needed to make her firm succeed. This is particularly true for growth-oriented firms where so many resources are needed. Be strategic in your networking strategy, and identify those individuals or groups who can help you secure the financing you will need to grow your firm. Be systematic and consistent, and nurture these relationships over time so they will be there when you need them. Further, develop backup and supplementary sources because you will probably need more capital than you think, and some of your "primary" sources may not materialize. Aside from the acquisition of external capital, networking can help you and your firm in a number of other ways as well. By networking you may identify additional individuals to fill out your management team, or you may establish connections with important customers who will be a source of needed revenues. Networking will also lead you to other successful entrepreneurs who can serve as mentors to help you avoid some of the most dangerous pitfalls of growth-oriented entrepreneurship. As a growth-oriented entrepreneur, you will need and rely on the networks you develop, so get out there and get started!

• Tips for Growth-Oriented Entrepreneurs

1. Have a long-term vision.
2. Find other successful growth-oriented entrepreneurs who can serve as role models and mentors.
3. Be prepared to raise substantial amounts of external capital.
4. Network strategically with individuals and groups that can provide the resources required to support firm growth.

Public Policy Issues

High-growth firms rely heavily on external sources of debt and, in particular, equity. The recent financial crisis has heavily damaged both the debt and equity markets threatening the launch, growth, and harvest of new high-growth firms. One of the side effects of the recent financial crisis and Great Recession was a severe "credit crunch." In 2009, U.S. banks posted their sharpest decline in lending since 1942 (*Wall Street Journal*, February 24, 2010). Thus, it has been very difficult for new firms to secure loans to finance facilities, equipment, vehicles, inventories, and working capital. A recent report on new U.S. firms issued by the Kauffman Foundation found that 89 percent of firms that were denied loans in 2009 felt that tougher lending standards contributed to their denial (Robb and Reedy, 2011). The good news is that as the economy and the financial system have begun to heal, there are signs that the credit markets are beginning to unfreeze and that debt capital is becoming more available and accessible to small and growth-oriented firms (*Wall Street Journal*, April 21, 2011).

Simultaneously, the venture capital industry has struggled due to economic difficulties, poor investment returns, and a weak market for initial public offerings. The number of VC firms in the United States declined from 1,023 in 2005 to 794 in 2009, a decline of over 20 percent (*Wall Street Journal*, March 9, 2010). In light of the fact that the VC industry requires a long lead time to raise new capital and fund new investments, there will be a lag in the availability of equity capital for growth-oriented firms.

The severity of the federal budget deficit also makes it increasingly likely that tax rates on personal income, corporate earnings, and capital gains will rise. Higher personal income tax rates will negatively affect entrepreneurs whose firms are organized as sole proprietorships or partnerships. These include many small, new, and even midsized firms. Simultaneously, higher corporate tax rates on larger firms will raise the cost of doing business in the United States. This could have the effect of making U.S. firms less competitive in global markets. One recent study conducted under the auspices of the National Bureau of Economic Research found that U.S. corporations face some of the highest effective tax rates in the world (Markle and Shackelford, 2011). Another study of 85 countries found that higher effective corporate tax rates have a substantial adverse effect on both investment and entrepreneurial activity (Djankov et al., 2010). Finally, higher taxes on capital gains may serve as an added deterrent on investment capital that seeks a return from growth rather than from current income.

Aside from taxation, governments also impose additional requirements and costs on businesses in the form of licensing and regulation. In the wake of a series of accounting scandals involving major firms such as Enron, WorldCom, and Tyco, Congress enacted the Sarbanes-Oxley Act (SOX) in 2002. The purpose of that act was to set new and enhanced standards for accuracy and disclosure for U.S. publicly held companies as well as for their senior managers, Boards of Directors, and accounting firms. In particular, SOX mandates the development of procedures to ensure the transparency and accuracy of financial reports. These procedures have the effect of raising costs associated with accounting, auditing, and compliance. Some researchers contend that these costs are overly burdensome to small firms and young firms (Kamar et al., 2007). Other sources contend that the high costs of compliance may encourage firms to remain private or to incorporate offshore rather than in the United States (*Wall Street Journal*, March 22, 2011).

To add to the complexity of the mix, there is currently a great deal of uncertainty regarding the future of certain growth-oriented industries, specifically health care, energy, and green or sustainable firms and technologies. If there's one thing investors don't like, it is uncertainty, so investment in these industries will, in all likelihood, be depressed until there is greater clarity regarding their prospects for the future.

Both the credit crunch and the recent weakness of the venture capital industry pose severe threats to the launch and development of growth-oriented firms. Tax policy also has the potential to either encourage or discourage the launch and investment in new growth-oriented firms. In addition to taxes, costs associated with regulation can make it either more or less attractive for growth-oriented firms to go public in this country. Finally, the current lack of clarity regarding economic priorities and the future of key industries discourages investment.

From a public policy perspective, our best response is to continue to make progress toward getting our economy back on track and healing the financial system. Further regulatory reform is needed to stabilize the banking system, restore it to health, and increase its willingness and ability to resume lending to smaller and newer firms. As the economy improves, the equity markets will continue to improve, as will prospects for investment returns and initial public offerings.

From the standpoint of economic policy, we are in dire need of greater clarity and the articulation of economic priorities going forward. In the words of one of our colleagues, "If everything's a priority, nothing's a priority." At the federal, state, and municipal levels we are no longer in a position where we can fund everything, so we and our elected officials need to make some difficult and often painful choices. Some of those choices will involve the size and cost of government, as well as the required levels of taxation on personal income, corporate earnings, and capital gains to support government.

Another set of decisions would weigh the costs of various types of regulations at all levels of government against their anticipated benefits. Finally, a third set of choices would determine the role and importance of new, growth-oriented firms that have the potential to employ substantial numbers of people, develop new products and services, and enter new markets. These firms can provide significant economic value to our economy. We need to establish policies that will encourage and nurture them rather than those that will stifle them in their infancy.

BRAVE NEW WORLD

Women and Technology-Based Firms

One of the most exciting areas of entrepreneurial opportunity in the last three decades has been technology-based entrepreneurship. Some of the firms that are household names today—Microsoft, Google, Yahoo!, eBay, and Apple Computer—were originally started as small ventures by youthful and inexperienced entrepreneurs—usually men. Women did not participate fully in this first wave of technological entrepreneurship, but they often played a supporting role. For example, in the Harvard Business School case on Amazon.com, Jeff Bezos played the starring role of founder and entrepreneur. Nevertheless, his chief financial officer, Joy Covey, also played a key role in preparing Amazon.com for its highly successful initial public offering ("Amazon.com—Going Public," 1999). Today we find ourselves not only in a new millennium but in the midst of a new wave of technology-based entrepreneurship, and women are raring to go this time around!

What has brought about this change? Why are so many women launching technology-based firms now? A number of factors have played a role. First, educational changes and innovations have contributed to the growing number of women seeking careers and entrepreneurial opportunities in technology-based fields. Traditionally, girls and young women have shied away from math and quantitative types of subjects, preferring instead to focus on the liberal arts, education, or "helping professions" such as nursing and social work (Correll, 2001; Staniec, 2004). Prior research reveals that women have less confidence in their ability to do well in quantitative types of courses, and they are "turned off" by the fact that most faculty and students in these courses are men. For the last decade, however, there has been a push to engage girls and young women more fully in the STEM fields (science, technology, engineering, and math). Programs to achieve this purpose have proliferated at the local, state, and federal levels with impressive results.

As an example, in 2004, the University of Hartford, in cooperation with the Capitol Region Education Council (CREC), established a magnet high school with a focus on science and technology. Forty percent of the students enrolled are young women, and they work side by side with high school and university faculty as well as with male students to prepare for college-level work and careers in these challenging fields. Other programs target girls who are even younger—those at the elementary school and junior high levels. These programs are designed to engage young women, help them develop their knowledge and skills, and give them confidence.

A second reason for the change is the growing number of women in technology-based fields who can serve as role models and mentors for those who follow. A simple prescription might be "if you want more women, get more women!" Many academic and professional groups are establishing women's special interest groups that provide women with the opportunity to network, share information, and learn from their peers. The Society of Women Engineers (SWE; http://societyofwomenengineers.swe.org), which embraces women in engineering, engineering technology, and computer science, is one of the more prominent examples of this trend. Its mission is to empower women to succeed and advance in the field of engineering through training and development programs, networking opportunities, scholarships, outreach, and advocacy activities.

In 2001, the National Science Foundation established the ADVANCE Program with the specific goal of increasing the number of women faculty in the STEM fields. To date, a number of major universities and a growing number of smaller universities and colleges have been recipients of ADVANCE grants. These institutions are helping to develop a new generation of women faculty in these fields who can serve as teachers and guides for thousands of female students in the years to come.

Finally, funding sources are beginning to open up more, albeit slowly, to women entrepreneurs in technology-based fields. Many of these firms have the potential for rapid growth, but they often require long lead times before they can begin to generate revenues. This necessitates substantial amounts of funding, typically from external providers of equity. In 2001, a talented group of women researchers (Brush et al., 2001a) conducted an extensive study that they called the "Diana Project," which revealed that only 5 percent of venture capital funding goes to women-owned firms, even though those firms represent a much higher percentage of the total. Brush and her colleagues (2004) also noted that venture capital firms with women managers tend to attract more women entrepreneurs. These scholars concluded that there is a need for more women who can serve as investors in women-owned firms and key decision makers in venture capital firms.

Technology-Based Firms

The term *technology-based firm* is widely used, and it has many different definitions and interpretations. Within the context of this book, firms were designated as "technology-based" using a definition based on an article written by Chapple and colleagues (2004). This article identifies a set of occupations that were science and engineering intensive, as well as industries where the number of employees in those occupations was three times the national average. For purposes of this research, we used this refined list of industries at the six-digit NAICS level provided by the Carnegie Mellon University Center for Economic Development (CED). These types of firms are often referred to as "technology employers." Firms were also designated as technology-based from a definition that uses industry data from the NSF's Survey of Industrial Research and Development. According to these data, firms were considered "primary technology generators" if they exceeded the U.S. average for both research and development expenditures per employee and for the proportion of full-time-equivalent R&D scientists and engineers in the industry workforce (Paytas and Berglund, 2004). There is quite a bit of overlap between firms that are defined as "technology employers" and those defined as "technology generators." When we speak of technology-based firms, we mean firms that fit either (or both) of these classifications. For a detailed list of NAICS codes that make up this technology-based firm definition, please see the appendix at the end of this chapter. A review of the industries covered in the appendix reveals that the term *technology-based* spans a broad range of industries from manufacturing to pharmaceuticals to electronics to computers to software to engineering and testing services and more. In other words, this is a wide field of opportunity for women entrepreneurs.

Technology-based firms frequently have some type of competitive advantage in the form of intellectual property—for example, a patent, license, or copyright. These protections serve as a barrier to entry for other competitors and provide the firm with a window of opportunity to establish itself within a new and growing market. In research using Kauffman Firm Survey data, the authors (Robb and Coleman, 2010) found that firms with some type of intellectual property had an advantage from a financing perspective as well. These firms were able to raise significantly higher levels of equity from external sources. In this sense, intellectual property can serve as a positive "signal" to outside investors.

• The Role of Business Incubators in Fostering the Development of Technology-Based Firms

Many technology-based firms have long lead times before they are able to bring a product to market and become profitable. During that often extended period of development, it is critically important for technology-based entrepreneurs to have access to financial resources, as well as the types of human and social capital that can help them launch their firms. This is where business incubators, many of which are supported by state and federal governments, come in. Business incubators are based on the "knowledge spillover theory of entrepreneurship," which states that locations that have a high density of networks to support the transmission of knowledge and information will also have higher levels of entrepreneurship (Amezcua, 2010). Treanor and colleagues (2010) defined a business incubator as "an effective support mechanism for nascent high-growth, high-risk enterprises, especially those related to SET—science, engineering, and technology."

Business incubators are often located on university campuses or in science or technology parks. Their purpose is to provide a shared venue for new firms that may include support services such as reduced rental rates, business support, mentoring and advice, and access to facilities and networks (Treanor and Henry, 2010). Prior research suggests that these services increase the likelihood of survival for new firms and help them grow more rapidly (Bollingtoft and Ulhoi, 2005). Prior research also indicates that women-owned firms are less likely to be housed in business incubators because, traditionally, women have been less likely to start firms in the areas of science, engineering, and technology (Treanor and Henry, 2010). As more women venture into technology-based entrepreneurship, one of our challenges will be to ensure that business incubators reach out to women entrepreneurs.

Financing Challenges for Technology-Based Firms

Prior research documents some of the challenges for technology-based entrepreneurs who seek financing (Brierley, 2001). Many such firms are based on intellectual rather than physical capital, so few tangible assets may be available to use as collateral for loans. Further, technology-based firms often create new products, new markets, and even new industries. This very "newness" can be a problem because there is no common body of knowledge to help potential investors evaluate the prospects of the firm. This lack of information is referred to as "asymmetric information," and it serves as a deterrent to both debt and equity investors.

So how do these firms get started? Typically they do so by relying on the personal financial resources of the entrepreneur. These come in the form of personal savings, loans secured by personal property, and even credit cards. In this sense, technology-based firms are not that different from entrepreneurial firms in general. The differences appear, however, when the firm begins to grow and its new product or technology takes hold. This has the potential to create an entirely new market accompanied by dramatic growth. That's where the need for large amounts of external financing kicks in!

Using Kauffman Firm Survey data, the authors (Robb and Coleman, 2010) tested the applicability of two major theories of financing for a sample of technology-based and non-technology-based new firms. The first theory, the "Pecking Order Theory" (Myers, 1984; Myers and Majluf, 1984), states that a financing hierarchy exists based on the cost of various sources of financing. Since outsiders have less information about the firm than insiders do, external sources of capital will be more costly than internal capital in the form of retained earnings. In the case of relatively new, technology-based firms, the cost of external equity, in particular, will be higher due to the combined problems of asymmetric information and a higher risk of failure. Equity holders are "in line" behind debt holders in terms of receiving cash flows from the firm. Thus, they bear greater risk and expect a higher return. Correspondingly, firm owners who do not wish to relinquish control to outsiders choose to use internal financing in the form of retained earnings and personal funds first, followed by external debt. They only use external equity as a last resort, because that typically entails sharing equity with outside investors.

The second theory is the "Life Cycle Theory" (Berger and Udell, 1998). This theory states that firms use different types of financing at different stages of firm growth. Thus, small, new firms will rely primarily on internal sources of financing, largely because it is difficult for outsiders to evaluate the prospects of the firm at this early stage. As the firm matures, however, and becomes less "informationally opaque," it can draw upon sources of external debt and equity.

Prior research has revealed that both the Pecking Order and Life Cycle theories apply in the case of small, new firms (Coleman, 2006; Coleman and Cohn, 2000). Robb and Coleman (2010) found, however, that they did not necessarily hold in the case of new technology-based firms. Their findings revealed that technology-based firms raised a substantially higher ratio of external equity to total capital even during their earliest stages of development. The authors concluded that the owners of technology-based firms are willing to trade off their concerns regarding the costs associated with external equity. Further, they are willing to share ownership and control in return for equity investments that will help the firm develop and grow in order to reach its full potential.

Table 8.1 provides a breakdown of financing sources for all firms included in the Kauffman Firm Survey—technology-based firms only and non-technology-based firms only—for 2004, the start-up year. It reveals that technology-based firms raised more than four times as much external equity as non-technology-based firms, even in their first year of operation!

TABLE 8.1 Start-up capital by technical status, 2004

	All (\$)	*High-tech* (\$)	*Non high-tech* (\$)	*All* (%)	*High-tech* (%)	*Non high-tech* (%)
Owner equity	32,728	30,200	32,884	28.5	21.2	29.1
Insider equity	2,041	2,404	2,019	1.8	1.7	1.8
Outsider equity	18,213	63,313	15,434	15.9	44.4	13.7
Owner debt	4,944	6,662	4,838	4.3	4.7	4.3
Insider debt	6,838	4,047	7,010	6.0	2.8	6.2
Outsider debt	49,929	36,065	50,783	43.5	25.3	45.0
Total financial capital	114,693	142,693	112,967	100.0	100.0	100.0

Source: Kauffman Firm Survey Microdata.

What do our findings regarding the financing strategies of technology-based firms mean for you? First, they mean that technology-based entrepreneurs should be aware that it may take a substantial amount of time for them to develop their product or service, bring it to market, and gain market acceptance. Second, they should also anticipate that if they don't move quickly enough through these early stages, some other enterprising entrepreneur will get there first. Thus, there is pressure to raise substantial amounts of capital quickly. Third, technology-based firms often require external capital in the form of both debt and equity to fund development and growth. In light of this technology-based entrepreneurs must be open to bringing in outside investors. Higher levels of external debt increase the riskiness of the firm, while higher levels of external equity often involve sharing ownership and control. These are the tradeoffs that many technology-based entrepreneurs accept in launching and growing their firms.

Table 8.2 provides a breakdown of the financing strategies for technology-based firms included in the KFS by gender. We can see that women-owned technology-based firms invested much less start-up capital in their firms

TABLE 8.2 Capital structure of new technology-based firms: Initial start-up capital and new financial injections

	All firms: 2004			
Start-up capital	*Female ($)*	*Male ($)*	*Female (%)*	*Male (%)*
Owner equity	20,967	31,857	32.2	20.4
Insider equity	1,993	2,482	3.1	1.6
Outsider equity	2,654	74,004	4.1	47.3
Owner debt	5,558	6,871	8.5	4.4
Insider debt	2,699	4,292	4.1	2.7
Outsider debt	31,317	36,981	48.0	23.6
Total financial capital	65,187	156,486	100.0	100.0
	Average annual new injections (2005–2008)			
	Female ($)	*Male ($)*	*Female (%)*	*Male (%)*
Owner equity	6,768	33,896	11.3	19.8
Insider equity	545	3,996	0.9	2.3
Outsider equity	16,999	77,893	28.4	45.5
Owner debt	7,396	5,581	12.4	3.3
Insider debt	2,624	6,088	4.4	3.6
Outsider debt	25,477	43,872	42.6	25.6
Total financial capital	59,809	171,326	100.0	100.0

Source: Kauffman Firm Survey Microdata.

compared to men ($65,187 vs. $156,486). Further, they invested lower levels in subsequent years as well. New financial injections averaged about $60,000 per year for women over the 2005–2008 period, compared with more than $170,000 for men. Interestingly, although women continued to use much lower levels of outsider equity (VC, angels, etc.) in subsequent years, it made up a much larger percentage of their overall funding (28 percent) than in the initial year (4 percent). Even so, technology-based firms owned by men continued to receive more than 45 percent of their funding from outsider equity on average over the same period, and they received nearly half (47.3 percent) of their start-up capital from this source of funding.

Why do we see different patterns in financing technology-based firms owned by women compared to those owned by men? Several theories have been put forth, some pertaining to women entrepreneurs' demand for capital and others pertaining to the supplies of capital that are available to them. In terms of demand, some researchers have found that women are more risk averse than men (Jianakoplos and Bernasek, 1998; Powell and Ansic, 1997). If this is the case, women entrepreneurs may tend toward more conservative financing strategies that are more reliant on internal sources of capital and less reliant on external debt.

Because Table 8.2 indicates that women entrepreneurs in the KFS actually used a higher percentage of outside debt than men, the theory of greater risk aversion does not appear to hold in this case. Other researchers contend, however, that women business owners are more concerned with retaining control of their firms and less willing to share ownership with outsiders (Watson et al., 2009). If this is the case, women entrepreneurs would show less reliance on external equity compared to external debt, as Table 8.2 illustrates.

From the perspective of supply, most recent research on bank borrowing indicates that women business owners are just as likely to be approved for loans as men (Coleman, 2002; Haynes and Haynes, 1999; Orser et al., 2006). Further, recent studies have found little evidence of a "finance gap" in bank loans for women when compared to men (Watson et al., 2009). In terms of external equity, however, researchers associated with the Diana Project contend that women entrepreneurs face structural barriers that deny them access to sources of external equity in particular. These researchers cite statistics pointing to the low percentage of venture capital that goes to women-owned firms, as well as the small number of women in key decision-making roles in venture capital firms (Brush et al., 2001a; Brush et al., 2004).

These conflicting supply findings for debt versus equity are borne out in our data from the KFS. Table 8.2 reveals that women were just as reliant—actually, more reliant—on external debt than men, suggesting that they did not experience problems of either demand, as we just saw, or supply. Alternatively, however, women were dramatically less reliant on external equity. This finding may be say something about women's concerns about control, or it may be indicative of supply problems in the area of external equity. Our minicase on DailyWorth in Chapter 4 documents the frustration of one woman entrepreneur who sought venture capital financing for her firm. She found the process much more time consuming and longer in duration than she ever anticipated. Nevertheless, our interviews with both growth-oriented and technology-based entrepreneurs indicate that they were willing and eager to secure external sources of equity. Their experience suggests problems of supply rather than of demand. Let's take a look at the experience of one of our technology-based entrepreneurs, Hilary DeCesare, the founder of Everloop.

Principles in Action: Everloop

Everloop (www.everloop.com) grew out of a venture called Girl Ambition, which started in 2007. Girl Ambition was a safe and secure online environment for girls to chat, post videos, and email one another. Hilary DeCesare cofounded the firm with two other women after seeing the potential dangers inherent in online networking websites like Facebook. Two years later, the founders approached Tim Donovan, a kids' media expert, to discuss the possibility of expanding their market to include boys. This paved the way for the launch of Everloop in June 2009. Prior to the launch of Everloop, Hilary spent more than ten years at Oracle Corporation in various sales management positions. She also had prior experience as an entrepreneur, having subsequently cofounded a management consulting firm that provided counseling to company executives in the areas of strategic planning and corporate development. As her track record demonstrates, Hilary is an accomplished entrepreneur and experienced in all aspects of launching and growing businesses.

In spite of her prior experience and many accomplishments, however, Hilary said that trying to raise funds in the summer and fall of 2009 during the financial crisis was the most stressful challenge she ever faced. At that time, bank loans were scarce, and VCs were hesitant to invest early. Hilary saw many businesses fail due to lack of funding. As she expressed it, her firm had to be "really scrappy" to survive and raise money in that environment. Nevertheless, when Hilary first spoke to us, she had just finished raising $500,000 of Everloop's first seed round that closed for $3.1 million. The first $1.5 million was raised from founders, friends, and family members. The three founders had also taken out a small business bank loan of $250,000 in their names for liquidity needs.

Hilary is currently raising her Series A round of funding and is oversubscribed at around $10 million. She is also in discussions with two to three investment groups who want to participate in this round. When we spoke with Hilary recently, she noted how dramatically the funding environment changed from 2009 to 2010.

It's amazing how we have gone from such a shortage of funding to such an abundance of funding in just a year! In the fall of 2009, we were scrambling for money, and now we are oversubscribed! It is a completely different funding environment, but we have retained the scrappy management strategies that we developed during those hard times.

Hilary is a big fan of groups like Springboard and Astia, which assist women entrepreneurs with their business models, help them to network with investors, and link them to a broad community of supporters. She joined Springboard just over a year ago and credits that organization as one of the reasons she was able to secure the funding for her seed round. Springboard reviewed her materials and presentation and had her go back and redo the presentation after giving her specific points to focus on. Springboard also introduced her to an attorney, whom Hilary subsequently hired, and introduced her to other potential funding sources. Even though she brings many years of experience to her new venture, Hilary feels that these types of programs can be helpful in broadening her network, as well as for fine-tuning her business model. When we first spoke with her, she was heading off to New York to pitch her business at an investor meeting for Springboard, and she had just found out she was selected to pitch her business as a finalist in the Women 2.0 pitch event in San Francisco the following month. She definitely took advantage of every opportunity!

When we interviewed Hilary, she was very confident that Everloop would be a very profitable venture. When asked to explain her reasoning, she was able to succinctly describe key drivers of the firm's success. First, there is an underserved market of parents who want a safe, secure environment for social networking for their children in the 8- to 13-year-old age range. Second, Everloop is designed to address that need, and in doing so, it will generate revenue streams from a variety of sources. These include sponsors of fan groups, private labels for sponsors at a higher tier, and a "virtual economy" where kids (through their parents) can buy Evercredits that they can use to purchase virtual assets such as stickers, interactive pranks called Goobs, games, and fun apps on demand. Finally, Hilary was able to estimate the purchasing power of her market. Children in this age group spend about $43 billion a year out of their own pockets, typically received through allowances, payment for chores, birthday gifts, and so on. These kids influence another $155 billion in purchases. The growth in virtual goods has been dramatic, reaching about $1.6 billion last year. Hilary has already tapped into the international potential for her firm by partnering with Mad Science Kids' Club to bring their 5 million members in Canada and the United States online into a social networking group of their own within the Everloop platform.

Based on her experience with Everloop, Hilary has several insights to share with potential entrepreneurs:

- Get involved with groups like Springboard, Women 2.0, and Astia to network and learn.
- Don't spend a ton of money on marketing until you are ready to launch, because things change as you get closer to launching, and you don't want to have a lot invested before you are close to entering the market.
- Don't do huge press events until the quarter after you've launched. Things happen, issues come up, and tweaking things is a necessary part of the process. Make sure you have all of those things fixed *before* you do a huge press event.
- Believe in yourself and in what you are doing. This belief and passion and the sense that there is a reason for what you are doing will help you get through the challenges you will surely face as you try to launch and grow your business.
- Assume you need double what you think you need in terms of cash. It always takes longer and costs more than you expect.

In addition to the sources of financing referenced in the case of Everloop, technology-based firms, by the nature of their products and services, have opportunities to draw upon other sources of financing. These include grants and contracts from government sources. Often these grants are designed to help the firm develop and commercialize new technologies. Two other important sources of funding are the SBIR (Small Business Innovation Research) Program and the STTR (Small Business Technology Transfer) Program. Both of these programs are federally funded programs administered by the U.S. Small Business Administration. Their intent is to ensure that the nation's small, innovative, high-tech firms are a part of the federal government's research and development efforts.

The Impact of Venture Capital Investments on Ownership and Control

Previously, we discussed the important role that venture capitalists play in funding the development of rapid growth and technology-based firms. From the standpoint of the entrepreneur, a venture capitalist has the potential to invest a relatively large amount of equity capital over a period of years. Since venture capital firms typically specialize by industry, they provide additional value in terms of expertise (human capital) and contacts (social capital). The downside of accepting venture capital is that it involves sharing ownership and control. Each time the venture capitalist provides an infusion of capital, she also takes a percentage of equity. This gives the VC a voice in decision making and management, and it entitles the VC firm to a share of future cash flows when the firm is sold or goes public. How does this work in practice? Let's use our Heavenly Chocolate Company as an example.*

As Figure 5.1 in Chapter 5 illustrates, Heavenly Chocolate had net income of $1.14 million in its most recent year of operation. When a venture capitalist invests in a firm, she typically does so with a five- to seven-year horizon. Thus, she is interested in the estimated value of the firm five to seven years out. Let's say that Heavenly Chocolate will experience a 500 percent increase in earnings over the course of the next five years and that firms in the candy industry typically sell at a multiple of ten times earnings. Thus, the estimated value of the firm in Year 5 will be $57 million:

Earnings today: $1.14 M

Earnings in five years: 5 × $1.14 M = $5.7 M

* The valuation and control method described in this section is based on "A Method for Valuing High-Risk, Long-Term Investments" by William A. Sahlman, Harvard Business School, July 2009.

$$\text{Value of the firm in Year 5, assuming a multiple of } 10 \times \text{earnings} = 10 \times \$5.7\text{ M} = \$57\text{ M}$$

During its first round of investment, the VC firm plans to invest $2 million in Heavenly Chocolate. What share of ownership will they receive in return? To answer this question, we need to know the VC's required rate of return on her investment and her time horizon. Since early-stage firms have a higher risk of failure, let's assume that the VC expects a return of 50 percent on this early-stage investment. Let's also assume that the VC anticipates that Heavenly Chocolate will either go public or be sold at the end of Year 5. We calculate the VC's ownership share as follows:

$$\text{Round 1 ownership share} = (1.50^5 \times \$2\text{ M})/\$57\text{ M} = 26.6\%$$

Thus, after Round 1, the VC owns 26.6 percent of the firm. Heavenly Chocolate continues to grow and expand both domestically and internationally. By the third year of operation, additional external capital is required to fund this growth. Heavenly Chocolate's founder goes back to her friendly venture capitalist for another round of funding. This round, provided in Year 3, is for another $2 million. Since Heavenly Chocolate is more firmly established and growing rapidly now, it is not as risky as in its first year of operation. Thus, the VC's required rate of return on this second round of financing is 35 percent. We can calculate the VC's additional ownership share for this second round as follows:

$$\text{Round 2 ownership share} = (1.35^3 \times \$2\text{ M})/\$57\text{ M} = 8.6\text{ percent}$$

After the second round of financing, the VC owns 35.2 percent (26.6 + 8.6) of the firm in total. On we go! In Year 5 we see Heavenly Chocolate preparing for an initial public offering. The firm needs one additional round of financing in the amount of $2 million to solidify its global position as a premier provider of candies and confections. Enter the VC, stage left! At this point, Heavenly Chocolate is a well-established, growth-oriented firm. The IPO, which is planned within the next 18 months, is expected to be very well received. This final round of financing is later-stage financing and involves considerably less risk than earlier rounds. Thus, the VC's required rate of return is 25 percent. The ownership share for this last round of financing is as follows:

$$\text{Round 3 ownership share} = (1.25^1 \times \$2\text{ M})/\$57\text{ M}$$
$$= 4.4 \text{ percent}$$

After three rounds of financing, the VC firm now owns 39.6 percent (26.6 + 8.6 + 4.4) of the firm.

As we review this progression, we can see the delicate balance between the interests of the entrepreneur and those of the venture capitalist. Obviously, the entrepreneur wants to retain as much ownership and control as possible. Conversely, the VC would like to gain a greater share of the company in order to provide a higher return to her investors when Heavenly Chocolate goes public. It is a tricky relationship to be sure! An entrepreneur can hang onto a larger share of the firm by postponing the point at which she needs to turn to VCs for financing. This can be done by bootstrapping, obtaining financing from family and friends, or using angel investors. At the same time, she does not want to smother the firm's opportunities for growth by not raising sufficient amounts of external capital.

As we will see in the minicases in this book, growth-oriented and technology-based entrepreneurs, in particular, often bite the bullet on accepting venture capital financing. They feel that the advantage of securing necessary capital outweighs the disadvantage of sharing ownership and control. In essence, they are willing to accept a smaller slice of what they hope will be a much larger pie.

Small Business Innovation Research Grants

Small Business Innovation Research (SBIR) grants represent another relatively unique source of financing for technology-based firms. The Small Business Innovation Research Program was originally authorized by Congress in 1982 to assist technology-based companies in the development of new products. Today, the SBIR program involves 11 federal agencies, of which the Department of Defense is the largest. Over $2 billion in funding is available each year, and firms must submit an application in order to secure funding.

SBIR grants are designed for technology-based firms that have fewer than 500 employees. The firm must be at least 51 percent U.S. owned, and all work under the grant must be done in the United States. SBIR grants are grants, not loans, so they do not have to be paid back. Further, an SBIR grant does not require the firm owner to give up any equity.

SBIR grants are awarded in three different "phases," and a single company can received multiple grants. Phase I provides funding up to $150,000 to conduct a feasibility study on the new product. Phase II, during which the company conducts research and development to design a prototype, can be funded at a level of up to $1 million. Finally, Phase III is the commercialization stage. At this stage the company is expected to secure outside funding in order to further develop and commercialize the product.

From the entrepreneur's perspective, the advantage of securing SBIR funding is not just the money but the access to expertise and key contacts as well. Researchers have also pointed out that securing an SBIR grant is like a Good Housekeeping Seal of Approval in the sense that firms that receive these grants are in a better position to attract other funding sources (Audretsch, 2002; Lerner, 1999).

According to Deb Santy, director of Connecticut's SBIR Program, SBIR grants are an underrecognized and underused source of funding for technology-based firms. She would love to see more women entrepreneurs apply for and use this valuable program. To learn more about the SBIR program in your state, go to the SBIR website at http://www.sbir.gov.

In addition to programs sponsored by the federal government, state and local governments may also offer incentives—often in the form of tax credits, loans, or grants—for the establishment of technology-based firms, particularly those that target certain industries. Check with your state's Department of Economic Development to determine if your firm or industry qualifies for any of these opportunities.

Strategic partnerships represent yet another financing strategy for technology-based firms. As just noted, it can take years to develop and test a new technology-based product or service. During that time, money continues to flow out, but nothing is flowing in yet! A strategic partnership could take the form of funding, laboratory space, key personnel, administrative support, or other resources provided by a larger and better-endowed firm. Not surprisingly, these arrangements come with various strings attached, but, nevertheless, a collaboration of this type may help you launch and develop your business.

Principles in Action: ElectroChem

Radha Jalan started out as what we might describe as a "reluctant entrepreneur" when her husband, Vinod, died suddenly in 1992. Vinod Jalan had founded ElectroChem (www.fuelcell.com) in 1986 in order to develop products and services in the area of hydrogen fuel cell technology. When he died, Radha, a stay-at-home mom, was faced with the prospect of either selling the company or running it herself (Amatucci and Coleman, 2007). She chose the latter for several reasons, and she has never regretted her decision.

First and foremost, following the death of her husband, Radha had to find a way to support herself and her family.

I had one daughter in high school and one in college, with no money for tuition. Because of the money my husband and I had personally invested in the firm, we had no money and no savings. I had to support us, and this was a way to do it.

A second motivation was Radha's desire for the flexibility that she would have by running her own firm. As she expressed it:

I still had a daughter at home, and she had just lost her dad. She needed me, and it was important at that time that I have the flexibility to be there for her.

Another important motivation for Radha was the fact that so many people in the very male-dominated fuel cell industry expressed the belief that she would not or could not manage the firm. Although Radha did not have a technical background, she was well educated, with a doctorate from the University of Florida, and she had grown up in an entrepreneurial family and culture in India. She believed she had many of the necessary attributes in the form of human resources to be a successful business owner. She also had social capital in the form of a network of friends and supporters, many of whom were members of the Indian community, who provided encouragement and advice. Ultimately, Radha decided to take the plunge and set out to prove the naysayers wrong.

I don't know if it was because I was a woman or if it was because I was a member of a minority group, but initially, many people in this industry didn't take me seriously. People didn't think I could do it, and I had a lot of pressure to sell the firm. Over the years I have proven myself, however, and they take me seriously today!

Today ElectroChem researches, develops, tests, and manufactures fuel cells and fuel cell testing equipment. Fuel cells generate electricity without burning fuel. Their advantage is that they do so without using hazardous materials. Thus, they represent a renewable and nonpolluting energy source (Amatucci and Coleman, 2007). Like the majority of firms in the fuel cell industry, ElectroChem is relatively small, with approximately ten employees and annual revenues in the range of $3 million. Although the fuel cell industry has been around for some time, it is still, in many ways, a fledgling industry and a developing technology. Most firms in the fuel cell industry are not profitable, and they depend on support in the form of government grants and contracts to do their research and development work. Radha's firm is no exception in this regard. Over the years, her firm has secured financing in the form of grants and contracts from NASA and the Department of Energy (DOE), as well as from the Electric Power Research Institute (EPRI). Radha noted that her relationship with NASA, in particular, has been very strong.

NASA knows our firm and trusts us. They value our relationship and recognize our leadership in the fuel cell industry, as well as the integrity of the firm and our results.

Radha has supplemented these sources of income with sales of her products to research facilities worldwide. She has also used home equity and business lines of credit but notes that "banks don't really understand high-tech companies."

At one point, Radha also brought in several angel investors to provide additional capital. Unfortunately, that was not a good experience for either her or the firm. Within months, the investors' goals diverged from Radha's, and they pressured her to break up the firm in order to allow them to take over one of the more promising lines of business. Radha refused, and relations continued to deteriorate. Eventually the investor group sued ElectroChem and Radha, claiming that she had misrepresented the condition of the firm in order to lure them into investing. After a considerable amount of time and expense, Radha settled the case by paying off the four angel investors (Amatucci and Coleman, 2007). This ordeal taught her to trust her instincts, and she also learned that having a reputation as an expert does not automatically make someone the right fit for a particular firm. One size does not fit all, to be sure. Radha also learned that she needed to be more cautious about trusting other people. Further, she had to ensure that future contracts were structured in such a way as to protect her interests, not just those of her investors.

Our industry is still developing, so funding is always a struggle. Banks do not really understand technology companies, and when you bring in outside investors, that can pose its own set of challenges, as can be seen from my experience.

One important source of funding for ElectroChem has been SBIR grants. Over the years, the firm has received a number of SBIR grants to develop new hydrogen fuel cell applications. A recent SBIR grant awarded by NASA will allow ElectroChem to develop a water removal membrane for fuel cells that will operate at high-current densities. This technology will help NASA develop lunar-type rovers and will also increase the efficiency and reduce the cost of fuels cells for automobiles and backup systems.

In 2011 ElectroChem celebrated its twenty-fifth year in business. Radha is widely known and respected in the fuel cell industry, and in 2009 she received a Lifetime Achievement Award for her leadership and success from the Mountain States Hydrogen Business Council. In assessing her entrepreneurial journey, Radha feels a sense of accomplishment and pride.

We have taken a role in developing a technology that will contribute to a clean and healthful environment. It is important to have a commitment to what you do. When things get tough, money alone will not sustain you; you have to believe in what you are doing. You also have to have both short-term and long-term goals for the firm; you need a vision. There were times when things were not going the way we wanted in the short term, and there was a temptation to just give up. At times like that, I would think about my longer-term goals, and that would keep me going.

Radha also expressed the belief that she has enjoyed the economic rewards of entrepreneurship and that ElectroChem has enabled her to achieve a flexible and comfortable lifestyle and quality of life while also providing employment for other people. Further, it has allowed her to become a role model for her daughters and for other women entrepreneurs.

If I just had financial success and my family did not turn out well, it would not be enough. But both of my daughters are strong, accomplished women. That is a big piece of my success.

• Angel Investors: The Devil Is in the Details

Angel investors are individual investors who invest their own money in entrepreneurial ventures with the goal of achieving a return on their investment. These investments can be in the form of debt or equity, and in the case of equity, the entrepreneur shares ownership and control with her angel investors. Angel investors invest for a variety of reasons. Often they are high-net-worth individuals seeking attractive returns. In other instances, they are successful entrepreneurs themselves and want to support new entrepreneurs in a specific industry. Although we tend to hear more about venture capital investing, there are far more angel investors than there are venture capital firms, and they invest far greater amounts in many more firms. Whereas only a tiny fraction of firms receive venture capital funding, many firms benefit from the involvement of angel investors. Unlike venture capital firms that tend to focus on a fairly narrow set of industries, such as high-tech and bioscience, angels invest across a broad range of industries. The Center for Venture Research at the University of New Hampshire reported that there were 265,400 active angel investors in 2010, representing a slight increase over 2009 (Sohl, 2011). Women angels represented 13 percent of that total.

Another difference between angel and venture capital investors is that angels tend to make smaller investments. In recent years, however, angel investors have been banding together into angel investment networks, which gives them the opportunity to invest larger amounts in aggregate while spreading risk across a number of investors. Individual angel investors and angel networks identify deals through a broad range of sources that come into contact with entrepreneurs and new ventures. These include accountants, attorneys, industry associations and contacts, other angel investors, and the like. Although research has shown that a relatively small percentage of women entrepreneurs actually seek angel financing, those who do are just as successful in obtaining it as men (Becker-Blease and Sohl, 2007). In general, however, entrepreneurs tend to seek financing from investors of the same sex. Since there are relatively few women angel investors, this poses a challenge for women entrepreneurs (Becker-Blease and Sohl, 2007).

As just noted, angel investors are individual investors and, as such, they may have individual goals and motivations. They may also have different requirements and expectations regarding their level of involvement and control in the company. Some angels are very hands-off, while others want to be directly involved in management and decision making. As Radha's example illustrates, it is important to address the issue of shared ownership and control to ensure that the goals of the entrepreneur are consistent with those of the angel investors. Even when such early discussions take place, however, there is still the risk of different "agendas."

What Have We Learned?

In this chapter we saw that technology-based entrepreneurship offers a wealth of opportunities to women entrepreneurs and aspiring women entrepreneurs. If you want to be a technology-based entrepreneur, however, you have to plan ahead and start early because it is essential to have the necessary human capital attributes in the form of education and experience.

We also discussed "asymmetric information," or the problem of incomplete information flows between the entrepreneur and potential investors. This problem is particularly acute in the case of technology-based firms because they are often based on new products, new markets, and new industries. A big part of your challenge as a technology-based entrepreneur is to reduce the level of asymmetric information by providing necessary information and sending positive signals. Examples of positive signals include having the right type of education and prior experience, including prior start-up experience; developing and protecting intellectual property; and securing financing from known sources who can then serve as signals to subsequent sources.

Finally, we saw that the technology-based entrepreneur has a very big bag of financing tricks at her disposal! In spite of the complexities associated with launching a technology-based firm, their very nature gives rise to a broader array of financing options than many other types of firms enjoy. Typically, technology-based firms are launched with the personal financial resources of the entrepreneur. They may go on to raise various types of bank debt (often secured by personal assets), angel, and venture capital financing. In addition, however, technology-based firms have opportunities to secure government grants, contracts, and tax credits, and they also have opportunities to establish strategic partnerships with larger firms that are eager to gain access to new technologies.

What Does All This Mean For Me?

Technology-based firms offer women the opportunity to develop new products, new services, and new markets. They may also provide the opportunity to satisfy personal goals such as finding a more effective way to administer life-saving drugs or sustaining the environment. Finally, because some technologies actually create whole new industries, they offer the opportunity for substantial growth and wealth. What are some of the keys to securing the financing that will allow you to go from Point A to Point B in these exciting new industries?

1. First, make sure that your leadership team has the proper mix of education and experience, because you may not have all these credentials on your own. Given the uncertainties surrounding new technologies and technology-based firms, it is important to send as many positive signals as you can to

potential investors. One way to do this is by assembling a leadership team that has the appropriate college and graduate degrees as well as a track record of achievement in the industry. Since the technology is often new and unknown, investors are essentially betting on you and the team you put together. Make it a good team!

2. Along the same lines, investigate the availability of business incubators in your area. These may be associated with individual universities or with science or technology parks. As we saw, business incubators offer their tenants a variety of services, including reduced rates for space, facilities and equipment, office support, mentoring and advisory services, and access to key contacts during those critical early months and years. A good place to start your search for business incubators in your state would be the state Department of Economic Development. There is also a National Association of Business Incubators (www.nbia.org).
3. Prepare for the long haul. It can take years for a technology-based product or service to go through the patenting process, clinical trials, or FDA approval. Be prepared for that, and understand that you will probably be spending a lot of your time raising money for a number of years. Further, the money, particularly equity investments, may come in tranches, which means that you get additional funding only after you have achieved certain benchmarks.
4. Recognize the value of intellectual property, and take the necessary steps to protect it. Intellectual property in the form of patents, formulas, copyrights, or trademarks acts as a barrier to entry against potential competitors. That can buy you some time while you get your firm up and running.
5. Take advantage of the education, services, and networks provided by organizations focused on the development of growth-oriented and technology-based firms. Although Hilary DeCesare, the founder of Everloop, had prior experience in both the technology field and entrepreneurship, she struggled to find investors until she began working with Springboard Enterprises. Membership in that organization opened doors not only to potential funding sources but also to other types of advice, training, and support.
6. Cast a wide net, and be doggedly persistent! Technology-based entrepreneurs use some of the traditional sources of financing for their firms (personal savings, family and friends, bank loans, angel and venture capital),

but they also have access to other types of financing, including government grants, contracts, and tax credits. If you are developing a new technology, you may also be a candidate for a strategic partnership with a larger, established firm that can provide a broad array of resources. Keep an open mind, and consider these various financing alternatives to determine if they will help you to achieve your longer-term goals for the firm. Finally, if one source of financing falls through, go after another! Be creative, persistent, and undaunted in your financing strategy!

• Tips for Technology-Based Entrepreneurs

1. Create a well-rounded leadership team.
2. Check out business incubators in your area.
3. Prepare for the long haul!
4. Protect your intellectual property.
5. Identify and become a part of networks that support technology-based entrepreneurs.
6. Cast a wide net for sources of financing.

Public Policy Implications

Technology-based entrepreneurship is critical for keeping the United States globally competitive. It is also critically important from a national security perspective. Further, technology-based entrepreneurship holds the keys to helping us address issues pertaining to health and wellness, quality of life, productivity, and sustainability. For too long, many women have been closed off from technology-based entrepreneurship due to educational, employment, financial, and structural barriers. Gradually, these barriers are being lifted, and an increasing number of women are acquiring the human, financial, and social capital that will equip them to be the technology-based entrepreneurs of tomorrow.

Much of this progress has been prompted by programs launched and funded at the state and federal levels. Some of these, such as the NSF ADVANCE Program, specifically target women. Others, such as the SBIR and

STTR Programs, target technology-based firms more generally but have the potential to benefit women as well as men. It is important, particularly in this environment of difficult and unattractive budget decisions, that funding for such programs continue. As previously noted, many technology-based firms have long development cycles, and they do not generate revenues for years. Simultaneously, however, their costs for research, product development, clinical trials, and approvals are high. Although angel and venture capital can close some of the funding gap, these sources are often not sufficient. Thus, government funding to support the development of new technologies and technology-based firms is essential.

It is also important for us to continue to develop and fund educational programs that engage girls and young women in the STEM fields at an early age. By doing so, we further enfranchise the next generation of entrepreneurial women, and, in doing so, we create new opportunities for both personal and economic empowerment.

Recently the Kauffman Foundation in cooperation with the Information Technology and Innovation Foundation published its *2010 State New Economy Index* (Atkinson and Andes, 2010). This report details the success factors that state economies need to drive innovation-based growth. These include economies that are knowledge-based, globalized, entrepreneurial, IT-driven, and innovation-based. The report goes on to rate the performance of the states in each of these factors as well as subsets within each factor. Policy recommendations for innovation-based growth include the following:

1. Aggressive innovation policies, including government support for research, STEM education, R&D tax credits, and strategic support for key industries.
2. Activities to boost infrastructure, educational levels, business support systems, and technology development and transfer systems.
3. Identification of best practices for innovative win-win policies adopted by states in areas such as education and workforce development, entrepreneurial development, research support, technology transfer and commercialization, and manufacturing modernization.
4. Initiatives to leverage private sector and industry funding to support government-funded activities.
5. Cluster initiatives and the creation of knowledge-based networks.
6. Regional innovation strategies.

The report concludes that the current fiscal environment provides states with an opportunity to focus on and reexamine the role of state government in supporting innovation. It is also an opportunity to make tough decisions that will allow us to use existing resources more effectively. Last, but not least, states can themselves serve as engines of innovation by focusing on performance, organizational innovation, and outcome-based rather than process-based accountability.

Appendix: NAICS Codes that Make Up a Technology-Based Category

NAICS 4	NAICS 6	NAICS Industry
2111	211100	Oil and Gas Extraction
2111	211111	Crude Petroleum and Natural Gas Extraction
3251	325100	Basic Chemical Manufacturing
3251	325110	Petrochemical Manufacturing
3251	325120	Industrial Gas Manufacturing
3251	325131	Inorganic Dye and Pigment Manufacturing
3251	325182	Carbon Black Manufacturing
3251	325188	All Other Basic Inorganic Chemical Manufacturing
3251	325192	Cyclic Crude and Intermediate Manufacturing
3251	325199	All Other Basic Organic Chemical Manufacturing
3252	325211	Plastics Material and Resin Manufacturing
3252	325212	Synthetic Rubber Manufacturing
3254	325400	Pharmaceutical and Medicine Manufacturing
3254	325411	Medicinal and Botanical Manufacturing
3254	325412	Pharmaceutical Preparation Manufacturing
3254	325413	In-Vitro Diagnostic Substance Manufacturing
3254	325414	Biological Product (except Diagnostic) Manufacturing
3332	333200	Industrial Machinery Manufacturing
3332	333210	Sawmill and Woodworking Machinery Manufacturing
3332	333220	Plastics and Rubber Industry Machinery Manufacturing
3332	333292	Textile Machinery Manufacturing
3332	333293	Printing Machinery and Equipment Manufacturing

NAICS 4	NAICS 6	NAICS Industry
3332	333294	Food Product Machinery Manufacturing
3332	333295	Semiconductor Machinery Manufacturing
3332	333298	All Other Industrial Machinery Manufacturing
3333	333300	Commercial and Service Industry Machinery Manufacturing
3333	333313	Office Machinery Manufacturing
3333	333314	Optical Instrument and Lens Manufacturing
3333	333315	Photographic and Photocopying Equipment Manufacturing
3333	333319	Other Commercial and Service Industry Machinery Manufacturing
3341	334100	Computer and Peripheral Equipment Manufacturing
3341	334111	Electronic Computer Manufacturing
3341	334113	Computer Terminal Manufacturing
3341	334119	Other Computer Peripheral Equipment Manufacturing
3342	334200	Communications Equipment Manufacturing
3342	334210	Telephone Apparatus Manufacturing
3342	334220	Radio and Television Broadcasting and Wireless Communications Equipment Manufacturing
3342	334290	Other Communications Equipment Manufacturing
3343	334300	Audio and Video Equipment Manufacturing
3343	334310	Audio and Video Equipment Manufacturing
3344	334400	Semiconductor and Other Electronic Component Manufacturing
3344	334412	Bare Printed Circuit Board Manufacturing
3344	334413	Semiconductor and Related Device Manufacturing
3344	334414	Electronic Capacitor Manufacturing
3344	334415	Electronic Resistor Manufacturing
3344	334417	Electronic Connector Manufacturing
3344	334418	Printed Circuit Assembly (Electronic Assembly) Manufacturing
3344	334419	Other Electronic Component Manufacturing
3345	334500	Navigational, Measuring, Electromedical, and Control Instruments Manufacturing

NAICS 4	NAICS 6	NAICS Industry
3345	334510	Electromedical and Electrotherapeutic Apparatus Manufacturing
3345	334511	Search, Detection, Navigation, Guidance, Aeronautical, and Nautical System and Instrument Manufacturing
3345	334512	Automatic Environmental Control Manufacturing for Residential, Commercial, and Appliance Use
3345	334513	Instruments and Related Products Manufacturing for Measuring, Displaying, and Controlling Industrial Process Variables
3345	334514	Totalizing Fluid Meter and Counting Device Manufacturing
3345	334515	Instrument Manufacturing for Measuring and Testing Electricity and Electrical Signals
3345	334516	Analytical Laboratory Instrument Manufacturing
3345	334517	Irradiation Apparatus Manufacturing
3345	334519	Other Measuring and Controlling Device Manufacturing
5112	511200	Software Publishers
5112	511210	Software Publishers
5413	541300	Architectural, Engineering, and Related Services
5413	541310	Architectural Services
5413	541330	Engineering Services
5413	541370	Surveying and Mapping (except Geophysical) Services
5413	541380	Testing Laboratories

Source: U.S. Census Bureau: Foreign Trade Statistics.

OUR PIECE OF THE PIE

Financing Minority-Owned Firms

The Attraction of Entrepreneurship

Women minority-owned firms are an important element of our entrepreneurial story, because their numbers are growing so rapidly! More rapidly, in fact, than the growth rate of women-owned firms overall. What are the reasons behind this dramatic growth? What factors motivate the growing number of women minority entrepreneurs? In speaking with women minority entrepreneurs, at least three types of motivations surface: opportunity, financial gain and economic independence, and family. Let's consider each of these in turn.

Starting with opportunity, many minority women entrepreneurs see an opportunity to put their skills to work filling an unmet need in their local communities (Levent et al., 2003). Other women minority entrepreneurs are motivated by financial gain and economic independence. These women who pursue entrepreneurship with strong endowments of human, social, and financial capital are able to establish growth-oriented firms, technology-based firms, or firms that require specialized skills, education, and training. One of our favorite such firms is Smith Whiley & Company, a women- and minority-owned investment management firm located in Hartford, Connecticut.

Principles in Action: Smith Whiley & Company

Gwendolyn Smith Iloani started thinking about launching her own investment firm in the mid-1990s after rising through the ranks of investment professionals at Aetna, a large insurance company located in Hartford, Connecticut. Gwen had both undergraduate and graduate degrees, and she had a strong track record of investment performance, having managed over $9 billion in assets. Her goal was to become a CEO. Nevertheless, as she looked around her own firm, she realized that no one at the top "looked like me."

I started to think about starting my own business as a result of the glass ceiling. When I looked at the CEO office, I wasn't sure where I would fit in or how long it would take me to get there. I decided to start my own business because I wanted the freedom to realize my ambitions and to control my destiny.

Smith Whiley & Company (www.smithwhiley.com) was established in 1994 to provide mezzanine and private equity funding to firms at the low end of the middle market. Based on her experience as an investment professional, Gwen felt that this was an underserved segment of the market.

I identified a niche in the marketplace that I could serve successfully. The opportunities were exceptional, and I could make a nice profit along the way.

One of Gwen's challenges was to raise enough financial capital to start. The sales cycle is much longer on the investment side, and she anticipated that she would need enough capital to stay in business for about three years until she successfully sold her investment funds to institutional investors. To secure this capital, she negotiated a strategic partnership with her former employer, who put in $2.5 million in a combination of start-up financing and support services in return for one-third of the firm. In turn, Gwen supplied "sweat equity" and an investment of approximately $10,000 of her own money. Gwen's strong track record and her relationships with investment professionals and key decision makers at Aetna was a critical factor in making the strategic partnership happen. Thanks to this source of financing, Gwen did not have to turn to other providers of external capital.

It was like a marriage of two people who knew each other, as opposed to an arranged marriage of two people who don't know each other. Aetna knew the quality of my work, and they trusted me. I had a history with them.

Gwen also secured financing from the Connecticut Development Authority (CDA), a quasi public-private entity that invests in new firms as a way to promote economic development for the state. CDA invested $1 million in Smith Whiley in return for a 10 percent ownership position in the firm.

Gwen established Smith Whiley as a series of funds. Investors include pension fund and endowment funds who hire Smith Whiley to execute their strategy for investing in firms within the niche that Smith Whiley has targeted. To date, the firm has launched three funds, each in excess of $100 million. Attractive earnings allowed Gwen to buy out the minority positions held by Aetna and the Connecticut Development Authority in the late 1990s. Today, Smith Whiley is 100 percent owned by Gwen and by other insiders.

Currently Gwen finances Smith Whiley with earnings from the firm and a bank loan.

With respect to bank financing, we operate in a complicated business, and banks have difficulty understanding the business and the economics. I always do my homework on the potential lender, and I go out of my way to make the analysis easy for them by giving them all of the supporting documents they will need; this is before they ask for it. I am also very patient with them.

As a woman entrepreneur in the field of finance, Gwen has faced challenges, and she has developed strategies for overcoming them.

The financial field is one of the last male bastions, and it is still not fully integrated. When people realize that I am a female, they are taken aback. Then they try to find out if there is a white Mr. Smith or a white Mr. Whiley. Gender is definitely an issue in the world of finance. As a female, I always have to work harder and be better to get the respect that I deserve. Men tend to gravitate and make eye contact with other men versus women. The challenge is to get them to acknowledge you, particularly when you are making an investment presentation and you are asking them to invest millions of dollars into your business as a client. I had to learn to be versatile in my style and approach, and I learned to use my femininity as a strength along with my size, height, and distinctive clothing.

In spite of the tough investment climate in the current economy, the firm is currently preparing to launch its fourth fund, the largest to date. Gwen continues to see investment opportunities in the marketplace, as well as both financial and personal rewards for her and her team.

A major advantage of operating a business is that I used my investment track record to identify an opportunity in the marketplace to sell a high-margin product. In a sense, I created my own opportunity, and at the same time I took control of my destiny. I like the risk taking that I do daily. The rewards for taking risk are apparent immediately. I also enjoy doing a great job for my investors, the recognition the firm receives in the form of awards and reputation, and the benefits that we reap as a result of these things.

Gwen Smith's story of success illustrates the important role played by both human capital in the form of education and relevant experience and social capital in the form of access to key contacts and networks. Both of these essential resource inputs helped Gwen to secure the financial capital needed to launch and grow her firm.

Gwen is a great example of an "opportunity-driven" entrepreneur. She saw an opportunity in the marketplace and put her human, social, and financial capital to work in order to take advantage of it. In contrast, many minority women entrepreneurs are "necessity-based" entrepreneurs who may experience difficulties in finding employment due to language or cultural differences (Davidson et al., 2010; Levent et al., 2003). Undaunted, these women pursue entrepreneurship with the goal of making a living and helping to support their families. Their firms are often smaller and may serve a more limited segment of the population or a limited geographic territory. Examples might include a neighborhood grocery store or a hairdressing salon that caters to black clients. Like Gwen, a part of their motivation is financial, but they are also motivated by a lack of attractive employment alternatives. Entrepreneurship offers these women a way to pursue the American dream, as well as a means to achieve goals that are important to them.

A third motivation for minority-owned firms is family and, more specifically, being able to employ other family members or have the flexibility to care for children and older relatives. Many minority-owned firms employ multiple generations, and it is not uncommon to go into a business establishment to find young children present. Minority women business owners may not have access to available and affordable child care, or cultural differences may dictate that mothers do not leave their children with nonfamily members. Starting a home-based firm or a firm where you can bring your young children solves this dilemma while also contributing to the family's income. Minority entrepreneurs often cite the importance of both formal and informal support provided by other family members. One of the key forms of support, in fact, is the provision of child care while the entrepreneur runs the business (Davidson et al., 2010; Levent et al., 2003). Table 9.1 provides information on the number of minority-owned firms, by gender, in the United States, as well as their revenues and the number of people they employ. It reveals that there were a total of 5.7 million minority-owned firms in 2007. Of these, 2.2 million or 38 percent were women-owned. Table 9.1 shows that women- and minority-owned firms generated $186 billion in revenues or 18 percent of total revenues generated by all minority-owned firms. As in the case of women-owned firms in general, only a small percentage of women- and minority-owned firms (8 percent) had employees in addition to the owner herself. Nevertheless, these employer firms generated jobs for 1.2 million individuals.

Bumps in the Road

In spite of the attractions and benefits of entrepreneurship, minority women entrepreneurs face a number of impediments and bumps in the entrepreneurial road. These often include barriers or gaps in the areas of financial, human, and social capital. Minority entrepreneurs, on average, have lower levels of income and wealth than nonminority entrepreneurs. Thus, they have smaller amounts of personal capital that can be invested into starting a firm (Rogers et al., 2001). They are also less likely to be a part of social and professional networks that would put them in touch with potential providers of capital or investors (Davidson et al., 2010; Levent et al., 2003).

Minority-owned firms are more likely to be located in urban areas. While this may provide opportunities because individuals living in urban communities need firms that can provide goods and services in close proximity to where they live, it can also be a disadvantage in that many urban areas face higher levels of crime combined with social and economic problems. In light of these types of problems, external providers of capital may be more reluctant to invest in firms located in urban communities.

Language and cultural differences can pose challenges for minority women entrepreneurs. Researchers have observed that most mainstream financing sources such as banks are still focused primarily on nonminority borrowers. In this sense, they can be less accepting of and willing to deal with entrepreneurs who do not fit that mold. In turn, minority entrepreneurs may be less willing to deal with banks and other formal providers of capital due to language difficulties, distrust, or a lack of understanding for the types of services they provide (Davidson et al., 2010).

Minority entrepreneurs also report barriers in the form of discrimination and negative stereotypes relating to their race and ethnicity (Davidson et al., 2010). These can make it even more challenging for minority women

TABLE 9.1 Firms, receipts, employment, and payroll by race and gender in 2007

Gender	Minority/ nonminority	Number of firms	Receipts ($ thousands)	Number of employer firms	Employer receipts ($ thousands)	Number of employees	Annual payroll ($ thousands)	Number of nonemployer firms	Nonemployer receipts ($ thousands)
Female-owned	Minority	2,212,777	186,180,130	180,100	141,430,873	1,211,151	31,087,414	2,032,678	44,749,256
Female-owned	Equally minority/ nonminority	13,722	2,917,875	3,413	2,446,231	27,092	909,185	10,310	471,644
Female-owned	Nonminority	5,565,615	1,007,509,999	726,149	870,489,243	6,281,878	182,676,801	4,839,466	137,020,756
Male-owned	Minority	2,903,966	710,789,124	457,892	613,626,786	3,697,690	114,123,646	2,446,074	97,162,338
Male-owned	Equally minority/ nonminority	52,952	42,132,100	18,311	39,763,628	215,609	9,544,427	34,641	2,368,472
Male-owned	Nonminority	10,943,636	7,725,275,376	2,753,871	7,255,760,511	37,138,139	1,386,782,737	8,189,764	469,514,865
Equally male-/ female-owned	Minority	642,466	127,832,704	128,541	105,434,459	907,272	18,853,536	513,925	22,398,244
Equally male-/ female-owned	Equally minority/ nonminority	368,050	63,413,213	64,176	49,756,091	453,750	11,830,717	303,874	13,657,122
Equally male-/ female-owned	Nonminority	3,591,676	1,083,411,353	857,515	936,435,138	6,693,973	184,764,482	2,734,161	146,976,215
All	Minority	5,759,209	1,024,801,958	766,533	860,492,119	5,816,114	164,064,596	4,992,676	164,309,839
All	Equally minority/ nonminority	434,725	108,463,188	85,900	91,965,951	696,450	22,284,328	348,825	16,497,237
All	Nonminority	20,100,926	9,816,196,729	4,337,535	9,062,684,893	50,113,990	1,754,224,020	15,763,391	753,511,836

Source: U.S. Census Bureau, *2007 Survey of Business Owners.*

entrepreneurs to acquire needed resources, gain access to key networks, and penetrate mainstream rather than local markets (Rogers et al., 2001).

In terms of financial capital, although the Community Reinvestment Act was passed over 20 years ago, a number of researchers have documented the difficulties of minority entrepreneurs in their attempts to secure both personal and business loans (Cavalluzzo et al., 2002; Coleman, 2003; Park and Coleman, 2009). These studies have shown that minority entrepreneurs are significantly less likely to have loans from banks. Further, some minority entrepreneurs are more likely to be turned down for loans or avoid applying entirely because they assume they will be turned down. On the equity side, regrettably, so few minority entrepreneurs receive external equity that very few studies address their experience.

Alternatively, researchers have noted that minority entrepreneurs typically rely heavily on personal sources of financing, such as personal savings and financial support provided by family members (Davidson et al., 2010; Rogers et al., 2001). From the perspective of Resource-Based Theory, this strategy is an advantage in that it often provides "patient" capital, or capital that is willing to wait for the entrepreneur's success. Alternatively, however, a strategy of heavy reliance on personal and family financing poses a risk in that it limits the amount of capital available to start a new firm, develop new products and services, and grow.

Financing Strategies of Minority Women-Owned Firms

One of the things we learned while writing this chapter is that we cannot necessarily lump together the experience of all minority women entrepreneurs (Kwong et al., 2009). In fact, the experiences of black Hispanic, and Asian women may differ considerably. From a financing perspective, Table 9.2 gives us some insights into these distinctions.

Table 9.2 provides a profile of the capital structures of minority entrepreneurs included in the Kauffman Firm Survey. It reveals differences in financing strategy, not only by race and ethnicity but also by gender. For women entrepreneurs, we can see that Asian entrepreneurs raised the largest amount of capital in the start-up year, followed by white (nonminority) entrepreneurs and Hispanic entrepreneurs. Black entrepreneurs raised dramatically smaller amounts of total capital to start their firms than the other three groups. For

TABLE 9.2 Initial capital structure by race and ethnicity

	Female							
	Black ($)	*Hispanic* ($)	*Asian* ($)	*White* ($)	*Black* (%)	*Hispanic* (%)	*Asian* (%)	*White* (%)
Owner equity	10,146	32,853	43,436	23,609	44.1	59.0	45.9	34.0
Insider equity	116	—	3,925	2,123	0.5	0.0	4.1	3.1
Outsider equity	893	265	524	981	3.9	0.5	0.6	1.4
Owner debt	887	5,354	4,434	4,135	3.9	9.6	4.7	5.9
Insider debt	3,517	1,049	11,366	4,797	15.3	1.9	12.0	6.9
Outsider debt	7,428	16,153	30,929	33,890	32.3	29.0	32.7	48.7
Total financial capital	22,986	55,674	94,614	69,535	100	100	100	100
	Male							
	Black ($)	*Hispanic* ($)	*Asian* ($)	*White* ($)	*Black* (%)	*Hispanic* (%)	*Asian* (%)	*White* (%)
Owner equity	26,095	34,311	62,724	36,158	57.8	41.1	26.6	26.0
Insider equity	656	3,003	8,132	1,891	1.5	3.6	3.4	1.4
Outsider equity	367	1,567	16,648	27,557	0.8	1.9	7.1	19.8
Owner debt	1,064	3,240	2,775	6,081	2.4	3.9	1.2	4.4
Insider debt	2,690	8,577	17,940	7,695	6.0	10.3	7.6	5.5
Outsider debt	14,306	32,798	127,526	59,502	31.7	39.3	54.1	42.8
Total financial capital	45,178	83,496	235,746	138,885	100	100	100	100

Source: Kauffman Firm Survey Microdata.

all three categories of minority women entrepreneurs, owner equity (personal savings) was the largest source of capital, followed by outsider debt (loans). In contrast, nonminority women entrepreneurs relied most heavily on outsider debt (48.7 percent), followed by personal sources of financing (34 percent). This finding suggests, consistent with prior research, that nonminority women entrepreneurs have greater familiarity and access to formal debt providers. This could include banks, credit unions, and other types of lenders.

Table 9.2 also reveals that black women entrepreneurs and Asian women entrepreneurs were more heavily reliant on insider debt than nonminority women entrepreneurs. Insider debt includes loans from family, friends, and other insiders. In fact, black entrepreneurs used insider debt for 15.3 percent of total financing during the start-up year, while Asian entrepreneurs used it for 12 percent of total financing. This finding suggests that some minority women entrepreneurs may be less willing or less able to use formal rather than informal sources of borrowing.

One of the most noteworthy aspects of Table 9.2 is the relatively minimal amount of outside equity used by any of the groups of women entrepreneurs. Black women entrepreneurs were the most reliant on outside equity at 3.9 percent of total financing, but even for them, outside equity represented a very small amount. Consistent with prior research, it appears that women entrepreneurs are largely closed out of the market for external equity (Brush et al., 2004). The University of New Hampshire's Center for Venture Research found that in 2010, minority investors represented only 2 percent of the total, while only 6 percent of minority entrepreneurs applied for angel investor capital (Sohl, 2011). These statistics suggest a lack of supply of angel investor capital for minority entrepreneurs as well as a lack of awareness and access on their part.

Table 9.2 also allows us to observe some marked differences in financing strategy by gender. For all four types of entrepreneurs, men raised dramatically larger amounts of capital than women. Like black and Hispanic women, black and Hispanic men relied most heavily on owner equity and outsider debt. It is noteworthy, however, that Hispanic men financed their firms with substantially higher amounts of outsider debt than Hispanic women (39.3 vs. 29 percent). Hispanic men also relied more heavily on insider debt than women (10.3 vs. 1.9 percent). Both of these findings suggest that Hispanic men were more willing to use debt provided by others, or, alternatively, that they have better access to networks and financial institutions that can serve as providers of debt.

Whereas for Asian women entrepreneurs, the dominant sources of financing were owner equity (45.9 percent) and outside debt (32.7 percent), the reverse was true for Asian men (26.6 and 54.1 percent). Asian men also used a higher percentage of outside equity than Asian women (7.1 vs. 0.6 percent). These findings would seem to indicate that Asian men have better access to networks that can provide external sources of capital than Asian women. It may also suggest that the types of firms that Asian men start are more attractive to outside providers of both debt and equity. Alternatively, the low reliance on external equity by Asian women may suggest that they are more concerned with maintaining control of their firms and more reluctant to share ownership with outsiders.

It is noteworthy that Asian men raised the largest amount of start-up capital for any of the groups represented in Table 9.2. In spite of that, however, we can still observe that nonminority men used dramatically higher percentages of outside equity (19.8 percent) than both minority entrepreneurs and nonminority women entrepreneurs. This reinforces the contention of researchers that the market for external equity is closely knit, nonfemale, and, as these findings reveal, to a large extent nonminority.

Principles in Action: Evay in Hartford, Connecticut

Entrepreneur Vivan Akuoko founded her company Evay in 1986 because she wanted to get off public assistance and stay off. Evay stands for "Excellence, Versatility, Absolutely for You." Vivian's company is a day spa and beauty salon located on Albany Avenue in Hartford. Evay provides skin and hair care services to customers and sells skin and hair care products that are produced by cosmetics laboratory partners in New York and New Haven. Evay prides itself on the fact that its products are never tested on animals.

Vivian's personal entrepreneurial journey is an inspiring one. She realized that she would have to acquire an education and marketable skills if she wanted to stay off welfare, so she tried to apply for hairdressing school. In the office of the school's owner, Vivan discovered that federal assistance would no longer pay for her to do so. Overcome by disappointment, Vivian was unable to hold back her tears. The school's owner, Mrs. Dressler, was so impressed by Vivian's desire to learn that she agreed to work with her to find grants that would cover the cost of her training. At the same time, she made Vivian promise that she would also get her high school general equivalency diploma, or GED, when she finished hairdressing school. Vivian did both, and since that time, she has engaged in at least one continuing education class in every year. She recognized the value of education, and she also recognized that as an entrepreneur, she had to continually learn new skills.

Mrs. Dressler also introduced Vivian to financial management. While Vivian was in hairdressing school, she advised her to bank her tips every day. Over time, they would add up to a substantial amount. True to form, Vivian opened up a bank account and faithfully deposited her tips, even during this early stage of her career.

After graduation, Vivian worked for a hair salon for seven years to acquire additional experience. In doing so, she gained insight into both good and bad business practices, and she learned the fundamentals of what it takes to succeed in that business.

When Vivian opened her own firm, she did so with $2,500 that was originally supposed to go to the IRS. One of her customers pointed out that she could pay the IRS in installments rather than in a lump sum. Vivian did not know that, but she immediately took advantage of this opportunity to apply her savings to starting her own salon. She used the $2,500 to rent space on Albany Avenue and set up her salon, and she paid the IRS in installments rather than all at once. Vivian tried to get a loan for her firm from several banks, but they all turned her down, even though she had good credit.

All the banks talk about supporting this neighborhood, but they don't really want to do it. Maybe they have had bad experiences in the past with getting repayments. I don't know.

Since its launch in 1986, the fortunes of Evay have risen and declined with the economy. When Vivian started, she was generating about $80,000 in revenues per year. This rose to $300,000 and eventually to $500,000. To accommodate the increase in business, Vivian bought a building that would provide her with more space. Her building was financed with a commercial mortgage provided by a bank. She also hired six employees. The "Great Recession," however, hit the Albany Avenue community hard. Many of Vivian's customers lost their jobs and could no longer afford her products and services. She expected to generate approximately $80,000 in revenues in 2010, and she had to lay off three employees.

Vivian is nothing if not resourceful, however, and she has found ways to use the tough economy to her advantage.

A lot of my customers have lost their jobs, but they still need to look good for their interviews to get new jobs. To accommodate their needs, I have offered a lot of specials, including Senior Citizen Days and lower prices. That means I have lower revenues now, but I am keeping my customers and building loyalty. When the economy gets better, and it will, people will remember that.

Vivian has also become vigilant about expense control during these tough times. She has identified the things that she really needs to run her company versus the extras, and she has eliminated and cut back on unnecessary expenses. She has improved her skills in inventory management, in particular. Whereas she used to create large batches of her products at a time, she now makes smaller batches more frequently to avoid having a lot of cash tied up in inventory that may not be sold for several months. Vivian has also found ways to generate additional revenues. The building she bought has two apartments that she rents for additional income to defray her expenses. She is also able to rent out some of her commercial space.

Vivian's major source of financing today is HEDCo, the Hartford Economic Development Corporation. This is an entity that provides both loans and training to small businesses in Hartford, as well as the 57-town Hartford Metropolitan Region.

HEDCo has been great because they understand this neighborhood, and they understand the needs of small businesses in this neighborhood.

Vivian has also benefited from her association with the University of Hartford's Micro Business Incubator. Students from the university have provided her with training and assistance in a variety of skill areas, including customer service, marketing, and web page design.

The students from the university have helped me a lot. Because they are young and in college, they are up on the latest knowledge and techniques for everything affecting a business. In particular, they know all about the latest technology and how you can use it for the business. So many of my customers want to work on their technology when they come in, their laptops or their cell phones. To accommodate that, I don't have a TV or loud music in here. I play soft music so people can do their work. That's something I have learned.

Constant innovation is a part of Vivian's success. She is always developing new products, new services, and new marketing approaches. She advises other women entrepreneurs:

Don't be afraid to do something new. You have to embrace new ideas and change with the times. Every year I have been in business, I have gone to at least one class to learn something new. It might be about my products or business, or it might be something like setting up spreadsheets or using the Internet. Every year I go to learn something new.

Vivian has also recognized the importance of community in these tough times. Her salon has become a haven of mutual support, serenity, and peace not only for her customers but also for people from the neighborhood in general.

People need to come together in times like this. I try to create an environment where people can come for quiet and support. They come in to listen to the music, read a book, or just eat a sandwich. We are here for each other.

Financing Programs and Support for Minority Women-Owned Firms

Respect has been growing for the important roles that minority entrepreneurs play. Their firms provide much needed products, services, employment, and tax receipts to urban communities. Minority-owned firms are also a means for fighting urban blight and improving the quality of inner-city neighborhoods. In light of their contributions, a number of local and regional programs have been developed to help minority entrepreneurs in general and minority women entrepreneurs in particular to secure sources of financing. The best of these combine not only financial support but also skill building and the development of networks that will connect, support, and sustain women entrepreneurs. Following we discuss a few such programs.

The University of Hartford's Micro Business Incubator

A number of colleges and universities have introduced educational and training programs that provide valuable outreach to their neighboring communities. One such program, based at the University of Hartford, is the Micro Business Incubator, or MBI. The Micro Business Incubator program was developed in 2002 by Upper Albany Main Street (www.upperalbany.com) in partnership with the Metro Hartford Alliance, the Barney School of Business at the University of Hartford, and the city of Hartford. The Upper Albany community is an urban neighborhood with a high concentration of minority-owned firms serving the local populations. Over the past five years, the MBI has evolved into a valuable community resource that actively stimulates economic development. The MBI provides training, resources, and support on a one-to-one basis to a minimum of 25 businesses in the target community.

Using a "train the trainers" approach, students from the University of Hartford help to develop Upper Albany entrepreneurs' business skills by applying concepts from the intellectual capital obtained at the Barney School of Business and a series of seminars devoted to small business management. Training is conducted on-site, at the business owners' location on topics such as business planning, loan applications, financial literacy/management, marketing, customer service, and technology training, among others. As part of the mutual learning experience, students obtain hands-on, real-world understanding about owning and operating a small business, as well as first-hand exposure to diversity through this service learning initiative. In 2004, the MBI was recognized as the "Best Economic Development Program" in the state of Connecticut by the Department of Economic and Community Development. The MBI is a unique, innovative, public-private partnership that has helped illuminate the Albany Avenue gateway as critical to the success of Hartford's overall revitalization.

Since its inception in 2002, the Micro Business Incubator has served a total of more than 62 different business clients. During that time period, the MBI has facilitated closing 20 low-interest loans totaling more than $765,000 for participating clients. The MBI has donated 26 computers to encourage greater access to technology and has provided 11,310 volunteer hours of training to Albany Avenue area entrepreneurs. From 2002 to 2010, MBI participating businesses added more than 130 new jobs to the neighborhood economy. The program, in conjunction with Upper Albany Main Street initiatives, has helped stimulate more than $88.1 million of private commercial development.

Microlending Programs: ACCION USA

Microloans are small loans made to help entrepreneurs launch their firms, develop their products and services, and acquire the resources needed to succeed. These entrepreneurs typically establish small firms, often in urban communities. They are primarily minorities and women, and they lack access to more traditional forms of business capital. According to a recent report published by the Aspen Institute, approximately 700 organizations were involved in microenterprise development in the United States in 2008 (Girardo and

Edgcomb, 2011). Only a fraction of these provided detailed data on their financial services, but the most common services were microloans accompanied by technical assistance and training. Approximately 130 organizations did provide detailed financial data, which revealed a total of over 6,000 loans averaging $11,000 each. This report also revealed that the ten largest microlenders accounted for 49 percent of the dollars loaned, compared with 51 percent for the remaining organizations. One of the largest and most enduring of these microlenders is ACCION USA (www.accionusa.org).

ACCION USA is the largest microlender in the United States and was launched in 1991 to provide access to both capital and financial education for microentrepreneurs. Since its establishment, it has provided over 19,500 loans totaling more than $119 million to small firms throughout the United States. In terms of borrower characteristics, 61 percent of ACCION USA's borrowers are Hispanic, 27 percent are African American, and 40 percent are female. The average loan size is $5,100. ACCION USA secures its funding through grants, loan repayments, and donations. To date, over 89 percent of ACCION USA borrowers have repaid their loans. Small business owners can apply for a small business loan at accionusa.org. In 1998, ACCION USA received the Presidential Award for Excellence in Microenterprise Development for Program Innovation.

Let's Not Forget the U.S. Small Business Administration!

In addition to information, advice, and assistance, the Small Business Administration (SBA) (www.sba.gov) has a variety of loan programs targeted to the needs of small firms. The best known of these are the 7(a) lending program and 504 loans. The 7(a) loan program provides loans of up to $5 million through a large network of participating lenders in each state. The SBA guarantees between 75 and 85 percent of these loans, depending on loan size. To qualify, a firm must fit the SBA criteria for a small business and must have been turned down for loans from two different lending sources. In Chapter 7, Table 7.1 reveals that the SBA guaranteed over 50,000 credit lines totaling over $12 billion in 2010. Approximately 14 percent of this amount was for loans secured by women.

Certified development companies (CDCs) provide 504 loans for amounts up to $5 million for the purchase of real estate or equipment. Table 7.1 reveals that almost 8,000 504 loans were granted in 2010 totaling over $4 billion. Of this amount, women-owned firms received $603 million or 13.6 percent of the total. Although the 7(a) and 504 programs are the SBA's largest and best-known loan programs, it has a number of other types of loan programs to support different small business needs. These include Patriot Express, which guarantees loans of $500,000 or less; a microloan program for loans of up to $50,000; and special 7(a) loan guarantee programs to support exporters. For further information on the broad array of programs and services available through the U.S. Small Business Administration, visit your district office or the SBA website at http://www.sba.gov.

What Have We Learned?

In this chapter we saw that minority women entrepreneurs are a diverse group with different types of motivations and varying levels of financial, human, and social capital. Some establish firms to take advantage of opportunities in their local community or to balance family needs and considerations. Others, such as Gwen Iloani, start firms on a larger scale, with the objective of putting specialized knowledge and skills to work to launch highly profitable and growth-oriented firms. Still other minority women entrepreneurs take the path of entrepreneurship because it offers them an attractive employment alternative and a way to help support their families. Minority entrepreneurs, such as Vivian Akuoko, who establish firms in urban communities, have unique opportunities to serve a market that needs and desires goods and services. At the same time, however, urban entrepreneurs face particular difficulties due to the perception of higher levels of crime combined with social and economic problems and issues.

On average, minority women entrepreneurs have lower levels of earnings and wealth than nonminority entrepreneurs. Thus, they have smaller amounts of capital to invest in their firms. Minority entrepreneurs also have higher failure rates and are more likely to have a history of credit difficulties, which makes it hard for them to attract external sources of debt. Aside from that, some research suggests that minority entrepreneurs continue to experience discrimination in the market for both personal and business debt.

The statistics we have provided in this book indicate that women entrepreneurs, in general, receive minimal amounts of external equity. This is also true for minority women entrepreneurs. Our findings show that minority women entrepreneurs rely most heavily on personal equity in the form of savings and external debt that may include loans and credit cards. Prior research also suggests that minority women entrepreneurs use both formal and informal financial support provided by other family members. Minority women entrepreneurs raise substantially smaller amounts of capital than minority men entrepreneurs. Further, black women entrepreneurs, in particular, raised dramatically smaller amounts of capital to start their firms than both other minority women entrepreneurs and black men.

All of this tells us that minority women entrepreneurs, in general, face greater capital constraints than minority men entrepreneurs. This is particularly true for black and Hispanic women entrepreneurs. The good news, however, is that an increasing number of governmental and community-based programs are available to assist women entrepreneurs in the areas of skill building, establishing networks and key contacts, and acquiring capital. These programs, combined with your own initiative, can help to launch you on your way to becoming a successful entrepreneur.

What Does All This Mean for Me?

If you are a minority woman entrepreneur, there is no shortage of opportunities for you. You can develop products and services that are targeted to specific segments of the population where there is an unmet need. Alternatively, you have the option of applying your specialized education, experience, and skills to developing a new product, service, or market. The potential opportunities and the many sources of support to get you started on the right path are out there waiting for you.

In terms of financing strategy, your ability to secure financing will be determined by the type of firm you start as well as by your resources in the form of human and social capital. In terms of human capital, do a personal inventory of the skills and knowledge you already have compared to what you think you will need. Find ways to develop your skills through workshops, seminars, short courses, assistance from the local chapter of SCORE, or the use of college interns. Our entrepreneur Vivian Akuoko has been diligent in acquiring new knowledge and skills on an ongoing basis. She recognizes the importance of constant improvement and innovation.

Many programs are available to provide support and technical assistance. See what is offered in your local area or your state. For example, in the state of California, the California Association for Microenterprise Opportunity (CAMEO) (www.microbiz.org) promotes economic opportunity and community well-being through microenterprise development by expanding resources and building the capacity of local microenterprise development organizations throughout California. In addition, CAMEO promotes best practices and public awareness of the economic impacts of microenterprise development and advocates at the state and federal levels for public policies that support microenterprise development in the state.

A number of national programs benefit minority entrepreneurs as well. The following are just a few examples:

1. The Association for Enterprise Opportunity is the principal trade association for microenterprise programs and serves as a forum for learning about innovations, developments, and best practices in this field (www.microenterpriseworks.org).
2. MicroMentor is a program that matches inexperienced entrepreneurs with experienced businesspeople who provide assistance to new business owners (www.micromentor.org/).
3. Count Me In for Women's Economic Independence Inc. is a nonprofit organization dedicated to helping women grow their microbusinesses into million-dollar enterprises through its Make Mine a Million initiative (www.makemineamillion.org/).

• Certification as a Path to Revenue Growth

Becoming certified as a woman- or minority-owned firm has great benefits. One of the most important ones is that certification can open up additional opportunities for revenue generation. The Minority Business Development Agency (MBDA) was established at the federal level in 1969 to support the needs of minority business owners. Currently, the MBDA is housed within the U.S. Department of Commerce and operates through a nationwide network of business centers and strategic partners. The MBDA provides assistance to business owners in a variety of areas, including access to financial capital and markets. It also helps firms become certified as minority-owned businesses and helps them to identify opportunities for contracts in both the public and private sectors. For further information on obtaining certification as a minority-owned business through the Minority Business Development Agency or to find a regional office for the MBDA near you, go to http://www.mbda.gov.

Like the Minority Business Development Agency, the U.S. Small Business Administration also assists small women- and minority-owned firms through its

8(a) Business Development Program. This program is designed to provide a broad scope of business assistance to firms that are at least 51 percent owned or controlled by socially and economically disadvantaged individuals. Firms certified under this program have additional opportunities for contracts at the city, state, and federal levels. Once certified, firms also receive further guidance and information on how to engage in government contracting. For further information on getting certified as an 8(a) woman- or minority-owned firm through the U.S. Small Business Administration, contact your district SBA office or go to http://www.sba.gov.

From the standpoint of financial capital, if you want to start a home-based firm or a relatively small business, you will need savings and other insiders who can provide debt or equity. You will also need good credit in order to get a line of credit or other type of business loan. Finally, if you anticipate the need for either external debt (loans) or equity (investors), you need to develop your social capital by becoming a part of those networks. For example, if you anticipate needing a bank loan, find a bank that specializes in loans to small businesses. Open checking and savings accounts, and talk to the bank manager about your business. Make sure you have organized financial statements (balance sheet, income statement, statement of cash flows), because you will need them if you ask for a loan. Also, try to anticipate a lender's concerns and ways in which you can turn potential negatives into positives. For example, lenders may be concerned with a firm's ability to generate sales in an inner-city community or in neighborhoods with high levels of crime. You can use these concerns as an opportunity to point out the ways in which your firm's products and services will meet the needs of the community as well as the ways in which it can generate revenues by doing so (Porter, 1995). You can also stress the efforts of citizens and community groups to reduce crime, stabilize neighborhoods, and support local businesses. All of these factors are positives that work in your favor.

If you anticipate a need for external equity in the future, identify angel or venture capital networks and organizations that would be appropriate for your type of firm. Most venture capital firms specialize by industry type, so if you are establishing a technology-based firm, there are specific VC firms that will be interested in you. Some VC firms, such as Golden Seeds and Illuminate Ventures, also specialize in funding women-owned firms. Don't forget that you will need not only financial statements but also a business plan for most sources of external equity. Educate yourself on your financing options, learn the pros and cons of each type, and network strategically!

One of the unique opportunities you have is the large number of government and community-based financing programs that help minority entrepreneurs launch and succeed. The best of these combine not only financing but also skill development and networks for ongoing advice and support. Some of the examples we provided in this chapter include local organizations such as the Hartford Economic Development Corporation (HEDCo) and the University of Hartford Micro Business Incubator, as well as national organizations such as ACCION USA. Research what's available in your community in terms of grants, loans, and informational or training programs, and take advantage of these programs. They were designed to help *you*!

• Tips for Inner-City Entrepreneurs

1. Continuously work to develop your knowledge and skills by participating in education and training programs.
2. Investigate local or national microlending programs that may provide small amounts of capital to help you get started.
3. Seek out local, state, and national programs that provide assistance or financial support for minority entrepreneurs or targeted geographic areas.
4. Find out what it takes to get certified as a "minority-owned firm."
5. Maintain good credit. Good credit is a key to securing both personal and business loans at a reasonable price. If you have a weak credit history, find a local program that will provide you guidance on how to repair your credit. Check with a local Small Business Development Center (SBDC) or with your regional SBA office.
6. In addition to your "regular" Chamber of Commerce, find out if there is a local chapter of the U.S. Hispanic Chamber of Commerce, the U.S. Pan Asian American Chamber of Commerce, or the National Black Chamber of Commerce. These groups may put you in touch with other entrepreneurs who can alert you to the availability of specific resources and opportunities.

Public Policy Implications

Fortunately we have already recognized the importance of minority entrepreneurship. According to a recent forecast, by the year 2050, nonminority whites will represent only 50 percent of the population in the United States (http://www.census.gov). This demographic trend suggests a vast future of opportunity for minority entrepreneurs and for the populations they serve.

In light of this trend, it is troubling that minority entrepreneurs still experience greater difficulties in securing sources of financing. It is important that we continue to work toward greater access to sources of both debt and equity. On the debt side, this can be achieved at least partially through regulation and partially through continued education of professionals in the lending community. On the equity side, access can be achieved by developing networks of angel and venture capital providers who are receptive to funding the firms of minority entrepreneurs.

Policies to promote entrepreneurship and business ownership among minorities are widespread. Nationwide, a growing number of both nonprofit and for-profit programs provide loans, training, and/or technical assistance to minority and disadvantaged entrepreneurs (Girardo and Edgcomb, 2011). The focus of many programs for minority and disadvantaged firms is on providing more access to financial capital. Perhaps the most well-known program is the U.S. Small Business Administration 7(a) Loan Guaranty Program, which provides government backing on loans by commercial lenders. The loans are awarded to businesses applying for loans that would not otherwise receive bank funding. Although the program is not targeted toward minority entrepreneurs, they are disproportionately affected.

As we have discussed in this chapter, a number of microlenders provide small loans to disadvantaged business owners (Girardo and Edgcomb, 2011; Servon, 1999). Clearly, improving access to capital for minority entrepreneurs is important, especially in light of the striking wealth inequality that exists in the United States. Wealth inequality may be directly addressed through expanding asset-building programs such as financial education programs, individual development accounts (IDAs), and first-time home ownership programs. It can also be addressed by continued educational innovations such as magnet and charter schools, which have been successful in raising the educational levels of students in urban communities. These programs have helped minority students to develop their human capital through increased access to higher education and, thus, to good-paying jobs and careers.

A few large, national programs exist that provide mentoring services to entrepreneurs. For example, the Small Business Administration runs the Mentor-Protégé Program for disadvantaged firms under the 8(a) Business Development Program. This program focuses on technical, management and financial assistance, subcontract support, and assistance in performing prime contracts through joint venture arrangements. Another mentoring program is provided by the Service Corps of Retired Executives. SCORE volunteers, who are both working and retired business owners, executives, and corporate leaders, provide free advice and training to entrepreneurs and small business owners.

In the face of current inequities, there is a continued need for both governmental and community-based programs that combine access to capital with skill building and the establishment of ongoing networks. The studies cited in this chapter attest to the fact that minority women entrepreneurs are often isolated and outside the networks leading to mainstream sources of financing. At the university level also, we can continue to develop programs that will pair college students and faculty with minority entrepreneurs to help with skill development in areas such as marketing and the development of financial systems and controls. Our minority women entrepreneurs are a bright part of our economic future, and it is in all our interests to ensure that they acquire the resources they need to thrive in the areas of financial, human, and social capital.

IT'S A SMALL WORLD AFTER ALL

A Global Perspective

Throughout this book, our primary focus has been on the financing strategies of women-owned firms in the United States. As we have attempted to demonstrate, there is more than enough to talk about in terms of the variety of motivations, firms, and their financing strategies! We did not want to leave you, however, without saying a few words about women's entrepreneurship globally. Although we cannot do justice to the financing strategies of women throughout the world in one small chapter, we would like to devote some attention to at least three important topics that show a link between women's entrepreneurship and financing strategy. Thus, we will start by discussing the growth rates of women's entrepreneurship globally and some of the motivations that drive women entrepreneurs in different parts of the world. We will see that, just as in the United States, these motivations help to determine the types of firms that women start and the financing strategies they use.

We will also discuss the opportunities available to U.S. women entrepreneurs for global entrepreneurship through exporting. In this section we review the extent to which women-owned firms in our own country are participating in the global economy through exporting, and we discuss some of the financing strategies they use to do so. Finally, we address the experience of immigrant women entrepreneurs, the particular difficulties that they may face in their attempts to secure financing in this country, and programs or strategies that have been especially helpful to them. As you may imagine, we could write another book on any one of these three topics, so what we present here is just a taste to whet your appetite and introduce some of the key financing issues and challenges.

A Global Perspective

Let's start with our first topic: the growth of women's entrepreneurship globally. Throughout the developed and developing world, women's entrepreneurship is flourishing. Nevertheless, men are still more likely to become entrepreneurs than women in countries representing a range in levels of economic development (Elam and Terjesen, 2010; Minitti, 2010). Table 10.1 reveals gaps in the levels of entrepreneurship between women and men in low- to middle-income countries in Europe and Asia, low- to middle-income countries in Latin American and the Caribbean, and high-income countries like the United States and Canada. The gap between women and men is smallest in low- to middle-income countries in Europe. This suggests that lower-income women may turn to entrepreneurship in these countries due to a lack of other employment opportunities; traditionally, European countries have had higher unemployment rates than the United States. Similarly, many European countries have well-developed and government-funded programs for child care. These may have the effect of "freeing up" a greater number of women to pursue entrepreneurship.

Table 10.1 also reveals that the gap between women and men is widest in low- and middle-income economies in Latin America and the Caribbean, where social and cultural norms may encourage women to assume more traditional roles in the home (Terjesen and Amoros, 2010). High-income countries also show a relatively large gap between women and men. These include countries such as the United States and Canada, where women have many

TABLE 10.1 Prevalence rates of business ownership across country groups by gender, 2007

	Business ownership	
	Men	*Women*
Low/middle-income countries (Europe/Asia)	19.89%	12.24%
Low/middle-income countries (Latin America/Caribbean)	31.76%	20.97%
High-income countries	16.08%	7.91%

Source: Allen et al. (2007). *Global Entrepreneurship Monitor: 2007 Report on Women and Entrepreneurship.*

other opportunities for paid employment and where structural barriers may discourage women from entrepreneurship (Elam and Terjesen, 2010). As noted throughout this book, women in developed economies may have different resource attributes in the form of education and experience than men. Similarly, they may have more difficulty accessing capital, particularly capital in the form of external equity. Finally, even in developed economies, women are less likely to have networks that include other women entrepreneurs who could serve as role models and mentors (Minitti, 2010).

Our findings in Table 10.1 are further reinforced by Table 10.2, which provides information on the prevalence rates for both men and women entrepreneurs in a variety of countries. This table reveals considerable variability across nations that may well be a reflection of each country's stage of economic development, the condition of its financial markets, its degree of political freedom, and social and cultural values that help to determine the role of women in society.

In developed countries, those women who choose to pursue the path of entrepreneurship often do so in order to take advantage of opportunities in the marketplace, to achieve a degree of economic and personal independence, to create a new product or service, to achieve financial gain, or to balance the demands of work and family. Just as in the United States, these developed-country women entrepreneurs start firms that are consistent with their motivations, and they select financing strategies based upon their motivations and firm type. This model, like the model in our country, assumes economic and political freedom, at least relative equality for all citizens, and well-developed financial markets. In other words, entrepreneurs can choose from a wide variety of financial service providers, products, and services.

Conversely, in developing countries, prior research reveals that women's motivations are often more basic; survival, better nutrition, better health care, and better education for themselves and their families (Hanson, 2009; Minitti, 2010). Many of these countries experience high levels of poverty, and educational opportunities, particularly for women, may be more limited than they are for men. A number of developing countries do not enjoy the economic and political freedom that we experience in the United States, and, in most instances, their financial markets are not fully developed. This limits the types of firms that women are able to start and further limits the availability of capital to fund their firms. One study found that women in developing nations with high levels of poverty were more likely to start subsistence firms such as

TABLE 10.2 Prevalence rates of entrepreneurial activity across countries by gender, 2007

	Early stage (nascent and new)		*Established businesses*		*All (nascent + new + established)*	
	Male (%)	*Female (%)*	*Male (%)*	*Female (%)*	*Male (%)*	*Female (%)*
Argentina	17.52	11.34	15.78	4.16	33.30	15.50
Austria	3.06	1.84	7.25	4.78	10.31	6.61
Belgium	4.30	1.98	1.86	0.93	6.16	2.91
Brazil	12.73	12.71	12.70	7.24	25.43	19.95
Chile	16.45	10.43	11.89	5.59	28.33	16.02
China	19.27	13.43	9.66	7.04	28.93	20.47
Colombia	26.91	18.77	15.49	7.84	42.41	26.60
Croatia	9.44	5.13	5.79	2.67	15.23	7.80
Denmark	6.21	4.56	8.54	3.43	14.75	8.00
Dominican Republic	14.50	8.96	6.12	27.88	20.62	18.91
Finland	8.96	4.81	10.31	4.80	19.27	9.60
France	4.14	2.21	2.52	0.95	6.66	3.16
Greece	7.96	3.46	14.59	12.04	22.56	15.51
Hong Kong	14.33	5.82	7.51	3.75	21.84	9.56
Hungary	9.29	4.52	5.88	3.81	15.17	8.33
Iceland	17.40	7.44	13.43	3.98	30.83	11.42
India	9.51	7.49	8.69	2.18	18.21	9.66
Ireland	10.57	5.87	12.66	5.38	23.22	11.25
Israel	7.12	3.75	3.61	1.10	10.72	4.84
Italy	6.69	3.30	8.87	2.17	15.56	5.48
Japan	3.47	5.22	8.72	8.57	12.20	13.79
Kazakhstan	11.17	7.64	6.80	4.80	17.97	12.44
Latvia	7.70	1.41	4.90	2.02	12.60	3.43
Netherlands	6.64	3.70	8.59	4.07	15.24	7.77
Norway	8.59	4.28	8.20	3.50	16.79	7.78
Peru	25.74	26.06	18.07	12.40	43.80	38.46
Portugal	11.70	5.92	9.79	4.44	21.49	10.36
Puerto Rico	3.16	2.97	4.05	0.89	7.21	3.87
Romania	4.95	3.09	3.34	1.70	8.30	4.79
Russia	3.79	1.64	1.63	1.73	5.41	3.37
Serbia	12.11	5.06	7.74	2.83	19.85	7.88
Slovenia	6.84	2.68	6.84	2.31	13.69	4.99
Spain	9.75	5.48	8.17	4.57	17.92	10.06
Sweden	5.78	2.47	6.87	2.48	12.65	4.95
Switzerland	7.59	4.92	8.56	4.60	16.15	9.52
Thailand	27.78	25.95	23.22	19.47	51.00	45.42
Turkey	8.65	2.41	9.47	1.32	18.12	3.73
United Kingdom	3.60	7.59	2.55	15.00	6.15	7.41
United States	11.98	7.25	6.47	3.48	18.45	10.73
Uruguay	17.33	7.19	8.63	4.54	25.96	11.73
Venezuela	23.50	16.81	5.87	4.90	29.37	21.71

Source: Allen et al. (2007). *Global Entrepreneurship Monitor: 2007 Report on Women and Entrepreneurship.*

small agricultural enterprises, street vending, or domestic service (Hanson, 2009). In contrast, another study found that women in developed economies with the goal of financial gain were more likely to start growth- or export-oriented firms (Hessels et al., 2008). Those are the women who are not worried about starving to death—at least not this week.

We have discussed the financing strategies of a number of different types of women entrepreneurs in a well-developed economy, the United States, throughout this book. Those differ quite dramatically from the financing sources and strategies that are available to women in developing countries. One researcher studied women entrepreneurs in Botswana, India, and Peru and found a combination of governmental programs, women's cooperatives, and NGO-sponsored initiatives (nongovernmental organizations) (Hanson, 2009). Many of these programs provided training and skill building combined with low-interest loans. This researcher stressed that microloans by themselves are not sufficient. Women entrepreneurs in developing economies also need grassroots programs to build women's skills and confidence, while providing them with ways to connect with other women business owners. These additional measures help to create a support system and a sense of community.

In many developing nations, including those in Africa, Southeast Asia, and Latin America, microfinance has become an emerging trend (Khavul, 2010). Microlenders provide small loans to borrowers to enable them to start or grow very small or "microbusinesses." Prior research has revealed that microlending programs result in the creation of a significantly greater number of new businesses, as well as improved profitability for existing businesses (Banerjee et al., 2009). Microloan borrowers are typically women, who use the proceeds from the business to support their families. Other research has noted that, in addition to providing financial capital, microlending programs help women entrepreneurs develop social capital by creating small groups of women entrepreneurs (Sanyal, 2009). These groups provide women entrepreneurs with a sense of community and empowerment.

• Grameen Bank

The Grameen Bank (www.grameen-info.org) in Bangladesh is one of the most well-known microlenders available to women in a developing country. Grameen, which stands for "rural" or "village," was established in 1976 by Professor Muhammad

Yunus, a Fulbright Scholar from Vanderbilt University. The bank's intent is to provide small, unsecured loans to the rural poor, a significant number of whom are women. Financing for the bank is provided by donors, support from the central bank of Bangladesh, and bond sales. The bank itself is owned by the rural poor whom it serves, with borrowers holding 90 percent of the shares and the government holding 10 percent.

The Grameen Bank's objectives include eliminating the exploitation of the poor by money lenders and creating opportunities for self-employment for the vast multitude of unemployed people in rural Bangladesh. The principles of the bank are based on a combination of personal empowerment and peer pressure and support (Yunus et al., 2010). Individual borrowers are personally responsible for the repayment of their loans, but they are also part of a small group that encourages each woman to pay the loan while developing sound financial practices and good credit. Traditionally, a high percentage of Grameen borrowers, more than 90 percent, have repaid their loans. Grameen also promotes the value and importance of education, so the majority of borrowers also enroll their children in local educational programs, thereby improving the prospects of the next generation. As of September 2010, the Grameen Bank had 8.32 million borrowers, 97 percent of whom were women. Through its 2,500 branches, the bank provides service to 97 percent of the villages in Bangladesh. It has made over $8 billion in loans since its inception. The success of the Grameen Bank has given rise to similar projects in other developing nations. In 2006, Professor Yunus and the Grameen Bank were jointly awarded the Nobel Peace Prize for their work to create opportunities and alleviate poverty.

The growing interest and demand for microcredit has given rise to an increasing number of both nonprofit and for-profit entities operating microlending programs (Hudon, 2008). Nonprofits or NGOs often emphasize the goals of community building and the alleviation of poverty. In contrast, for-profit entities typically place greater emphasis on loan volume, repayment, and the generation of returns. In spite of the many positive outcomes associated with microlending programs, some researchers have expressed concerns about their unintended consequences. One such criticism is that such programs focus on microbusinesses and do not encourage women to start larger ventures that would provide more substantial economic rewards. A second concern relates to the collection policies of some microlenders that boast high repayment rates in order to attract investors. In some instances these repayment rates are the result of threats or intimidation or encouraging borrowers to take out additional loans to repay the earlier ones (Taylor, 2002; *Wall Street Journal,* October 23–24, 2010). A third concern is that microloans do not necessarily help women entrepreneurs if the funds are coopted and used for other purposes by males in the household (Taylor, 2002). This is a distinct possibility in male-dominated cultures where women have limited personal and financial freedom.

Unfortunately, recent research indicates that women entrepreneurs throughout the world still have a more difficult time raising financing than men do (Muravyev et al., 2009). Fewer women obtain loans, and when they do, they pay higher interest rates and have higher collateral requirements. These unfavorable lending conditions have the effect of discouraging women from borrowing or, even worse, discouraging them from entrepreneurship entirely. This same study found, however, that evidence of discrimination disappeared in countries with well-developed and highly competitive financial markets because banks in highly competitive markets cannot afford the "luxury" of taste-based discrimination (Becker, 1957). Another recent study of British firms (Roper and Scott, 2009) found that if women even perceived higher financial barriers, they were less likely to go forward with starting a firm. Both of these studies suggest that if women are discouraged in the capital acquisition process, they are also more likely to be discouraged from entrepreneurship entirely.

If the story on the debt side is somewhat discouraging, it is even more so on the equity side. Most foreign countries do not have well-developed markets for either angel or venture capital. Thus, the prospects for securing external equity are bleak. The good news is that many of these markets are developing rapidly, and there is also a strong appetite in the U.S. private equity market for foreign investment at the present time. All of this is good news for our global entrepreneurs!

Principles in Action: Razoss Ltd.*

Following an innovative idea for a web browser, Gali Ross became a high-tech entrepreneur in her native Israel because of the opportunities she saw for young entrepreneurs like herself. In 2008, she established her Internet browser firm, Razoss (www.razoss.com), to provide hundreds of custom-made applications designed for specific browsing needs.

---

* We are indebted to our friend and colleague Dr. Dafna Kariv at the College of Management in Israel for interviews with Gali Ross of Razoss Ltd. and Hilla Ovil-Brenner of WhiteSmoke, Inc.

On a personal level, a young, first-time entrepreneur in the field of high-tech (especially in Israel) has the opportunity to try and attempt business maneuvers and operations we would not normally be able to do at our age. The Internet arena is one that is built and based upon people who are relatively young, making it a natural habitat for people with new ideas and out-of-the-box thinking.

Gali was well equipped with both human and social capital when she launched her firm. She served as an intelligence officer in the Israeli Defense Forces and studied information systems engineering at the Technion, Israel's version of MIT. Subsequently, Gali gained both high-tech and entrepreneurial experience as a project manager at eWave and later as the chief operating officer of Clementina, where she worked with a number of Israeli and non-Israeli start-ups.

Gali and cofounder Rami Raz initially financed their firm with less than $100,000, most of which went to cover salaries and basic expenses. They were fortunate in finding a prominent angel investor who was well-known for funding early-stage start-ups. Since that time, Gali has obtained financing from three additional angel investors and has also established a strategic partnership.

The second round of investors were much more demanding than our first investors. Investment was made in return for preferred shares in the company. Negotiating the strategic partnership was not easy either, since at that time Razoss had not yet launched or acquired a significant user base. At that point, investments were made based on the company's technology, vision, and team.

In spite of her impressive background and strong credentials, Gali has found it difficult to be a woman in a mostly male-dominated field.

It's a man's industry. There is a major advantage to being a geek, . . . a quality far more common amongst guys than girls.

Nevertheless, she advises other aspiring women entrepreneurs to take chances and "just do it."

Expanding Our Reach

Our second topic under the headline of globalization is the extent to which women entrepreneurs in the United States participate in exporting and, if they do export, how they finance those transactions. Exporting creates additional opportunities for women entrepreneurs because it opens new markets and provides insights into possibilities for new products and services. In this sense, exporting has the potential to dramatically increase revenues.

Figure 10.1 highlights the appeal of exporting from an entrepreneur's perspective. In 2009, U.S exports totaled over $1 trillion, and major trading partners include developed economies such as Canada, Germany, and the United Kingdom, as well as rapid-growth economies such as China, Mexico, and other parts of Asia and Latin America.

The Kauffman Firm Survey reveals that about 13.8 percent of male-owned firms exported in 2007, compared with 10.9 percent of female-owned firms. By 2008, the percentage of exporting firms increased to 14.2 and 12.7 percent,

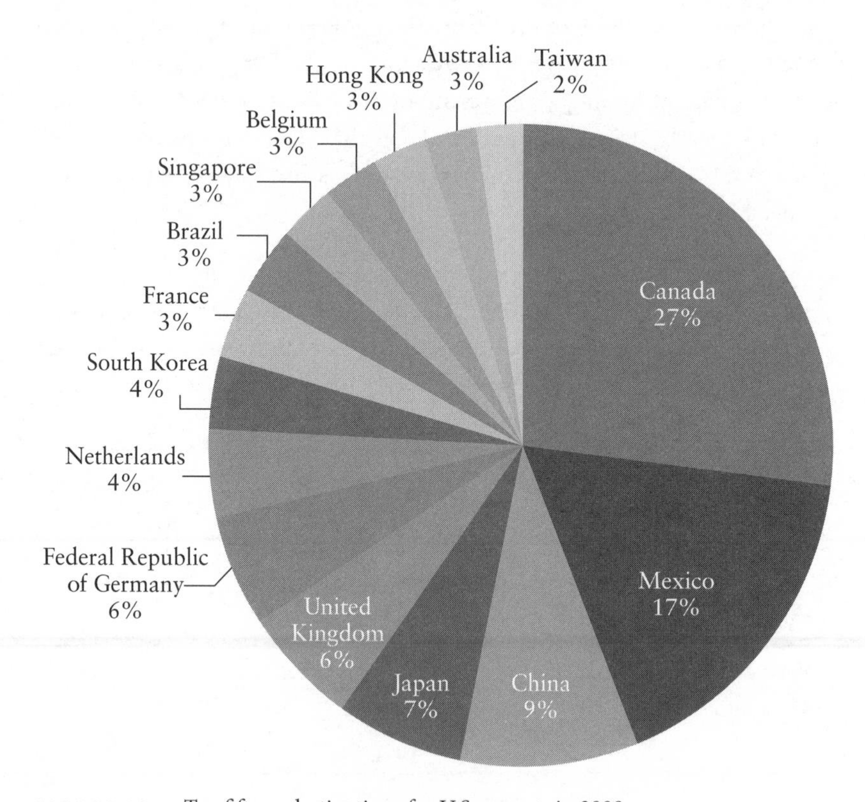

FIGURE 10.1 Top fifteen destinations for U.S. exports in 2009
Source: U.S. Census Bureau, Foreign Trade Statistics.
Note: In 2009, U.S. exports totaled $1.06 trillion. Of that amount, exports to the top fifteen destinations accounted for $760 billion (72 percent).

respectively. While firms that export are in the minority, they tend to be larger on average in terms of sales and employment. Further, the financing strategies of exporting firms also differ from firms that do not export.

Table 10.3 includes data from the KFS, specifically on exporting firms. Data are only included for the years 2007 and 2008 because those were the first years that questions about exporting were asked. Table 10.3 reveals that women-owned firms relied heavily on new injections of outsider debt to finance their activities. Outsider debt represented 71.7 percent of new financial capital raised by women in 2007 and 52.5 percent in 2008. This confirms the theory that women entrepreneurs turn to exporting as a growth-oriented strategy, as a means to increase sales and penetrate new markets. These findings also reveal that women entrepreneurs, on average, are unable to finance growth through exports by relying solely on internal sources of capital. External debt may be the most attractive alternative because it does not require them to relinquish control to external equity investors. Further, as just noted, exporting firms tend to be larger, and as such, they are more attractive to banks and other lenders.

In spite of its many attractions, exporting poses some challenges for women entrepreneurs, not the least of which is that they are doing business with customers in countries having different languages, different financial systems, and different currencies. How does one finance such initiatives? And

TABLE 10.3 Financial capital injections for exporting firms, 2007–2008

	Female ($)	*Male ($)*	*Female (%)*	*Male (%)*
2007				
Owner equity	7,403	12,481	18.4	9.8
Insider equity	—	496	—	0.4
Outsider equity	—	43,820	—	34.5
Owner debt	2,877	3,213	7.1	2.5
Insider debt	1,047	5,164	2.6	4.1
Outsider debt	28,871	61,852	71.7	48.7
Total financial capital	40,245	127,026	100	100
2008				
Owner equity	20,799	25,207	33.3	16.0
Insider equity	—	2,478	—	1.6
Outsider equity	—	33,541	—	21.3
Owner debt	6,464	5,886	10.3	3.7
Insider debt	978	4,355	1.6	2.8
Outsider debt	32,806	85,728	52.5	54.5
Total financial capital	62,510	157,195	100	100

Source: Kauffman Firm Survey Microdata.

how does one get paid by a customer in, say, China? One of the most frequently used financial instruments to secure payment for exported goods and services is a letter of credit.

• Letters of Credit

A letter of credit is a financial instrument used to facilitate payment by a customer in one country to a supplier in another (*Trade Finance Guide*, 2008). Let's say that Customer A in France wants to buy goods from Supplier B in the United States. Customer A would approach her bank to issue a letter of credit with Supplier B as the beneficiary. Customer A's bank then forwards a copy of the letter of credit to Supplier B's bank. Supplier B's bank notifies Supplier B that payment is in place, so the merchandise can be shipped to Customer A. Documents pertaining to the shipment of goods are forwarded to Customer A's bank, which then transfers payment to Supplier B's bank. Some of the documents typically specified in a letter of credit include a bill of exchange, an invoice, a packing list, a bill of lading, and an insurance policy. Finally, Supplier B's bank credits Supplier B's bank account with the designated payment amount.

A letter of credit provides an added level of protection to both importers and exporters. From the exporter's perspective, a letter of credit is helpful when reliable credit information about a foreign buyer is difficult to obtain. From the importer's standpoint, it ensures that documentation is in place to verify the shipment of goods before payment is made. A letter of credit also helps to alleviate differences in language, cultural practices, and time zones. If you are considering exporting, you may wish to explore letters of credit as a means of payment. To do so, speak with the International Department of your bank. If you currently do business with a relatively small, local bank, it may not provide these services. Your bank may, however, be able to recommend a larger bank that does provide services to support international transactions. We also recommend that you participate in seminars or training programs offered by your district office of the U.S. Department of Commerce to learn more about exporting and services to support firms that export.

Contributions and Challenges of Immigrant Entrepreneurs

Our third topic under the umbrella of globalization and women's entrepreneurship is the role of immigrant entrepreneurs and their strategies for financing their firms. Each year thousands of individuals come to the United States in search of the "American Dream." Some of these are women who start their own businesses, either by themselves or with other family members. What are their motivations? Many immigrants, both women and men, come to this country seeking freedom and the benefits of democracy, education and opportunity for their children, and financial wealth through the fruits of their labors. Some come from countries where women have limited personal and economic freedom, and others may come to escape corrupt or repressive political regimes. Many, who arrive with limited or no resources, are prepared to work for survival, just as they did in their own country. Overall, these immigrant entrepreneurs come for a better way of life, and they are prepared to work unbelievably hard to achieve it.

Within the context of Resource-Based Theory, the resources that women immigrant entrepreneurs bring to the table include courage, initiative, a willingness to work hard, and often specific skills or talents that can be employed within an entrepreneurial context, but they also face daunting challenges. As newcomers to the American way of life, they are unfamiliar with financial products and financial service providers in this country. Many also arrive with limited financial capital and, in some instances, limited human capital in the form of education and experience. Finally, language differences make it even more difficult to start a firm and secure external sources of financing.

What types of firms do these courageous women start? As with other types of women-owned firms discussed in this book, their selection of firm type is typically driven by a combination of motivation and resources. If their motivation is survival and their resources in the form of financial, human, and social capital are limited, they may start small retail or service businesses that require minimal amounts of financial capital. Examples might include crafts or products manufactured in the home, street vending, nail salons, massage parlors, domestic service firms, and neighborhood restaurants or grocery stores. Typically these immigrant entrepreneurs put in long hours, and the firm may also employ other members of the family. In fact, that may be one of the primary motivations. When we speak with these women entrepreneurs, another important motivation is to provide educational opportunities for their children so they can have a better life. One woman entrepreneur from Vietnam who operates a nail salon told me proudly that her son was attending MIT. Another has shared stories about her son and daughter studying at the University of Connecticut. A woman entrepreneur from Poland who operates a cleaning service told me after cleaning four non-air-conditioned houses on a 90° day, "I want my children to have an easier life. I do this for them."

Often these small firms and microbusinesses start and operate without support from the formal financial system. These entrepreneurs may lack assets that can serve as collateral on loans or a track record of accomplishment in the United States. They are also hampered by language and cultural differences, and they are not a part of networks that would give them access to formal financial service providers. Alternatively, many of these immigrant entrepreneurs start their firms with their own financial capital or financial capital provided by other family members, sometimes from earnings from paid employment. Due to resource constraints, many start firms with minimal capital requirements and then finance their ongoing needs with earnings from the firm. Since a number of immigrant-owned firms are service firms, they have a constant flow of cash once they are up and running. Thus, they do not have to secure financing for receivables, inventories, or fixed assets. Once their firms are established, they can be very profitable.

• Kiva: Investing in Women Microentrepreneurs

Kiva's (www.kiva.org) mission is "to connect people, through lending, for the sake of alleviating poverty." It accomplishes this mission by using the Internet to bring together lenders and borrowers in both developing and developed nations, including the United States. Microlending organizations like Kiva have been established to respond to the credit needs of microentrepreneurs who typically do not have access to bank loans. Their firms are small and often new, and their loan requests are not big enough to make them profitable for banks. Further, many small borrowers have limited levels of financial literacy combined with nonexistent or poor credit histories.

The Kiva website states:

> Access to credit allows poor people to take advantage of economic opportunities. While increased earnings are by no means automatic, clients have overwhelmingly demonstrated that reliable sources of credit provide a fundamental basis for planning and expanding business activities.

As of April 2011, Kiva had provided $200 million in loans to borrowers in 210 countries (Jackley, 2011). Over 80 percent of these borrowers have been women. The average loan granted to a Kiva borrower is $381, and Kiva has a 98 percent repayment rate. From a lender's perspective, Kiva allows lenders to target their investments to specific entrepreneurs featured on their website. In this way, lenders are able to track the performance and success of "their" borrower over time. To date, almost 500,000 lenders in over 200 countries have funded loans averaging $216. In some instances, lenders form groups to target the needs of specific populations, types of firms, or geographic areas. For example, members of a book club might decide to make loans to a woman-owned business in Somalia. In doing so, they feel a sense of ownership and community (Jackley, 2011). In addition to these small lenders, Kiva has also been funded by larger grants and donations. Recently it announced a million-dollar grant from Visa (*Wall Street Journal,* October 22, 2010).

During a recent visit to the University of Hartford, Kiva.org cofounder Jessica Jackley (2011) observed the following:

> Around the world, women do a lot of the work, but they don't have access to a lot of resources. Often success is a matter of logistics—getting the right resources to the right people at the right time. That's the goal of Kiva: to provide small amounts of capital at key points for our entrepreneurs. Kiva is also about creating social capital through a community of worldwide support. By creating a community, we can help to bring out that which is remarkable in all people.

In 2011, Jessica Jackley launched a second entrepreneurial venture called ProFounder (www.profounder.com). ProFounder is an online platform that allows for-profit firms in the United States to raise both debt and equity directly from investors, thereby increasing access to financial capital and reducing costs.

Other immigrant entrepreneurs come with specific skills and human capital in the form of education and experience. These entrepreneurs are in a better position to establish growth-oriented or technology-based firms that provide opportunities for significant financial gain. Our friend Radha Jalan came to the United States from India. She was well educated and came from a successful entrepreneurial family in her home country. When she took over her husband's fuel cell company after his death, she did not know the specifics of the fuel cell industry, but she understood the entrepreneurial process, she was smart and willing to learn, and she knew how to develop strong networks of friends and advisors both within and outside the industry. In her case, her high levels of both human and social capital enabled her to identify and develop sources of external financial capital. These included not only bank loans secured by personal assets but also private equity from investors and government grants.

Table 10.4 includes data on the initial capital structure of immigrant entrepreneurs, both women and men, from the Kauffman Firm Survey. It reveals that women immigrant entrepreneurs raised approximately the same amount of capital to start their firms as native-born entrepreneurs. The sources of financing, however, differ substantially. Specifically, women immigrant entrepreneurs raised more capital from internal sources, including owner equity, insider equity, owner debt, and insider debt (67 vs. 47 percent). Conversely, they raised smaller amounts of capital from either outsider debt or equity. Thus, immigrant women, as just noted, relied less heavily on loans for the business or outside equity investors, possibly because they experience greater difficulty in dealing with financial institutions in this country or because they do not have access to networks that could provide equity capital.

Table 10.4 also allows us to compare the experience of women and men immigrant entrepreneurs. In doing so, we can observe several important distinctions. First, immigrant men raise dramatically more capital on average to start their firms than women: $186,119 compared to $70,283. Second, male entrepreneurs are able to contribute substantially larger amounts of personal capital in the form of owner equity: $57,360 versus $34,632. Male immigrant entrepreneurs also raise larger amounts of external capital in the form of outsider debt and equity. The gap between women and men in terms of the amount of outsider equity is particularly large: $168 versus $35,989. These differences in levels of external financing suggest that immigrant men are more adept at using formal financial service providers such as banks and that they have better access to networks that can provide sources of external debt and equity.

TABLE 10.4 Start-up capital structure for native-born and immigrant entrepreneurs

	Native-born ($)		*Immigrants ($)*	
	Female	*Male*	*Female*	*Male*
Owner equity	23,095	33,496	34,632	57,360
Insider equity	1,863	1,654	2,062	5,701
Outsider equity	1,000	21,512	168	35,989
Owner debt	3,802	5,633	5,117	3,648
Insider debt	4,716	6,719	5,482	14,901
Outsider debt	37,214	54,742	22,822	68,520
Total financial capital	71,690	123,756	70,283	186,119

Source: Kauffman Firm Survey Microdata.

• Tips for Immigrant Entrepreneurs

1. Learn English. Although you may conduct business with many of your customers, suppliers, and buyers in your native language, English remains the dominant language in the United States. By learning English you can expand your universe of potential customers and geographic territories. Also, most financial service providers in this country conduct business in English, so English-language fluency will help you to secure sources of financing. Many local school systems and community groups offer low-cost or free English-language programs. Find out what is available in your community.
2. Learn how the financial system works in the United States, and develop financial literacy. The financial system of any country has its own complexities and characteristics, and the financial system of the United States is no exception. As an entrepreneur you and your firm may benefit from the use of a variety of financial products and services, such as checking accounts, credit cards, personal and business loans, mortgages, and the like. A number of community organizations, government entities, and even churches provide classes to help you gain an understanding of the financial system and how to use it in this country.
3. Develop a support network. This can include other successful immigrant entrepreneurs who have "learned the ropes" for doing business in the United States, as well as individuals, groups, and civic or governmental entities that can provide you with guidance, information, resources, and support. Examples might include your local chapter of the National Association of Women Business Owners, your local chapter of the Service Corps of Retired Executives, and your local office of the U.S. Small Business Administration.
4. Seek out governmental and quasi-public sources of financing and support that may target your specific needs as an immigrant entrepreneur. For example, if you are launching a high-tech firm that has the potential to create a substantial number of jobs, there may be state or local programs that can provide assistance in the form of loans, equity investments, tax credits, training grants, or other benefits. Similarly, if you plan to launch a business in an urban community, there may be governmental programs that provide additional support.
5. Remember that the courage, determination, and ability that brought you to the United States can also be applied to launching your own firm and achieving success!

Principles in Action: WhiteSmoke, Inc.

In founding her company, WhiteSmoke (www.whitesmoke.com), South African native Hilla Ovil-Brenner took a page from American history by noting that Native Americans communicated across vast distances and language barriers by sending up puffs of smoke. Her firm develops software that allows native and nonnative speakers from around the world to communicate clearly and effectively in English. Initially, Hilla and her husband Liran started the firm in their apartment with a small investment of personal funds and a vast amount of enthusiasm. Today, WhiteSmoke has over 50 employees and boasts millions of users worldwide. Hilla explains:

WhiteSmoke has a very broad "target group": anyone writing in English! We designed it to cater to any level of English proficiency, but we also know that writers in different professional fields have specific needs. That's why our R&D teams developed specially tailored versions for business, legal, medical, creative, and academic writing styles.

As the firm grew, Hilla had to turn from using her own financial resources to external investors. Although she has raised thousands of dollars by doing so, it has often been a struggle. She advises other women entrepreneurs to persist and to be confident. In addition to equity investors, Hilla also uses bank loans for credit. She has taken steps to defend her revenues against potential competitors by patenting the technology behind WhiteSmoke.

The beauty of WhiteSmoke is that it uses state-of-the-art technology unique only to us. Other text editing software programs are based on a predictated list of grammar and spelling rules. They simply compare the user's text to these and mark basic mistakes. But we've challenged this approach by creating smart artificial intelligence algorithms that perform both rule- and statistical-based analysis of real mistakes users actually make in real life.

One of the challenges and opportunities for Hilla and WhiteSmoke is the need for constant innovation to stay ahead of the market and to provide new and improved products and services to users.

What Have We Learned?

We saw in this chapter that women entrepreneurs participate in the global economy in a variety of ways: by establishing firms in their home countries, some developed and some developing; by exporting their goods and services; and by starting new firms in the United States as immigrant entrepreneurs. We also saw that women's global entrepreneurship brings additional financial challenges. Women who establish firms in their own countries may or may not have access to well-developed financial markets and the products and services they can provide. Women in developing countries, in particular, can benefit from grassroots programs that provide financing, as well as programs that help build their skills and confidence. It is also important to develop networks of women entrepreneurs to share advice and support on an ongoing basis. Similarly, women immigrant entrepreneurs who come to the United States may not understand our financial system or be able to use it due to language or cultural differences. They could benefit from information and advice on how to use the financial system in this country to meet their companies' needs. As newcomers to this country, immigrant entrepreneurs can also benefit from the establishment of networks of women entrepreneurs to provide skill building, information, and support.

Finally, we saw that exporting can provide opportunities for growth for women entrepreneurs. Currently, only a small percentage of women entrepreneurs in the United States are involved in exporting, but the number is growing. Major impediments to growth include lack of information, lack of key contacts, and lack of financing alternatives. Many women entrepreneurs do not know the first thing about how to get started with exporting or who the recipients of their products and services will be. As an added challenge, they know that exporting will require additional financial resources, and they are uncertain as to how to acquire them. Women entrepreneurs need an "Exporting 101" course to help them determine if their products are suitable for export and, if so, which markets are most promising. Further, they need assistance in identifying and joining networks that will provide information and support to exporting firms through seminars, training programs, trade missions, and individual contacts. Finally, they need information about how and when they will get paid if they do business internationally, as well as guidance on how to finance their international activities.

What Does All This Mean For Me?

What exactly does this mean for you as a woman entrepreneur or as an aspiring women entrepreneur? If you are a woman starting a firm in another country or an immigrant entrepreneur starting a firm in the United States, this chapter highlights the importance of establishing and using networks. Your networks can provide information, key contacts, and access to sources of financing. Further, they can help you to develop new skills that will contribute to the success of your firm. Last, but not least, they can provide you with an ongoing source of emotional support so you know you are not alone in your entrepreneurial journey. If you are an immigrant entrepreneur, your networks will help you gain a better understanding of the U.S. financial system, as well as greater access to both informal and formal sources of capital.

If you are a native-born woman entrepreneur in the United States and you are not yet participating in the global economy by exporting, get the lead out! Exporting can be an exciting pathway to firm growth and new business opportunities. Attend some seminars or workshops offered by your district office of the U.S. Department of Commerce or one of your area's business associations to learn if your firm's products or services are appropriate for export. Start building your export-oriented network to include organizations that can provide information and assistance, other exporting firms, and financial service providers. Talk to other women entrepreneurs who are engaged in exporting to learn from their experiences. Ask important questions like "How do I get paid?"; "When do I get paid?"; "What are the additional costs associated with exporting?"; "How can I finance my growth through exporting?"; and "What financial products and service providers are appropriate for my exporting needs?" Learn the risks as well as the benefits associated with exporting, and, by all means, network with other women who are doing it and doing it successfully.

As a woman entrepreneur in the United States, you can also take steps to ease the path of women entrepreneurs in other countries or immigrant entrepreneurs in this one. Include them in your networks, share your experience and expertise, and learn from them as well. As an example, a church at which one of the authors is a parishioner—Saint Patrick–St. Anthony in Hartford, Connecticut—has a sister parish relationship with St. Genevieve in Haiti. As a part of our activities, we provide financing for women entrepreneurs in that parish. These women travel to the local marketplace to sell their goods. Simple as it may sound, they need shoes to make the walk and notebooks and pencils to write down orders. That's what our donations help to pay for. There are many other nonprofit organizations, some located in your own community, that provide similar types of financing and other forms of support to women entrepreneurs throughout the world. It's not a big sacrifice for us, but it can make a tremendous difference to the women we help. We have made them a part of our network, and none of us is alone.

Similarly, if you have women immigrant entrepreneurs in your community (and you do!), make it a point to reach out to them and connect them with networks that may be beneficial to them. Make them aware of local business organizations that could provide information, contacts, and support. Offer to take them to their first meeting or function, and introduce them to your friends and contacts. Share information about local programs or seminars that may help them build their skills and gain additional information about doing business in the United States. Introduce them to the U.S. financial system by taking them to a bank and having someone explain different types of business and personal products. Be an advisor, advocate, and friend. As women entrepreneurs from different countries, we are different, but we are similar in so many ways! Build upon those similarities, and you will find that over time you will benefit as much personally and professionally as the women immigrant entrepreneurs you befriend.

Public Policy Implications

In this chapter we looked at three ways in which women can become involved in entrepreneurship. We discussed women who establish firms in countries outside of the United States, women entrepreneurs in this country who engage in exporting to other countries, and immigrant entrepreneurs who come to our country in search of the "American Dream." Following we provide public policy recommendations for each type of entrepreneur.

Public Policy Recommendations to Increase the Level of Women's Entrepreneurship Globally

A number of public policy measures have been suggested to increase the flow of capital to global entrepreneurs in general and global women entrepreneurs in particular:

1. Antidiscriminatory policies in both business and the private sector. These measures will allow women access to both educational and employment opportunities, as well as sources of financial capital.

2. Policies that recognize the value of women in society, as well as the value of the economic contributions that women entrepreneurs can make. As in the United States, women entrepreneurs worldwide have a role to play in the development of new products and services, as well as in the economic development of their communities and nations.
3. Policies to develop competition within the financial sector, since discrimination is less prevalent in highly competitive markets. Many developing nations have financial markets that are also still developing. A well-developed financial sector provides greater transparency, as well as a wider choice of both debt and equity alternatives for all entrepreneurs.
4. Policies to link sources of financing with the establishment of grassroots organizations to support women entrepreneurs through skill and confidence building and the establishment of networks of women entrepreneurs for ongoing support. As we have seen in our own country, in the case of women entrepreneurs, it's not just about the money. Many women entrepreneurs can also benefit from education and training in financial literacy and financial management. Similarly, this book is full of the stories of women entrepreneurs who have found both business and personal support through their participation in both formal and informal networks and business organizations.

Public Policy Initiatives to Increase the Number of Women-Owned Firms Involved in Exporting

From a public policy perspective, it is important to encourage and assist women entrepreneurs who are considering exporting their products and services. The Information and Technology Innovation Foundation's *2010 State New Economy Index* points out that exports as a percentage of gross domestic product have increased dramatically in recent decades and that workers in exporting industries enjoy higher earnings than workers overall (Atkinson and Andes, 2010). For women entrepreneurs, assistance with exporting can come in the form of identifying appropriate products and markets for export, establishing linkages with buyers in foreign markets, and advice on how to structure foreign transactions including financing.

Many women entrepreneurs may not consider exporting because, if you will excuse the term, it is just too "foreign" to them. They need information as well as assistance and support, and they need to be connected with the appropriate networks in the United States and in the country to which they are exporting. In terms of financing, exporting will require additional financial resources, so women entrepreneurs can benefit from guidance on either governmental or private sources such as banks that have expertise in international trade.

Public Policy Initiatives to Support Immigrant Entrepreneurs

Women immigrant entrepreneurs would benefit from public policy initiatives designed to help them to integrate into their local communities and find appropriate forms of financial support. As in the case of women entrepreneurs in other countries, immigrant entrepreneurs need sources of advice and support as well as sources of financing to identify attractive business opportunities, develop their skills, and establish networks, including those with sources of financial capital. The KFS data cited in this chapter suggest that women immigrant entrepreneurs have less familiarity with and access to the formal financial system in this country. In light of that, financial service providers should make a special effort to reach out to women immigrant entrepreneurs and to educate them on products and services that are appropriate for their firms.

From the perspective of public policy, immigrant entrepreneurs also have the potential to make a substantial contribution to job creation and economic growth. Our minicase on Hilla Ovil-Brenner, the founder of WhiteSmoke, provides an example of the opportunities that are available in the United States for highly educated and highly skilled immigrant entrepreneurs who establish growth-oriented and technology-based firms. In light of the role that such entrepreneurs can play in the creation of new firms, new products and services, and new technologies, some researchers have called for changes in U.S. immigration law that would make it easier for highly skilled immigrants to establish residency and launch firms in the United States (Tyler and Shuck, 2011).

IT'S A WRAP!

What Have We Learned?

In *A Rising Tide: Financing Strategies for Women-Owned Firms*, we attempted to highlight the financial issues, challenges, and opportunities facing women entrepreneurs. As noted in Chapter 1, women business owners are a growing economic force. Today, women are better educated and better employed than ever before. Nevertheless, although women constitute half of the population, they represent only about one-third of entrepreneurs in the United States. This gap in entrepreneurship between women and men is true not only for the United States but for most other countries as well. Since we are the type of people who prefer to see the glass half full, this discrepancy in participation rates represents a tremendous opportunity for both current and potential women entrepreneurs going forward.

In this book, we used a life cycle approach to develop the themes, examples, and lessons about women entrepreneurs. We included firms that represented a wide variety of industries at various stages of development to show that women entrepreneurs use different financial strategies depending on the type of firm and the stage of development of the business involved. A home-based firm such as Cookies Direct focuses on developing sales through effective use of the Internet combined with careful expense control and some extraordinarily creative bootstrapping. Alternatively, a growth-oriented firm such as FirstRain devotes a considerable amount of time and attention to raising a substantial amount of external equity. New firms such as Everloop face different types of challenges than firms such as ElectroChem, which celebrated its twenty-fifth anniversary in 2011. Whereas Amanda Steinberg is still seeking out and evaluating the sources of financing that are most appropriate for her firm, Radha Jalan has become an expert in securing government contracts and grants to develop her fuel cell company. Radha has also acquired "reputational capital" through a long track record of performance.

Resource-Based Theory Revisited

This book is grounded in both Resource-Based Theory and Motivational Theory. Resource-Based Theory tells us that the task of the entrepreneur is to identify, secure, and utilize the resources necessary to make her venture successful. Motivational Theory asserts that the types of firms that entrepreneurs start will be determined by their motivations. This, in turn, will dictate the types of resources required. In essence, the entrepreneur's motivations will drive her search for and selection of resources.

We have provided examples of women entrepreneurs with a broad array of motivations. Some, like the founders of Pioneer Telephone, W3 Partners, and Smith Whiley, have been driven by opportunities in the marketplace and a desire to realize significant financial gain. Others, such as Kate Meyers at Brown & Meyers, have been driven by a desire to be their own boss and have control over their financial destinies. Some, such as Jude Workman of MediaWorks and Melanie Downey of Wilava, have been motivated by a desire to balance work and family. Several, such as Radha Jalan of ElectroChem, Debbie Godowsky of Cookies Direct, and Vivian Akuoko of Evay, have been driven by a specific economic goal or need. This highly diverse set of examples illustrates that an important first step for an entrepreneur is to assess her own goals in order to determine what is most important for her. Goals that we have cited include opportunity, financial gain, being one's own boss, self-realization, balancing work and family, or a lack of desirable employment opportunities.

As we said, the entrepreneur's goals and the type of venture she selects to achieve those goals largely determine the nature of the resources required. A home-based firm such as Cookies Direct, Wilava, or Marilyn Steinmetz's financial advisory firm can be launched with relatively modest resources. Alternatively, growth-oriented firms such as DailyWorth, FirstRain, and W3 Partners require substantial resources to launch and grow.

In assessing women entrepreneurs from a Resource-Based Theory perspective, we identified three primary resource areas: human capital, social capital, and financial capital. Human capital refers to the entrepreneur's level of education, as well as her prior work, industry, managerial, and entrepreneurial experiences. Prior research reveals that entrepreneurs with higher levels of human capital are more likely to succeed. Similarly, they are often in a better position to raise both internal and external sources of capital. In terms of internally provided sources of capital, women with higher levels of education and experience tend also to have higher levels of income and wealth that can be devoted to an entrepreneurial venture. From the perspective of external capital, the educational and experiential qualifications of the entrepreneur often act as a "signal" to external investors, thus dispelling some of the uncertainties or "asymmetric information" typically associated with newer or privately held firms.

Many of our successful entrepreneurs demonstrate a good understanding of the importance of human capital. Kate Meyers put herself through court reporting school before starting her firm, and Vivian Akuoko went to hairdressing school and completed her GED. Marilyn Steinmetz "apprenticed" herself to a financial advisor and worked without pay to learn the business. The founders of W3 Partners accumulated many years of experience in the commercial real estate industry before starting their own firm. The lesson to be learned for aspiring women entrepreneurs is that acquiring needed education and experience is a prerequisite for entrepreneurial success. When you have determined the type of firm you want to start, take the time to research the types of education, training, certifications, and employment or entrepreneurial experiences that will help you succeed in your chosen field. The first step in your entrepreneurial journey may be devoting a few years to closing the gap between your current level of human capital and the level that is required.

Human capital requirements are particularly important for women who want to launch growth-oriented or technology-based firms. Although many women participate in the workforce, they continue to be clustered at the middle management and "worker bee" levels. Thus, they do not obtain the senior management skills and credentials that would equip them to manage a growth-oriented firm. This picture is starting to change as more women climb the leadership ranks, but it is changing too slowly. Companies need to do more to identify high-potential women employees early on and provide them with a range of experiences that will prepare them for the ranks of senior management. Some companies are already doing this, and they are reaping the benefits of a more diverse and productive workforce.

We also encountered the issue of human capital in Chapter 8 where we discussed technology-based firms. As we noted, the majority of technology-based firms are established by men because men are more likely to have educational and experiential backgrounds in technology-related fields. This represents an area of significant opportunity for young women and aspiring women entrepreneurs going forward, because technology industries offer some of the most attractive prospects for firm growth and financial rewards. Eager to "ride the wave," more women are getting degrees and advanced degrees in technology-related disciplines, working in technology-based firms, and taking the plunge into technology-based entrepreneurship (Table 11.1). As a nation, we can continue to accelerate this trend by developing and funding educational programs that attract girls and young women into technology and science fields, thereby helping to equip them for careers in these growth-oriented sectors.

Human capital can also be acquired through entrepreneurial teams. One entrepreneur will not necessarily have all of the necessary educational and experiential requirements. This is particularly true in growth-oriented or technology-based firms, where coverage of different functional areas is usually required. Take an inventory of your own human capital and determine where the gaps and weaknesses are. We all have them! Then, when you start to build your firm, identify members of your founding or management team who can fill in these gaps. Similarly, identify outside advisors who can provide expertise in specific areas. These may include attorneys, accountants, financial

TABLE 11.1 Number of degrees conferred to women by degree-granting institutions, by type of degree

	Number			*Percentage conferred to women*		
Type of degree and race/ethnicity	*1997–1998*	*2002–2003*	*2007–2008*	*1997–1998*	*2002–2003*	*2007–2008*
Associate's	558,555	634,016	750,164	61.0	60.0	62.3
Bachelor's	1,184,406	1,348,811	1,563,069	56.1	57.5	57.3
Master's	430,164	513,339	625,023	57.1	58.8	60.6
First professional[1]	78,598	80,897	91,309	42.9	48.2	49.7
Doctoral[2]	46,010	46,042	63,712	42.0	47.1	51.0

Source: U.S. Department of Education, National Center for Education Statistics, 1997–1998, 2002–2003, and 2007–2008 Integrated Postsecondary Education Data System (IPEDS), "Completions Survey" (IPEDS-C:98) and Fall 2003 and 2008.

[1] Includes first professional degrees such as M.D., D.D.S., and law degrees.

[2] Includes Ph.D., Ed.D., and comparable degrees at the doctoral level.

professionals, or members of a Board of Directors. When Sue Bouchard founded Pioneer Telephone, she had a strong background in financial services, while her husband Peter had a similarly strong background in sales, marketing, and telecommunications. The Bouchards have been a strong management team because each has continued to focus on her or his area of expertise. Smith Whiley provides us with another example of a strong management team. When Gwen Iloani established her firm, she convinced Collette Nakhoul to join her as her senior managing director. In that capacity, Collette is responsible for analyzing, pricing, and valuing deals. Although both women have strong financial and quantitative skills, having Collette on board from the start has allowed Gwen to spend more time on marketing her funds and identifying and developing potential investors.

Our second resource category, social capital, refers to key networks and contacts. These can either provide resources directly or access to resources in the form of information, talent, specific skills, managerial ability, or financial capital. Prior research suggests that this is an area where women entrepreneurs are at a disadvantage when compared to men. Women tend to have "lower-tier" networks, and they are more likely to network with other women. Further, their networks are less likely to include individuals who have senior management skills and experience or access to substantial levels of financial capital. Women entrepreneurs' lower levels of social capital lead to correspondingly lower levels of financial capital.

What can women entrepreneurs do to remedy this gap in social capital? Many are already doing something about it by establishing networks that will provide women with access to key contacts and decision makers, other successful entrepreneurs, and providers of financial capital. We have given several examples of organizations that provide such support, including Springboard Enterprises, Astia, Echelon Circles, and Women 2.0. Networks of this type are critical for women entrepreneurs because they provide guidance, role models, and access to resource providers. Networks can also provide emotional support for women entrepreneurs who, like Kate Meyers at Brown & Meyers, may feel isolated at times. In addition to Kate, several of the entrepreneurs we profiled in this book, including Sue Bouchard at Pioneer Telephone and Hilary DeCesare at Everloop, stressed the benefits of being associated with a network focusing on the needs and experiences of women entrepreneurs.

On the subject of networking, several of our entrepreneurs stressed the importance of networking "strategically." In other words, you want your network to include the individuals and organizations that can help you advance your goals for your firm. The quality of your network, rather than its size, is the point. From the standpoint of financial strategy, if you know that your firm will need angel or venture capital, you should be networking with individuals and groups who can provide you access to those types of resources. Alternatively, if your objective is to secure government funding to support firms in specific industries or geographic territories, that should be your focus. Our technology-based entrepreneur Radha Jalan has become an expert in securing government grants and contracts to fund her fuel cell company, ElectroChem. Similarly, our inner-city entrepreneur Vivian Akuoko was able to access government sources of support to finance her education and to help finance the growth of her firm, Evay.

Our third resource area is financial capital, and as we saw, the entrepreneur's levels of human and social capital often pave the way for securing financial capital. In Chapter 2 we highlighted the fact that women entrepreneurs have different financial strategies than men. They tend to rely more heavily on internal rather than external sources of capital, and they raise smaller amounts of capital both at start-up and in subsequent years. In particular, women entrepreneurs use significantly smaller levels of external equity capital than men. This is an important distinction, especially in the case of growth-oriented and technology-based firms that often depend on substantial infusions of external equity from angel investors or venture capitalists. In some instances women use lower levels of external equity by choice because they prefer to retain control, because they have a specific vision for the firm, or because they want to preserve a specific firm culture or environment. Our technology-based entrepreneur Patty Sue Williams who founded Telesis is a case in point. She chose to avoid venture capital funding and sought alternative means when she found out how much ownership and control she would have to relinquish.

In other instances, however, women do not use external equity because they simply cannot get it. The Diana Project researchers pointed out that there are very few women venture capitalists, and women entrepreneurs are typically not a part of the VC network (Brush et al., 2001a, 2004) Nascent entrepreneur Amanda Steinberg expressed frustration over the fact that she saw other firms like hers being funded by venture capitalists but could not secure funding herself in spite of multiple meetings and presentations to VC firms.

Venture capitalist Cindy Padnos stresses the benefits of investing in women-owned firms in her white paper. She points out that many VC firms will miss out on attractive investment opportunities if they do not broaden their horizons to include firms launched by women. One way to do so would be to recruit more women investment professionals into the venture capital industry and to help them advance their careers. Prior research suggests that women angel investors and venture capitalists are more likely to attract and consider firms owned by women entrepreneurs (Becker-Blease and Sohl, 2007; Harrison & Mason, 2007). Thus, to attract women, you have to have women on your investment team.

Key Takeaways and Lessons Learned

Each chapter of this book ended with sections entitled "What Have We Learned?" and "What Does All This Mean for Me?" In these sections we attempted to integrate the theories and real-world examples presented and make them applicable for our readers. These are your "takeaways" or "lessons learned." As our time together draws to a close, we would like to summarize and highlight some of those takeaways in order to leave you with some of the guiding principles that we have encountered across the diverse array of women entrepreneurs whom we have interviewed. These are themes that have emerged again and again.

"Doing something I love . . ."

Several common themes have emerged from our research and interviews with "real-life" women entrepreneurs. First, we were impressed with how happy most of them seemed to be. They are doing something they love and have a passion for, and they are doing it on their terms. In her article on women's entrepreneurship, Helen Ahl (2006) suggests that women often have to become "honorary men" in order to succeed. Our entrepreneurs have not done that. They have found ways to be successful by carving out their own path. Further, they have defined success in their own terms, not necessarily in Wall Street's terms or in the terms of their male counterparts. Often their success is measured by personal satisfaction, independence, and balance rather than in solely financial and economic terms. When we spend time with Radha Jalan of ElectroChem or Vivian Akuoko of Evay, we come away with a sense of serenity and peace. When we enter Gwen Iloani's office, we can hear her booming laugh from the other end of the hall. When we sit with Nancy Hansen and Patty Sue Williams, they beam with happiness, and when we leave Kate Meyer's office, we can't help chuckling because she is so excited about all of her opportunities that she can barely sit still. This is a story that has had many happy endings, with even more to come. These are not "honorary men" but women who have arrived.

"It takes a village . . ."

A second theme relates to the importance of women establishing networks to help and encourage other women. For a period of time, there were so few women in leadership and decision-making roles in business that they often ascribed to what we somewhat acerbically called the "queen bee syndrome." They saw success as a zero-sum game. In other words, there is room for only one woman at the top, and if it's going to be me, then it can't be you. Thank goodness we have evolved! Today, although there are still relatively few women CEOs, the ranks of women in senior management are growing. This trend allows women to accumulate the human, social, and financial capital that will equip them for entrepreneurship or, alternatively, for investment in entrepreneurial firms. These are major gains that will help women acquire skills and experience in the areas of leadership and financial management while also providing access to networks that can lead to the acquisition of other resources including financial resources.

This type of experience and access is particularly important for women who aspire to start growth-oriented firms. Recognition of the support that can be provided by networks of women entrepreneurs has given rise to nationally known organizations such as Springboard Enterprises and Astia, as well as to more local and regional groups that play a similar role on a smaller scale by helping women entrepreneurs acquire information, skills, and valuable contacts. Equally important, networks provide women entrepreneurs with sources of support, role models, and confidence, all of which help in crafting financial strategies or seeking out and negotiating with providers of capital.

"You have to know when to hold 'em, know when to fold 'em . . ."

A third theme that has emerged is the theme of risk-taking. Any time you start a new firm, there is an element of risk, and prior research suggests that women are less willing to take risks than men (Jianakopolos and Bernasek, 1998; Powell and Ansic, 1997). We did not find this to be the case in our interviews with successful women entrepreneurs. In fact, some of them took extraordinary risks in starting their firms. Several launched firms as single parents with dependent children and limited financial resources. Others left lucrative and successful careers to strike out on their own. These women were not shrinking violets. In fact, they were uniformly courageous and unflinching in confronting the challenges they faced. They took risks, and in some instances, they took really big risks by staking their homes and personal livelihoods on their firms. They did not, however, take stupid risks; they took calculated risks. In doing so, they carefully thought through the various risk factors and tried to control for as many as possible. This sometimes led to a more conservative financial structure or set of strategies because that was something the entrepreneur could control.

A good example is Debbie Godowsky of Cookies Direct, who squeezed every nickel until it screamed and refused to buy anything for her firm that she didn't absolutely need. She became a bootstrapper par excellence—even asking the Catholic church down the street if she could use their ovens. This diligent level of expense control was a deliberate strategy on Debbie's part, and it allowed her to maximize earnings (revenues minus expenses). This, in turn, was consistent with her goal of raising the capital required to finance two college educations for her children. Similarly, when Gwen Iloani left a fast-track investment management position in a major insurance company, she left with impressive credentials and a track record of success. These attributes enabled her to secure her former employer's financial backing in order to provide start-up financing for her firm. Our experience suggests that our entrepreneurs were less concerned with avoiding risk than with managing it scrupulously.

"To thine own self be true . . ."

Another thing that impressed us about our entrepreneurs was that they had a very clear understanding of their priorities and goals. Each of our entrepreneurs was able to clearly and succinctly articulate what was most important to her. There was no hemming and hawing or scratching of collective heads. These women had an almost laser-like focus. Their firms, in turn, were a reflection of those priorities and values. Sue Bouchard wanted to have it all: a successful business and work/family balance. Twenty years later, her firm still accommodates those goals, not only for the firm's owners but for the employees as well.

The founders of W3 Partners wanted to create a company culture and management style that was a reflection of their values, even in the heavily male-dominated commercial real estate investment industry. Vivian Akuoku wanted to get off welfare and took it upon herself to learn the tools of both personal and business financial management step by step. That strength of purpose has helped her to succeed as an entrepreneur, and her skills in the area of financial management have enabled her firm to survive through economic ups and downs. She is always thinking about how the financial pieces of her firm fit together to make an integrated whole. For example, the current economic downturn has led her to completely revamp her system for ordering and managing inventories, thereby freeing up cash for other purposes.

"Try, try, and try again . . ."

Another quality we saw in our successful women entrepreneurs was their dogged persistence in crafting financial strategies and seeking sources of financing. Instead of "The buck stops here," we could justifiably say, "The buck starts here" when it came to these entrepreneurs. In different ways, several of them said essentially the same thing: your firm's destiny rests in your own hands, and you have to take responsibility for making things happen. In the realm of finance, this means that investors will not fund you just because you have a good idea. You have to be doggedly persistent in selling your idea to potential investors, following up, and negotiating for your own best deal. Although you may have a management team or a group of trusted friends and advisors, no one can do that for you, because, ultimately, you are in the driver's seat.

When Patty Sue Williams of Telesis tried to sell her idea for a software testing firm to major insurance companies, she didn't get any takers. Undaunted, she began to talk to venture capitalists—until she realized how much of the firm's equity they would demand. Ultimately, she settled on start-up financing provided by her parents, using her home as collateral. Initially Amanda Steinberg of Everloop also tried the venture capital route with no success. She shifted her focus to angel investors, who proved to be a more reliable source of start-up financing for her.

In addition to seeking out sources of financing, our entrepreneurs also had to learn to negotiate to maintain their ownership position and defend their interests. This is particularly true for growth-oriented and technology-based entrepreneurs seeking external equity. Other entrepreneurs, such as Sue Bouchard at Pioneer Telephone, deliberately chose to finance with debt rather than with external equity in order to maintain ownership and control. Nevertheless, they had to be fairly nimble in mustering the financial capital required to pursue opportunities. When Pioneer Telephone had the opportunity to acquire two other firms, the Bouchards needed to move quickly to close the deal. They used fairly expensive debt in the form of a private placement, but they later refinanced with bank debt at a lower interest rate.

An Inventory of Financial Strategies

Our review of research on financing women-owned firms and our conversations with women entrepreneurs highlighted several financial strategies that "work." Since our time together is drawing to a close, this would seem to be a good place to summarize them:

1. Develop your own level of financial literacy and skills. Several of our entrepreneurs had backgrounds in finance or in the financial services industry, but many did not. Thus, a successful woman entrepreneur must identify gaps in her level of financial knowledge and skills and then find ways to close those gaps through education, training, finding a mentor, becoming part of a network, or creating a management team with individuals who have those skills. One of our best examples of an entrepreneur who did that is Vivian Akuoko at Evay, who found a mentor, learned from her, and followed her advice in completing her GED. Vivian has continued to take courses and seminars every year for the last 25 years she has been in business.

2. Identify your goals, and align your financial strategies with your goals. If your goal, like Sue Bouchard's at Pioneer Telephone, is to develop and preserve a particular type of company culture, you may have a preference for financing sources that allow you to maintain ownership and control. Similarly, if your goal is manageable growth to accommodate the needs of young children, you may, like Melanie Downey at Wilava, choose to deliberately limit the size of your company. Alternatively, if your goal is significant size, growth, and wealth, you may, like Penny Herscher at FirstRain, recognize the need for external equity investors who can provide expertise, contacts, and substantial amounts of capital.

3. Cash is king (or queen, as the case may be). Companies do not go out of business because they don't have good ideas, customers, or revenues. They go out of business because they run out of cash. This has several implications for women-owned firms. First, find ways to maximize your cash position and accelerate cash inflows. Debbie Godowsky and Kate Meyers were aggressive users of bootstrapping techniques to minimize expenses. Initially Debbie also established her firm as a buying club in which customers prepaid for an entire year.

She purchased and learned to use a financial management software program to set up financial statements and create a system for tracking income and expenses. Software programs like QuickBooks, Quicken, or Peachtree Accounting are readily available, affordable, and easy to learn and use, even for entrepreneurs who do not have prior training in finance or accounting. Programs of this type can help you get a handle on your company's revenues, expenses, and cash.

Second, prior research suggests that women entrepreneurs may not raise enough capital to adequately fund their firms at start-up or during the growth phase (Amatucci and Sohl, 2004). Cindy Padnos at Illuminate Ventures refers to women as being "capital efficient," but there is often a fine line between being capital efficient and just not having enough capital to achieve your objectives. The successful growth-oriented entrepreneurs we spoke with were not afraid to go after substantial amounts of capital when they needed it. Patty Sue Williams borrowed money from her parents and put up her house as collateral with every intention of losing it if it came to that. Sue Bouchard did private placements of debt to finance two acquisitions. Gwen Iloani (Smith Whiley), and Diane Olmstead and Susan Sagy (W3 Partners) entered into strategic partnerships with much larger firms in order to launch their companies. Fully aware of the implications for growth, ownership, and control, Penny Hersher raised over $40 million in venture capital. These women were not risk averse. They didn't sit on the sidelines. They knew what they wanted, and they pursued sources of capital in sufficient amounts to allow them to achieve their goals.

4. Closely related to the theme of managing cash is the theme of managing your working capital accounts in general. Working capital is another name for current assets that include cash, accounts receivable, and inventory. Entrepreneurs are often so busy running their business that they forget to manage these three critically important accounts. We already talked about the importance of cash, and it is just as important to manage your receivables and inventory. Accounts receivable don't actually do you any good until you collect them. That's when you get the cash. In light of that, you need to monitor your receivables to ensure that you are getting paid and getting paid on time. If your customers are not paying, you may need to take additional steps to accelerate payment. Examples include letters, emails, phone calls, penalty charges for late payments, discounts for early payments, or, if worse comes to worse, dropping that customer because they don't pay. Jude Workman of MediaWorks stressed the

importance of getting paid. As the owner of a small firm, she cannot wait six months for her money, so she makes sure to include provisions for monthly or biweekly payments in her agreements with customers.

The other important working capital account is inventory. It is not uncommon for business owners to have 25 to 50 percent of their assets in the form of inventory. This is an enormous chunk of your balance sheet! Further, every asset on your balance sheet has to be paid for with either debt or equity. Thus, if you are carrying too much inventory, or if you are inefficient in managing your inventory, you are generating unnecessary costs. Vivian Akuoko tackled this issue during the recent financial crisis. She realized that she had to find a way to cut costs in a tough economy, so she revamped the way she managed her inventories of skin and hair care products. Rather than producing products in larger batches, she now does them in small batches to minimize her inventory holdings and the amount of cash she has tied up in inventories.

5. Don't be afraid to try something new. Most of our entrepreneurs were innovators in one way or another, and innovation is a way to generate additional revenues by introducing new products, entering new markets, or taking advantage of new technologies. This is an important point, because as we have noted throughout this book, earnings from sales are a major source of financing for most firms. You can maximize earnings by either controlling expenses or by increasing revenues. A number of our successful women entrepreneurs have used both strategies. Radha Jalan merged with another firm to increase ElectroChem's scope and capabilities. Sue Bouchard did two acquisitions to expand the nationwide reach of Pioneer Telephone. Debbie Godowsky and Melanie Downey turned to the Internet to market their products and reach a broader customer base. Similarly, Kate Meyers went to a web-based platform for legal and medical transcription services, thereby making it possible for her to serve customers throughout the country. Vivian Akuoko is working with her cosmetics lab partner to develop a new eye cream to target the needs of mature customers. In essence, our successful entrepreneurs are constantly reinventing themselves to stay abreast of the market and ahead of the competition.

6. If you have a problem, confront it promptly, deal with it, and move on. Women often fall into the role of nurturers and caretakers. As such, they prefer to avoid conflicts and give others second chances. These are wonderful qualities, but they can sometimes be taken too far to the detriment of the firm. By her own admission, Radha Jalan tolerated the nonperformance of a manager

for too long because he had been highly recommended by one of her equity investors. Sue Bouchard, who has worked hard to develop a positive and family-friendly company culture, said it best in pointing out that there are times when you need to be flexible and understanding, but there are other times when you need to be tough. Many of our entrepreneurs had to lay off employees in periods of lower demand or fire them for nonperformance. Failure to address these needs in a timely fashion adds to company costs and sometimes reduces revenues because of the negative impact on other employees.

7. Identify the individuals, networks, and organizations that can help you gain access to needed resources in the form of human, social, and financial capital. Several of our entrepreneurs, including Marilyn Steinmetz (Mutual Service Associates), Gwen Iloani (Smith Whiley), and Vivian Akuoku (Evay), identified mentors who provided direction, guidance, advice, and support. Many, including Kate Meyers (Brown & Meyers), Sue Bouchard (Pioneer Telephone), and Hilary DeCesare (Everloop), identified either local or national networks of women business owners or entrepreneurs that provide information, role models, contacts, and access to providers of financial capital. A number of our entrepreneurs also indicated that they are active and involved in their industry or trade associations. These groups provide information, contacts, and resources that are specific to individual industries and are thus more targeted in their focus.

8. Be on the lookout for funding and support services targeted at particular types of firms, industries, or geographic regions. Several of our entrepreneurs have been able to tap into these. Examples include Radha Jalan's use of SBIR grants, which are designed to support firms developing innovative technologies. Springboard Enterprises and Astia are both organizations that help growth-oriented women entrepreneurs develop skills, make contacts, and connect with potential investors. ACCION USA has provided over $100 billion in microloans to entrepreneurs who are predominantly Hispanic and African American. Vivian Akuoko's firm, Evay, has found ways to benefit from more localized sources of support, including loans provided by the Hartford Economic Development Corporation (HEDCo) and services provided by the University of Hartford's Micro-Business Incubator. Take the time to do your research, network, and find out what's out there for you and your firm. You may be surprised by the number of funding and support opportunities available to you.

9. Be confident. This may not sound like a financial strategy, but it is. Prior research reveals that women are less likely to apply for loans because they assume they will be turned down. Most recent studies show, however, that there is no significant difference between loan approval rates for women and men. Similarly, in the area of equity funding, prior research reveals that women may not ask for enough capital to adequately fund their firms. They also feel less confident of their ability to negotiate with equity investors and less confident in their level of financial skills overall.

How do you gain confidence? Many of the strategies for raising capital that we discussed in this book are also strategies that will help you build confidence. First, develop your level of business and financial literacy. This will help you to understand financial issues, challenges, and opportunities, and defend your interests with financial service providers. Second, develop human capital in the form of education and experience in your chosen field. These attributes send out signals that you "know your stuff." Third, develop social capital in the form of mentors, key contacts, and involvement in relevant groups and organizations. Like human capital, social capital also acts as a signal, and your contacts can pave the way for membership in the "club." Finally, stop focusing on all your shortcomings and start focusing on your strengths and accomplishments. Our successful entrepreneurs are optimistic, can-do people. They have not ignored their weaknesses, but they have leveraged their strengths to find ways to address them.

10. Last, but not least, pay it forward. If more women help other women, then more women will succeed. Remember that "rising tide" thing we have been talking about for the last 11 chapters? This book is full of examples of women entrepreneurs who have gained inspiration, knowledge and advice, contacts, and emotional support from other successful women entrepreneurs. Sometimes this has occurred on a "person-to-person" basis, as in the examples of Vivian Akuoko and Marilyn Steinmetz. Their stories illustrate the importance of getting a mentor and, by extension, being a mentor for other women. In other instances support has come through membership in a group that focuses on bringing together women business owners and entrepreneurs. As a whole, we are greater than the sum of our parts. Networks of this type provide opportunities to share your questions and concerns as well as the lessons you have learned as an entrepreneur.

Another area where women can help other women is in the area of financial capital. We discussed the difficulties that women entrepreneurs who are launching growth-oriented or technology-based firms encounter, particularly in their attempts to secure external equity financing. Some researchers contend that this is true because there are so few women angels and venture capitalists (Brush et al., 2004; Harrison and Mason, 2007). As women continue to rise in the ranks of corporations, and as they experience success with their own entrepreneurial ventures, they will accumulate significant amounts of wealth. As those successful women consider investment alternatives, it will be important for them also to consider investing in the firms launched by other women. Venture capitalist Cindy Padnos has noted that women-owned firms are a largely untapped area of investment opportunity. We need more women angels, venture capitalists, and investors to start taking a serious look at this area of opportunity.

• A Summary of Financial Strategies for Women Entrepreneurs

1. Develop financial literacy and skills.
2. Match your financial strategies to your goals.
3. Learn to manage cash flows.
4. Keep a close watch on your working capital accounts.
5. Explore new sources of revenue.
6. Confront and deal with problems promptly.
7. Network strategically to gain access to key information, advice, and resources.
8. Look for targeted funding opportunities.
9. Be confident in your abilities.
10. Pay it forward.

Public Policy Priorities

We discussed the implications of our findings for public policy throughout this book. If we are going to encourage and promote women's entrepreneurship, we need the right public policy environment to do so. As we said, public policy can encourage the development of specific industries and geographic regions.

Conversely, it can discourage entrepreneurship by imposing regulations and costs that stifle fledgling ventures. As we come to the end of this book, what are some of our priorities from a public policy perspective?

First, we need to encourage and equip the next generation of women entrepreneurs to enter industries that have significant opportunities for growth and wealth accumulation. These include growth-oriented fields such as math, science, engineering, computer science, health care, and bioscience. One of the reasons for the gap between women and men entrepreneurs in these growth-oriented fields is that women are less likely to have the requisite levels of education and experience. Further, they are less likely to be attracted to fields that are heavily male-dominated. Currently, there are programs at the local, state, and national levels to attract an increasing number of girls and women into the STEM fields and help them advance their careers in these fields. We need to continue with these initiatives to ensure that women have both equal access and equal opportunity.

Second, we need to develop a higher level of financial literacy among our citizens. This is particularly true for individuals from lower-income brackets and recent immigrants. Our research has shown that successful women entrepreneurs invest the time to increase their level of financial knowledge and understanding. This, in turn, helps them to make better financial decisions and avoid serious mistakes, while also building confidence. Conversely, it is difficult to be a successful entrepreneur if you don't understand the basics of finance or the workings of the financial system in this country. That's the place to start, as many community-based programs operated out of schools, libraries, community centers, and churches have recognized. Many of the individuals who participate in programs of this type are women seeking an escape from poverty for themselves and their children, or women trying to integrate into a new country and culture. We should make it a priority to develop curricula, teaching materials, and delivery systems for programs of this type.

Third, we need to develop policies and practices that recognize the role of entrepreneurship in general and women's entrepreneurship in particular at the local, state, and national levels. Currently, most elected officials and decision makers give lip service to the importance of launching and developing new firms. Often, however, legal, regulatory, and tax policies have just the opposite effect. We need greater consistency between our avowed commitment to economic development and job growth and the policies that will encourage those outcomes.

Fourth, we need to ensure that financial capital is available and affordable to small and entrepreneurial firms. Throughout the recent financial crisis, our focus has been on the survival of large institutions, whether they be banks, insurance companies, or automobile manufacturers. It has not been on small or new firms. Even now, as we embark on the path to economic recovery, small and new firms are constrained in their attempts to secure both debt and equity capital. In light of the fact that small firms provide the majority of net new jobs, it is in our interest to find ways to keep capital flowing, particularly during the most difficult economic times.

Finally, although women entrepreneurs have made good progress in terms of their ability to secure debt capital, there continues to be a structural imbalance in the area of external equity. As other researchers have pointed out, women receive only a small fraction of the total amount of venture capital funding (Brush et al., 2004). Further, there are currently very few women angel or venture capital investors. We need a better balance between women and men at the more senior levels of angel investor networks and venture capital firms. This will open the door for more growth-oriented women entrepreneurs, while also increasing the opportunities and returns of firms that invest in them.

Going forward, we need to prepare women better to be both participants and investors in women-owned ventures. Although women have advanced into management positions in major corporations, they are still relatively scarce at the most senior ranks. We need more women to reach the top of the pyramid, where they will gain experience in leadership and decision making at the highest levels. This experience, in turn, will provide valuable networks and the skills to launch their own growth-oriented firms. Simultaneously, women need to achieve the financial rewards that come with success at that level. This will provide them with the means to invest in other firms, including high-potential firms owned by women.

What Does Our Crystal Ball Tell Us?

Although we have reached the end of this book, we prefer to think of it as a beginning. According to U.S. Census data, there were 7.8 million women-owned firms in the United States in 2007. This represented over a 40 percent increase from 1997. During that time, the number of women-owned firms grew more rapidly than the number of firms overall, a trend that we anticipate will continue into the future as women continue to make gains in the areas of education, experience, earnings, and wealth. The number of women entrepreneurs will also increase as we emerge from a severe recession, and a gradual return to economic health creates opportunities for new products, services, and technologies.

Going forward, women's entrepreneurship will benefit from an increasing number of women who are capable of launching growth-oriented and technology-based firms, thanks to programs designed to attract girls and young women into these fields. We will also benefit from the growing number of minority entrepreneurs. Demographic forecasts for the United States indicate that the growth rate for minorities will exceed that of Caucasians (www.census.gov). This is an important trend, because black and Hispanic women are more likely to pursue entrepreneurship than their Caucasian counterparts. Finally, new immigrant women will continue to embrace entrepreneurship as a way to realize the American dream.

All of this bodes well for women's entrepreneurship and for the financial products, services, and institutions that support women's entrepreneurship. An increasing number of women entrepreneurs will create opportunities and support systems for an even greater number of women entrepreneurs. Going forward, women will have increased access to resources in the form of human, social, and financial capital that will help them launch and grow successful firms.

In terms of human capital, women have already made significant gains in education, and today over half of college graduates are women (*National Center for Education Statistics Fast Facts*, 2009). As shown in Table 11.1 and Figure 11.1, the proportion of women enrolling in degree-granting institutions has risen over the course of the last decade. Further, an increasing number of advanced degrees that typically lead to specialized knowledge and skills are being awarded to women. We predict that women will continue to embrace education at all levels as a pathway to personal and economic empowerment. In particular, we predict that the next generation of women entrepreneurs will be better educated and better prepared in growth-oriented fields such as science, technology, engineering, and math, thanks to efforts currently underway at the local, state, and national levels.

Women entrepreneurs have also recognized the importance of social capital in the form of mentors, role models, and networks of women entrepreneurs. They are actively seeking mentors, and this next generation of women

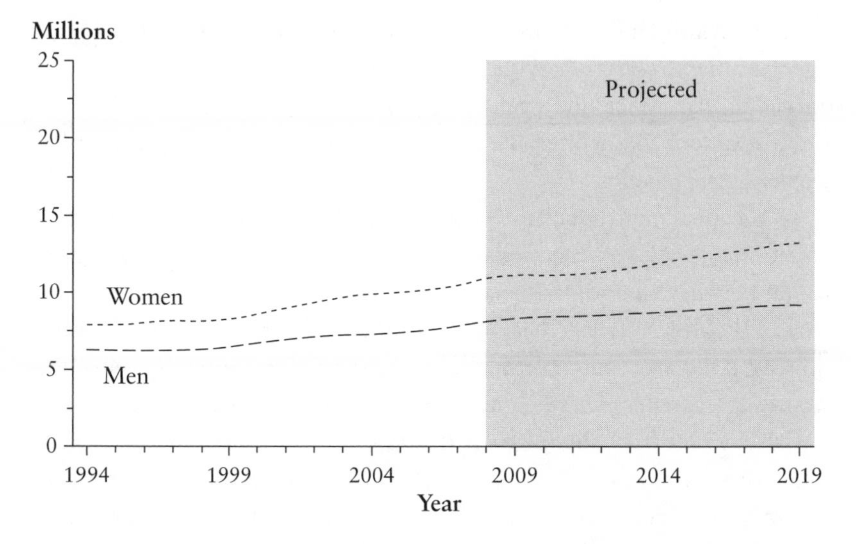

FIGURE 11.1 Actual and projected numbers for enrollment in all degree-granting institutions, by sex (Fall 1994 through Fall 2019)
Sources: U.S. Department of Education, National Center for Education Statistics, Integrated Postsecondary Education Data System, "Fall Enrollment Survey" (IPEDS-EF:94–99), and Spring 2001 through Spring 2009; and Enrollment in Degree-Granting Institutions Model, 1973–2008. (This graph was prepared in April 2010.)

entrepreneurs will be equipped to serve as mentors for other women. Networks that include other women entrepreneurs will provide contacts with financial service providers and potential investors, as well as information and advice on financial strategies that work. Further, we predict that women entrepreneurs will continue to develop their own networks while also penetrating key networks that have previously been dominated by males.

In the area of financial capital, prior research suggests that many of the financial institutions supporting entrepreneurship have been "gendered" in character or biased toward the needs of male rather than female entrepreneurs (Marlow and Patton, 2005). This characteristic has the effect of discouraging women entrepreneurs from seeking sources of financing or making it more difficult for them to obtain financing. We predict that the gendered nature of financial institutions and providers of capital will lessen over time for at least three important reasons. First, the growing number of women entrepreneurs and growth-oriented women entrepreneurs will make it increasingly difficult to marginalize them. Second, in an increasingly competitive global economy, financial institutions with any kind of a profit motive cannot afford to ignore opportunities to serve half of the population. Finally, as women make gains in education, experience, and wealth, they will assume leadership roles in financial institutions that will enable them to recognize, encourage, and support women entrepreneurs.

What about motivation? How does that fit into this forecast for the future? One of the best takeaways from our interviews with women entrepreneurs is that they have found diverse and rewarding ways to define entrepreneurship in their own terms. They have not become "mini-men," nor have they mimicked the motivations or financial strategies of male entrepreneurs. Our women entrepreneurs have found ways to be true to themselves and to their goals, and they have shaped their financial strategies and sources accordingly. This is just as true for our small home-based entrepreneurs as it is for our growth-oriented entrepreneurs. In each case, they have been creative, resourceful, strategic, and persistent. They have done it their way, and they have come into their own.

So, dear readers, we have come to the end of our journey together. As we do so, we would like to thank you for your interest, engagement, and support. In parting, we leave you with a reminder that this is not a book about a happy ending but a book about a happy beginning.

REFERENCES

Acs, Joltan J., Pia Arenius, Michael Hay, and Maria Minitti. 2005. *Global Entrepreneurship Monitor 2004 Executive Report*. Wellesley, MA: Babson College, and London: London Business School.

Ahl, Helene. 2006. "Why Research on Women Entrepreneurs Needs New Directions." *Entrepreneurship Theory and Practice* 30 (5): 595–621.

Alesina, Alberto F., Francesca Lotti, and Paolo Emilio Mistrulli. 2008. "Do Women Pay More For Credit? Evidence from Italy." Working Paper Series, Vol. w14202. Cambridge, MA: NBER. Accessed at http://ssrn.com/abstract=1190351.

Allen, I. Elaine, Amanda Elam, Nan Langowitz, and Monica Dean. *Global Entrepreneurship Monitor 2007 Report on Women and Entrepreneurship*. Wellesley, MA: Babson College, and London: London Business School.

Alsos, Gry Agnete, Espen John Isaksen, and Elisabet Ljunggren. 2006. "New Venture Financing and Subsequent Business Growth in Men- and Women-Led Businesses." *Entrepreneurship Theory and Practice* 30 (5): 667–86.

Altman, C. L., L. M. Crothers, and K. A. Blair. 2007. "The Relationship Between Girls' Academic Achievement and Academic Self-Concept: The Implications for School Psychologists." *The School Psychologist* 61: 113–19.

Amatucci, Frances M., and Susan Coleman. 2007. "Radha Jalan and ElectroChem, Inc.: Energy for a Clean Planet." *Entrepreneurship Theory and Practice* 31 (6): 971–94.

Amatucci, Frances, and Daria Crawley. 2010. "Financial Self-Efficacy Among Women Entrepreneurs." *International Journal of Gender and Entrepreneurship* 3 (1): 23–37.

Amatucci, Frances M., and Jeffrey E. Sohl. 2004. "Women Entrepreneurs Securing Business Angel Financing: Tales from the Field." *Venture Capital* 6 (2/3): 181–96.

Amatucci, Frances M., and Ethne Swartz. 2010. "Through a Fractured Lens: Women Entrepreneurs and the Private Equity Negotiation Process." Paper presented at the Annual Conference of the United States Association of Small Business and Entrepreneurship, Nashville, Tennessee, January 15, 2010.

American Family Business Survey. 2003. Springfield, MA: MassMutual Financial Group.

Amezcua, Alejandro S. 2010 "Performance Analysis of Entrepreneurship Policy: Which Business Incubators Generate the Highest Levels of Economic Performance?"

Frontiers in Entrepreneurship Research 30 (18), Article 1. Retrieved at http://digitalknowledge.babson.edu/fer/vol30/iss18/1.

Amit, R., and P. Schoemaker. 1993. "Strategic Assets and Organizational Rent." *Strategic Management Journal* 14 (1): 33–46.

Anderson, Ronald C., and David M. Reeb. 2003. "Founding-Family Ownership and Firm Performance: Evidence from the S&P 500." *The Journal of Finance* 58 (3): 1301–28.

Ang, James S. (1992). On the Theory of Finance for Privately Held Firms. *The Journal of Small Business Finance* 1 (3): 185–203.

Anna, Alexandra L., Gaylen N. Chandler, Erik Jansen, and Neal P. Mero. 1999. "Women Business Owners in Traditional and Non-Traditional Industries." *Journal of Business Venturing* 15: 279–303.

Astrachan, Joseph H., and Melissa C. Shanker. 2003. "Family Businesses' Contribution to the U.S. Economy: A Closer Look." *Family Business Review* 16 (3): 211–19.

Atkinson, Robert D., and Scott Andes. 2010. *The 2010 State New Economy Index: Benchmarking Economic Transformation in the States.* Washington D.C.: Information Technology and Innovation Foundation.

Audretsch, David B. 2002. "The Dynamic Role of Small Firms: Evidence from the U.S." *Small Business Economics* 18: 13–40.

Avery, Robert B., Raphael W. Bostic, and Katherine A. Samolyk. 1998. "The Role of Personal Wealth in Small Business Finance." *Journal of Banking and Finance* 22 (6–8): 1019–61.

Ballou, J., T. Barton, D. DesRoches, F. Potter, E. J. Reedy, and A. Robb. 2008. *Kauffman Firm Survey: Results from the Baseline and First Follow-up Surveys.* Kansas City, MO: Kauffman Foundation.

Banerjee, Abhijit, Esther Duflo, Rachel Glennerster, and Cynthia Kinnan. 2009. "The Miracle of Microfinance? Evidence from a Randomized Evaluation." Working Paper Series no. 31. Chennai, India: Institute for Financial Management and Research Centre for Micro Finance.

Barber, Brad M., and Terrance Odean. 2001. "Boys Will Be Boys: Gender, Overconfidence, and Common Stock Investment." *The Quarterly Journal of Economics* 116 (1): 261–92.

Becker, Gary S. 1957. *The Economics of Discrimination*. Chicago: University Press.

Becker-Blease, John R., Susan Elkinawy, and Mark Stater. 2010. "The Impact of Gender of Voluntary and Involuntary Executive Departure." *Economic Inquiry* 48 (4): 1102–18.

Becker-Blease, John R., and Jeffrey E. Sohl. 2007. "Do Women-Owned Businesses Have Equal Access to Angel Capital?" *Journal of Business Venturing* 22 (4): 503–21.

———. 2010. "The Effect of Gender Diversity on Angel Group Investment." *Entrepreneurship Theory and Practice* (July): 1–25.

Berger, Allen N., and Gregory F. Udell. 1995. "Relationship Lending and Lines of Credit in Small Firm Finance." *Journal of Business* 68 (3): 351–81.

———. 1998. "The Economics of Small Business Finance: The Roles of Private Equity and Debt Markets in the Financial Growth Cycle." *Journal of Banking & Finance* 22: 613–73.

Bergmann Lichtenstein, Benyamin M., and Candida G. Brush. 2001. "How Do 'Resource Bundles' Develop and Change in New Ventures? A Dynamic Model and Longitudinal Exploration." *Entrepreneurship Theory and Practice* 5: 37–58.

Biddle, Tabby. 2010. *DailyWorth: Transforming Women's Relationship with Money*. http://www.huffingtonpost.com. Posted April 20, 2010.

Block, Jorn, and Phillipp Sandner. 2007. "Necessity and Opportunity Entrepreneurs and Their Duration in Self-Employment: Evidence from German Micro Data." Discussion Paper 2007–10. Munich School of Management. http://epub.ub.uni-muenchen.de/.

Bobbitt-Zeher, Donna. 2007. "The Gender Income Gap and the Role of Education." *Sociology of Education* 80 (1): 1–22.

Boden, Richard J. Jr. 1999. "Flexible Working Hours, Family Responsibilities, and Female Self-Employment: Gender Differences in Self-Employment Selection." *The American Journal of Economics and Sociology* 58 (1): 71–83.

Boden, Richard J. Jr., and Alfred R. Nucci. 2000. "On the Survival Prospects of Men's and Women's New Business Ventures." *Journal of Business Venturing* 15 (4): 347–62.

Bollingtoft, Anne, and John P. Ulhoi. 2005. "The Networked Business Incubator: Leveraging Entrepreneurial Agency." *Journal of Business Venturing* 20 (2): 265–90.

Bordo, Michael, and Harold James. 2010. "The Great Depression Analogy." *Financial History Review* 17 (2): 127–40.

Brau, James C., and Jerome S. Osteryoung. 2001. "The Determinants of Successful Micro-IPOs: An Analysis of Issues Made under the Small Corporate Offering Registration SCOR Procedure." *Journal of Small Business Management* 39 (3): 209–27.

Brierley, Peter. 2001. "The Financing of Technology-based Small Firms. A Review of the Literature." *Bank of England Quarterly Bulletin* 41 (1): 64–76.

Bruett, Tillman. 2007. "Cows, Kiva, and Prosper.Com: How Disintermediation and the Internet Are Changing Microfinance." *Community Development Investment Review* 3 (2): 44–50.

Brush, Candida G. 1992. "Research on Women Business Owners: Past Trends, a New Perspective, and Future Directions." *Entrepreneurship Theory and Practice* 16 (4): 5–31.

Brush, Candida, Nancy Carter, Elizabeth Gatewood, Patricia Greene, and Myra Hart. 2001a. *The Diana Project: Women Business Owners and Equity Capital: The Myths Dispelled*. Kansas City, MO: Kauffman Center for Entrepreneurial Leadership.

———. 2004. *Gatekeepers of Venture Growth: A Diana Project Report on the Role and Participation of Women in the Venture Capital Industry*. Kansas City, MO: Kauffman Center for Entrepreneurial Leadership.

———. 2006. "The Use of Bootstrapping by Women Entrepreneurs in Positioning for Growth." *Venture Capital* 8 (1): 15–31.

Brush, Candida G., Nancy M. Carter, Patricia G. Greene, Myra M. Hart, and Elizabeth Gatewood. 2002. "The Role of Social Capital and Gender in Linking Financial Suppliers and Entrepreneurial Firms: A Framework for Future Research." *Venture Capital* 4 (4): 305–23.

Brush, Candida G., Linda F. Edelman, and Tatiana S. Manolova. 2008. "The Effects of Initial Location, Aspirations, and Resources on Likelihood of First Sale in Nascent Firms." *Journal of Small Business Management* 46 (2): 159–82.

Brush, Candida G., Patricia G. Greene, and Myra M. Hart. 2001b. "From Initial Idea to Unique Advantage: The Entrepreneurial Challenge of Constructing a Resource Base." *Academy of Management Executive* 15 (1): 64–78.

Butter, E. H., and D. P. Moore. 1997. "Women's Organizational Exodus to Entrepreneurship: Self-Reported Motivations and Correlates with Success." *Journal of Small Business Management* 35 (1): 34–46.

Canizares, Sandra Ma Sanchez, and Fernando J. Fuentes Garcia. 2010. "Gender Differences in Entrepreneurial Attitudes." *Equality, Diversity, and Inclusion: An International Journal* 29 (8): 766–86.

Carter, Nancy M., Mary Williams, and Paul D. Reynolds. 1997. "Discontinuance Among New Firms in Retail: The Influence of Initial Resources, Strategy, and Gender." *Journal of Business Venturing* 12: 125–45.

Carthy, Roi. 2009. *Three Israeli Femme-preneurs to Keep an Eye On.* http://techcrunch.com/2009/08/02.

Cassar, Gavin. 2004. "The Financing of Business Start-ups." *Journal of Business Venturing* 19: 261–83.

Catalyst. 2009. *Catalyst Census.* http://www.catalyst.org.

Cavalluzzo, Ken, Linda Cavalluzzo, and John Wolken. 2002. "Competition, Small Business Financing, and Discrimination: Evidence from a New Survey." *The Journal of Business* 75 (4): 641–79.

Chapple, Karen, Ann Marjusen, Greg Schrock, and Daisaku Yamamoto. 2004. "Gauging Metropolitan 'High-Tech' and 'I-Tech' Activity." *Economic Development Quarterly* 18 (1): 10–29.

Cliff, Jennifer E. 1998. "Does One Size Fit All? Exploring the Relationship Between Attitudes Toward Growth, Gender, and Business Size." *Journal of Business Venturing* 13: 523–42.

Clinton, Hillary Rodham (1996). *It Takes a Village: And Other Lessons Children Teach Us.* New York: Simon & Schuster.

Cohoon, J. McGrath, Vivek Wadhwa, and Lesa Mitchell. 2010. *Are Successful Women Entrepreneurs Different from Men?* Kansas City, MO: Kauffman Foundation.

Cole, Rebel A., and John D. Wolken. 1995. "Financial Services Used by Small Businesses: Evidence from the 1993 National Survey of Small Business Finances." *Federal Reserve Bulletin* (July): 629–67.

Coleman, Susan. 2000. "Access to Capital and Terms of Credit: A Comparison of Men and Women-Owned Small Businesses." *Journal of Small Business Management* 38 (3): 37–52.

———. 2002a. "Characteristics and Borrowing Behavior of Small Women-Owned Firms. Evidence from the 1998 Survey of Small Business Finances." *Journal of Business and Entrepreneurship*, 14 (2): 151–66.

———. 2002b. "Constraints Faced by Women Small Business Owners: Evidence from the Data." *Journal of Developmental Entrepreneurship* 7 (2): 151–74.

———. 2003. "Borrowing Patterns in Small Firms: A Comparison by Race and Ethnicity." *Journal of Entrepreneurial Finance & Business Ventures* 73 (3): 87–108.

———. 2006. "Capital Structure in Small Manufacturing Firms: Evidence from the Data." *Journal of Entrepreneurial Finance & Business Ventures* 11 (3): 105–22.

Coleman, Susan, and Richard Cohn. 2000. "Small Firms' Use of Financial Leverage: Evidence from the 1993 National Survey of Small Business Finances." *Journal of Business and Entrepreneurship* 12 (3): 81–98.

Coleman, Susan, and Alicia M. Robb. 2009. "A Comparison of New Firm Financing by Gender: Evidence from the Kauffman Firm Survey Data." *Small Business Economics* 33: 397–411.

Constantinidis, Christina, Annie Cornet, and Simona Asandei. 2006. "Financing of Women-Owned Ventures: The Impact of Gender and Other Owner- and Firm-Related Variables." *Venture Capital* 8 (2): 133–57.

Cooper, Arnold C., F. Javier Gimeno-Gascon, and Carolyn Y. Woo. 1994. "Initial Human and Financial Capital as Predictors of New Venture Performance." *Journal of Business Venturing* 9: 371–95.

Correll, Shelley J. 2001. "Gender and the Career Choice Process: The Role of Biased Self-Assessments." *The American Journal of Sociology* 106 (6): 1691–1730.

Davidson, Marilyn J., Sandra L. Fielden, and Azura Omar. 2010. "Black, Asian and Minority Ethnic Female Business Owners: Discrimination and Social Support." *International Journal of Entrepreneurial Behavior and Research* 16 (1): 58–80.

Davidsson, Per, and Magnus Henrekson 2002. "Determinants of the Prevalence of Startups and High-Growth Firms." *Small Business Economics* 19: 81–104.

Davidsson, Per, and Benson Honig. 2003. "The Role of Social and Human Capital Among Nascent Entrepreneurs." *Journal of Business Venturing* 18 (3): 301–31.

Delmar, F., and P. Davidsson. 2000. "Where Do They Come From? Prevalence and Characteristics of Nascent Entrepreneurs." *Entrepreneurship & Regional Development* 12: 1–23.

Diochon, Monica, Teresa V. Menzies, and Yvon Gasse. 2005. "Canadian Nascent Entrepreneurs' Start-up Efforts: Outcomes and Individual Influences on Sustainability." *Journal of Small Business and Entrepreneurship* 18 (1): 53–75.

———. 2008. "Exploring the Nature and Impact of Gestation-Specific Human Capital Among Nascent Entrepreneurs." *Journal of Developmental Entrepreneurship* 13 (2): 151–65.

Djankov, Simeon, Tim Ganser, Caralee McLiesh, Rita Ramalho, and Andrei Shleifer. 2010. "The Effect of Corporate Taxes on Investment and Entrepreneurship." *American Economic Journal: Macroeconomics*, 2 (3): 31–64.

Dohmen, Thomas, Armin Falk, David Huffman, Uwe Sunde, Jurgen Schupp, and Gert G. Wagner. 2005. "Individual Risk Attitudes: New Evidence from a Large, Representative, Experimentally Validated Survey." Discussion Paper no. 511. Berlin: German Institute for Economic Research.

Ebben, Jay J. 2009. "Bootstrapping and the Financial Condition of Small Firms." *International Journal of Entrepreneurial Behavior & Research* 15 (4): 346–63.

Elam, Amanda, and Siri Terjesen. 2010. "Gendered Institutions and Cross-National Patterns of Business Creation for Men and Women." *European Journal of Development Research* 22 (3): 331–48.

Fabowale, Lola, Barbara Orser, and Allan Riding. 1995. "Gender, Structural Factors, and Credit Terms Between Canadian Small Businesses and Financial Institutions." *Entrepreneurship Theory and Practice* (Summer): 41–65.

Fairlie, Robert W. 2011. *Kauffman Index of Entrepreneurial Activity: 1996–2010*. Kansas City, MO: Ewing Marion Kauffman Foundation.

Fairlie, Robert W., and Alicia M. Robb. 2009. "Gender Differences in Business Performance: Evidence from the Characteristics of Business Owners Survey." *Small Business Economics* 33: 375–95.

Fitzgerald, Margaret A., and Mary Winter. 2001. "The Intrusiveness of Home-Based Work on Family Life." *Journal of Family and Economic Issues* 22 (1): 75–92.

Ford, Matthew W., and Daniel W. Kent. 2010. "Gender Differences in Student Financial Market Attitudes and Awareness: An Exploratory Study." *Journal of Education for Business* 85: 7–12.

Gatewood, Elizabeth J., Candida G. Brush, Nancy M. Carter, Patricia G. Greene, and Myra M. Hart. 2009. "Diana: A Symbol of Women Entrepreneurs' Hunt for Knowledge, Money, and the Rewards of Entrepreneurship." *Small Business Economics* 32: 129–44.

Gatewood, E. J., K. J. Shaver, J. B. Powers, and W. B. Gartner. 2002. "Entrepreneurial Expectancy, Task Effort and Performance." *Entrepreneurship Theory and Practice* 27 (2): 187–206.

Girardo, William, and Elaine L. Edgcomb. 2011. *Key Data on the Scale of Microlending in the U.S.* Washington, D.C.: Field at the Aspen Institute.

Gundry, Lisa K., and Harold P. Welsch. 2001. "The Ambitious Entrepreneurs: High Growth Strategies for Women-Owned Enterprises." *Journal of Business Venturing* 16: 453–70.

Habbershon, Timothy G., and Mary L. Williams. 1999. "A Resource-Based Framework for Assessing the Strategic Advantages of Family Firms." *Family Business Review* 12 (1): 1–25.

Hanlon, Dennis, and Chad Saunders. 2007. "Marshaling Resources to Form Small New Ventures: Toward a More Holistic Understanding of Entrepreneurial Support." *Entrepreneurship Theory and Practice* 31 (4): 619–41.

Hanson, Susan. 2009. "Changing Places Through Women's Entrepreneurship." *Economic Geography* 85 (3): 245–67.

Harrison, Richard T., and Colin M. Mason. 2007. "Does Gender Matter? Women Business Angels and the Supply of Entrepreneurial Finance." *Entrepreneurship Theory and Practice* 31 (3): 445–72.

Hart, Myra. 2002. *Zipcar*. Harvard Business School Case #9-802-085. http://www.hbsp.harvard.edu.

Haynes, George W. 2010. "Income and Wealth: How Did Households Owning Small Businesses Fare from 1998 to 2007?" Accessed at http://www.sba.gov/advo.

Haynes, George W., and Deborah C. Haynes 1999. "The Debt Structure of Small Businesses Owned by Women in 1987 and 1993." *Journal of Small Business Management* 37 (2): 1–19.

Haynes, George W., Barbara R. Rowe, Rosemary Walker, and Gong-Soog Hong. 2000. "The Differences in Financial Structure Between Women- and Men-Owned Family Businesses." *Journal of Family and Economic Issues* 21 (3): 209–26.

Hessels, Jolanda, Marco van Gelderen, and Roy Thurik. 2008. "Entrepreneurial Aspirations, Motivations, and Their Drivers." *Small Business Economics* 31: 323–39.

Hill, Napoleon. 1960. *Think and Grow Rich*. New York: Fawcett Books.

Hisrich, Robert D., and Candida Brush. 1984. "The Woman Entrepreneur: Management Skills and Business Problems." *Journal of Small Business Management* 22 (1): 30–37.

Hudon, Marek. 2008. "Norms and Values of the Various Microfinance Institutions." *International Journal of Social Economics* 35 (1/2): 35–48.

Hughes, K. 2006. "Does Motivation Matter? Women's Entrepreneurship and Economic Success." Paper presented at the Annual Meeting of the American Sociological Association, Montreal, Canada, August 10, 2006.

Hustedde, Ronald J., and Glenn C. Pulver. 1992. "Factors Affecting Equity Capital Acquisition: The Demand Side." *Journal of Business Venturing* 7 (5): 363–74.

Jackley, Jessica. 2011. Ellsworth lecture presented at the University of Hartford, West Hartford, Connecticut, April 12, 2011.

Jensen, Elizabeth J., and Ann L. Owen. 2001. "Pedagogy, Gender, and Interest in Economics." *Journal of Economic Education* 32 (4): 323–43.

Jianakoplos, Nancy A. and Alexandra Bernasek. 1998. "Are Women More Risk Averse?" *Economic Inquiry* 36 (4): 620–30.

Kamar, Ehud, Pinar Karaca-Mandic, and Eric Talley. 2007. "Sarbanes-Oxley's Effects on Small Firms: What Is the Evidence?" Harvard Law School John M. Olin Center for Law, Economics and Business Discussion Paper Series, Discussion Paper no. 588.

Kelly, L. M., N. Ahtanassiou, and W. F. Crittenden. 2000. "Founder Centrality and Strategic Behavior in the Family-Owned Firm." *Entrepreneurship Theory and Practice*, 25 (2): 27–42.

Kepler, Erin, and Scott Shane. 2007. "Are Male and Female Entrepreneurs Really That Different?" SBA Office of Advocacy. http://www.sba.gov/advo.

Khavul, Susanna. 2010. "Microfinance: Creating Opportunities for the Poor?" *Academy of Management Perspectives* (August): 58–72.

Kim, Philip H., Howard E. Aldrich, and Lisa A. Keister. 2006. "Access (Not) Denied: The Impact of Financial, Human, and Cultural Capital on Entrepreneurial Entry in the United States." *Small Business Economics* 27 (1): 5–22.

Kirkwood, Jodyanne, and Beth Tootell. 2008. "Is Entrepreneurship the Answer to Achieving Work-Family Balance?" *Journal of Management & Organization* 14 (3): 285–302.

Kor, Y. Y., and J. T. Mahoney. 2000. "Penrose's Resource-Based Approach: The Process and Product of Research Creativity." *Journal of Management Studies* 37 (1): 109–39.

Kwong, Caleb C. Y., Piers Thompson, Dylan Jones-Evans, and David Brooksbank. 2009. "Nascent Entrepreneurial Activity Within Female Ethnic Minority Groups." *International Journal of Entrepreneurial Behavior & Research* 15 (3): 262–81.

Leach, J. Chris, and Ronald W. Melicher. 2009. *Entrepreneurial Finance*, 3rd ed. Ohio: South-Western Cengage Learning.

Lee, S., and D. Denslow. 2004. "A Study on the Major Problems of U.S. Women-Owned Small Businesses." *Journal of Small Business Strategy* 15 (2): 77–89.

Lerner, Josh. 1999. "The Government as Venture Capitalist: The Long-Run Impact of the SBIR Program." *Journal of Business* 72 (3): 285–318.

Levent, Tuzin Baycan, Enno Masurel, and Peter Nijkamp. 2003. "Diversity in Entrepreneurship: Ethnic and Female Roles in Urban Economic Life." *International Journal of Social Economics* 30 (11/12): 1131–61.

Liao, Kianwen, Harold Welsch, and Chad Moutray. 2004. "Start-up Resources and Entrepreneurial Discontinuance: The Case of Nascent Entrepreneurs." *Journal of Small Business Strategy* 19 (2): 1–15.

Lopez-Gracia, Jose, and Sonia Sanchez-Andujar. 2007. "Financial Structure of the Family Business: Evidence From a Group of Small Spanish Firms." *Family Business Review* 20 (4): 269–87.

Loscocco, Karyn, and Andrea Smith-Hunter. 2004. "Women Home-Based Business Owners: Insights From Comparative Analysis." *Women in Management Review* 19 (3): 164–73.

Lusardi, Annamaria, and Olivia S. Mitchell. 2006. "Planning and Financial Literacy: How Do Women Fare?" University of Michigan Retirement Research Center Working Paper 2006-136.

Lusardi, Annamaria, Olivia S. Mitchell, and Vilsa Curto. 2009. "Financial Literacy Among the Young: Evidence and Implications for Consumer Policy." Working Paper no. w15352. Cambridge, MA: NBER.

Mann, Ronald J. 1998. "Comment on Avery, Bostic and Samolyk." *Journal of Banking and Finance*, 22: 1062–66.

Manolova, T. S., C. G. Brush, and L. F. Edelman. 2008. "What Do Women Entrepreneurs Want?" *Strategic Change* 17: 68–82.

Markle, Kevin, and Douglas A. Shackelford. 2011. "Cross-Country Comparisons of Corporate Income Taxes." Working Paper no. w16839. Cambridge, MA: NBER.

Marlow, Susan, and Dean Patton. 2005. "All Credit to Men? Entrepreneurship, Finance, and Gender." *Entrepreneurship Theory and Practice* 29 (3): 526–41.

McConaughy, Daniel L., and G. Michael Phillips. 1999. "Founders Versus Descendants: The Profitability, Efficiency, Growth Characteristics, and Financing in Large, Public, Founding-Family-Controlled Firms." *Family Business Review* 12 (2): 123–31.

Minitti, Maria. 2010. "Female Entrepreneurship and Economic Activity." *European Journal of Development Research* 22 (3): 294–312.

Mishkin, Frederic S. 2011. "Over the Cliff: From the Subprime to the Global Financial Crisis." *Journal of Economic Perspectives* 25 (1): 49–70.

Mishra, Chandra S., and Daniel L. McConaughy. 1999. "Founding Family Control and Capital Structure: The Risk of Loss of Control and the Aversion to Debt." *Entrepreneurship Theory and Practice* (Summer): 53–64.

Moon, John. 2009. "Small Business Finance and Personal Assets." *Community Investments* 21 (3): 9–10, 39.

Morris, Michael H., Nola N. Miyasaki, Craig E. Watters, and Susan Coombes. 2006. "The Dilemma of Growth: Understanding Venture Size Choices of Women Entrepreneurs." *Journal of Small Business Management* 44 (2): 221–44.

Morrissette, Stephen. 2007. "A Profile of Angel Investors." *The Journal of Private Equity* 10 (3): 52–66.

Muravyev, Alexander, Oleksandr Talavera, and Dorothea Schafer. 2009. "Entrepreneurs' Gender and Financial Constraints: Evidence from International Data." *Journal of Comparative Economics* 37: 270–86.

Myers, Stewart C. 1984. "The Capital Structure Puzzle." *Journal of Finance* 39 (3): 575–92.

Myers, Stewart C., and Nicholai S. Majluf. 1984. "Corporate Financing and Investment Decisions When Firms Have Information that Investors Do Not Have." *Journal of Financial Economics* 13 (2): 187–221.

National Center for Education Statistics Fast Facts. 2009. http://www.nces.ed.gov.

National Science Foundation ADVANCE Program. http://www.nsf.gov.

Neeley, Lynn, and Howard Van Auken. 2010. "Women and Men Entrepreneurs: Different Relationships to Bootstrap Finance." Paper presented at the 2010 Annual Conference of the United States Association of Small Business and Entrepreneurship, January 16, 2010, Nashville, Tennessee.

Olson, J. M., N. J. Roese, and M. P. Zanna. 1996. "Expectancies." In *Social Psychology: Handbook of Basic Principles*, edited by E. T. Higgins and A. W. Kuglanski, 211–38. New York: Guilford Press.

Orser, Barbara, and Sandra Hogarth-Scott. 2002. "Opting for Growth: Gender Dimensions of Choosing Enterprise Development." *Canadian Journal of Administrative Sciences* 19 (3): 284–300.

Orser, Barbara J., Sandra Hogarth-Scott, and Allan Riding. 2000. "Performance, Firm Size, and Management Problem Solving." *Journal of Small Business Management*, 38 (4): 42–58.

Orser, Barbara J., Allan L. Riding, and Kathryn Manley. 2006. "Women Entrepreneurs and Financial Capital." *Entrepreneurship Theory and Practice* (September): 643–65.

Padnos, Cindy. 2010 *High Performance Entrepreneurs: Women in High Tech*. White Paper. http://www.illuminate.com.

Park, Yongjin, and Susan Coleman. 2009. "Credit Rationing and Black-Owned Firms: Is There Evidence of Discrimination?" *Journal of Developmental Entrepreneurship* 14 (3): 1–17.

Parker, Simon C., and Yacine Belghitar. 2006. "What Happens to Nascent Entrepreneurs? An Econometric Analysis of the PSED." *Small Business Economics* 27: 81–101.

Patel, Pankaj C., James O. Fiet, and Jeff Sohl. 2011. "Mitigating the Limited Scalability of Bootstrapping through Strategic Alliances to Enhance New Venture Growth." *International Small Business Journal* 29 (5): 421–47.

Paytas, Jerry, and Dan Berglund. 2004. *Technology Industries and Occupations for NAICS Industry Data*. Pittsburgh, PA: Carnegie Mellon University Center for Economic Development.

Pellegrino, Eric T., and Barry L. Reece. 1982. "Perceived Formative and Operational Problems Encountered by Female Entrepreneurs in Retail and Service Firms." *Journal of Small Business Management* 20 (2): 15–24.

Penrose, Edith T. 1959. *The Theory of the Growth of the Firm*. New York: John Wiley.

Petersen, Mitchell A., and Raghurum G. Rajan. 1994. "The Benefits of Lending Relationships: Evidence from Small Business Data." *The Journal of Finance* 49 (1): 3–38.

Porter, Michael. 1995. "The Competitive Advantage of the Inner City." *Harvard Business Review* (May–June): 55–71.

Powell, Melanie, and David Ansic. 1997. "Gender Differences in Risk Behavior in Financial Decision-Making: An Experimental Analysis." *Journal of Economic Psychology* 18: 605–28.

Randoy, Trond, and Sanjay Goel. 2003. "Ownership Structure, Founder Leadership, and Performance in Norwegian SMEs: Implications for Financing Entrepreneurial Opportunities." *Journal of Business Venturing* 18 (5): 619–37.

Reinhart, Vincent. 2011. "A Year of Living Dangerously: The Management of the Financial Crisis in 2008." *Journal of Economic Perspectives* 25 (1): 71–90.

Reynolds, Paul D. 1997. "Who Starts New Firms? Preliminary Explorations of Firms-in-Gestation." *Small Business Economics* 9: 449–62.

Reynolds, P. D., S. M. Camp, W. D. Bygrave, E. Autio, and M. Hay. 2002. *Global Entrepreneurship Monitor 2001 Executive Report*. Babson Park, MA: Babson College, and London: London Business School.

Reynolds, Paul D., Nancy M. Carter, William B. Gartner, and Patricia G. Greene. 2004. "The Prevalence of Nascent Entrepreneurs in the United States: Evidence from the Panel Study of Entrepreneurial Dynamics." *Small Business Economics* 23 (4): 263–84.

Riding, Allan L., and Catherine S. Swift. 1990. "Women Business Owners and Terms of Credit: Some Empirical Findings of the Canadian Experience." *Journal of Business Venturing* 5: 327–40.

Robb, Alicia M., and Susan Coleman. 2009. "The Impact of Financial Capital on Business Performance: A Comparison of Women- and Men-Owned Firms." Paper presented at the Annual Conference of the Western Economic Association International, Vancouver, British Columbia, July 1, 2009.

Robb, Alicia, and Susan Coleman. 2010. "Financing Strategies of New Technology-Based Firms: A Comparison of Women-and Men-Owned Firms." *Journal of Technology Management and Innovation* 5 (1): 30–50.

Robb, Alicia, and E. J. Reedy. 2011. *An Overview of the Kauffman Firm Survey: Results from 2009 Business Activities*. Kansas City, MO: Kauffman Foundation of Entrepreneurship.

Robb, Alicia M., and David T. Robinson. 2010. "The Capital Structure Decisions of New Firms." Working Paper no. 16272. Cambridge, MA: NBER.

Robb, Alicia, and John Watson. 2011. "Gender Differences in Firm Performance: Evidence from New Ventures in the United States." *Journal of Business Venturing*, available online November 12, 2011. ISSN 0883-9026.

Robb, Alicia M., and John Wolken. 2002. "Firm, Owner, and Financing Characteristics: Differences between Female- and Male-Owned Small Businesses." Working Paper no. 2002-18, FEDS. http://www.federalreserve.gov/.

Rogers, Craig D., Michael J. Gent, George M. Palumbo, and Richard A. Wall. 2001. "Understanding the Growth and Viability of Inner City Businesses." *Journal of Developmental Entrepreneurship* 6 (3): 237–54.

Romano, Claudio A., George A. Tanewski, and Kosmas X. Smyrnios. 2000. "Capital Structure Decision Making: A Model for Family Business." *Journal of Business Venturing* 16: 285–310.

Roper, Stephen, and Jonathan M. Scott. 2009. "Perceived Financial Barriers and the Start-up Decision: An Econometric Analysis of Gender Differences Using GEM Data." *International Small Business Journal* 27 (2): 149–71.

Ross, Stephen A., Randolph W. Westerfield, and Bradford D. Jordan. 2008. *Fundamentals of Corporate Finance,* 8th ed. Boston: McGraw-Hill Irwin.

Rugman, A. M., and A. Verbeke. 2002. "Edith Penrose's Contribution to the Resource-Based View of Strategic Management." *Strategic Management Journal* 23 (8): 769–80.

Sabarwal, Shwetlena, and Katherine Terrell. 2008. "Does Gender Matter for Firm Performance? Evidence from the East European and Central Asian Region." Working Paper Series no. 73, IPC. http://ssrn.com/abstract=1223454.

Sahlman, William A. 2009. *A Method for Valuing High-Risk, Long-Term Investments: The "Venture Capital" Method.* Harvard Business School Note 9-288-006.

Sanyal, Paromita. 2009. "From Credit to Collective Action: The Role of Microfinance in Promoting Women's Social Capital and Normative Influence." *American Sociological Review* 74: 529–50.

Schillinger, Liesl. 2006. "Start Something Big." *The Oprah Magazine* (January).

Scott, Robert H. III. 2009. *The Use of Credit Card Debt by New Firms.* Kansas City, MO: Kauffman Foundation.

Servon, Lisa. 1999. *Bootstrap Capital: Microenterprises and the American Poor.* Washington, D.C.: Brookings Institution Press.

Sirmon, D. G., and M. A. Hitt. 2003. "Managing Resources: Linking Unique Resources, Management, and Wealth Creation in Family Firms." *Entrepreneurship Theory and Practice* (Summer): 339–58.

Smyrnios, Kosmas X., Claudio A. Romano, George A. Tanewski, Paul I. Karofsky, Robert Millen, and Mustafa R. Yilmaz. 2003. "Work-Family Conflict: A Study of American and Australian Family Businesses." *Family Business Review* 16 (1): 35–51.

Sohl, Jeffrey. 2011. "The Angel Investor Market in 2010: A Market on the Rebound." http://www.unh.edu/news/docs/2010angelanalysis.pdf.

Sonfield, Matthew C. and Robert N. Lussier 2004. "Family Business Ownership and Management: A Gender Comparison." *Journal of Small Business Strategy* 15 (2): 59–75.

Staniec, J. Farley Ordovensky. 2004. "The Effects of Race, Sex, and Expected Returns on the Choice of College Major." *Eastern Economic Journal* 30 (4): 549–62.

Still, Leonie V., and Elizabeth A. Walker. 2006. "The Self-Employed Woman Owner and Her Business." *Women in Management Review* 21 (4): 294–310.

Taylor, Celia R. 2002. "Microcredit as Model: A Critique of State/NGO Relations." *Syracuse Journal of International Law and Commerce* 29 (2): 303–38.

Terjesen, Siri, and Jose Ernesto Amoros. 2010. "Female Entrepreneurship in Latin America and the Caribbean: Characteristics, Drivers, and Relationship to Economic Development." *European Journal of Development Research* 22 (3): 313–30.

Trade Finance Guide. 2008. Washington, D.C.: International Trade Administration.

Treanor, Lorna, and Collette Henry. 2010. "Gender in Campus Incubation: Evidence from Ireland." *International Journal of Gender and Entrepreneurship* 2 (2): 130–49.

Treanor, Lorna, Collette Henry, and Farzana Miah. 2010. "Supporting Women-Led New Venture Creation in the Bio-Sciences: The Role of the Incubator." Paper presented at the 2010 Diana International Conference on Women's Entrepreneurship, Banff, Alberta, August 3–4, 2010.

Treichel, Monica Zimmerman, and Jonathan A. Scott. 2006. "Women-Owned Businesses and Access to Bank Credit: Evidence from Three Surveys Since 1987." *Venture Capital* 8 (1): 51–67.

Tyler, John E., and Peter Schuck. 2011. *U.S. Policy Regarding Highly Skilled Immigrants: Change Whose Time Has Come in Rules for Growth: Promoting Innovation and Growth Through Legal Reform*. Kansas City, MO: Kauffman Foundation for Entrepreneurship.

U.S. Census. 2002. *Survey of Business Owners*. http://www.census.gov/econ/sbo/02.

U.S. Census. *Survey of Small Business Owners, 2007 and 2002*. http://www.census.gov.

U.S. Census. 2004. *U.S. Interim Projections by Age, Sex, Race, and Hispanic Origin*. http://www.census.gov.

U.S. Small Business Administration Office of Advocacy. 2011. *Frequently Asked Questions about Small Business Finance*. Retrieved from http://www.sba.gov/advocacy.

Van Auken, Howard, and Lynn Neeley. 1996. "Evidence of Bootstrap Financing Among Small Start-up Firms." *Journal of Entrepreneurial and Small Business Finance* 5: 233–47.

Vroom, V. H. 1964. *Work and Motivation*. New York: John Wiley & Sons.

Walker, Elizabeth, Calvin Wang, and Janice Redmond. 2008. "Women and Work-Life Balance: Is Home-based Business Ownership the Solution?" *Equal Opportunities International* 27 (3): 258–75.

Walker, Elizabeth, and Beverley Webster. 2004. "Gender Issues in Home-Based Businesses." *Women in Management Review* 19 (7/8), 404–12.

Watson, John. 2006. "External Funding and Firm Growth: Comparing Female- and Male-Controlled SMEs." *Venture Capital* 8 (1): 33–49.

Watson, John. 2007. "Modeling the Relationship Between Networking and Firm Performance." *Journal of Business Venturing* 22: 852–74.

Watson, John. Forthcoming. "Networking: Gender Differences and the Association with Firm Performance." *International Small Business Journal*.

Watson, John, Rick Newby, and Anna Mahuka. 2009. "Gender and the SME 'Finance Gap.'" *International Journal of Gender and Entrepreneurship* 1 (1): 42–56.

Wennekers, Sander, Andre van Stel, Roy Thurik, and Paul Reynolds. 2005. *Nascent Entrepreneurship and the Level of Economic Development*. Discussion Papers on Entrepreneurship, Growth and Public Policy. Jena, Germany: Max Planck Institute for Research into Economic Systems Group Entrepreneurship, Growth, and Public Policy.

Wernerfelt, B. 1984. "A Resource-Based View of the Firm." *Strategic Management Journal* 5: 171–80.

Wong, Poh Kam, Yuen Ping Ho, and Erkko Autio. 2005. "Entrepreneurship, Innovation and Economic Growth: Evidence from the GEM Data." *Small Business Economics* 24: 335–50.

Wu, Zhenyu, Jess. H. Chua, and James J. Chrisman. 2007. "Effects of Family Ownership and Management on Small Business Equity Financing." *Journal of Business Venturing* 22: 875–95.

Yunus, Muhammad, Bertrand Moingeon, and Laurence Lehmann-Ortega. 2010. "Building Social Business Models: Lessons from the Grameen Experience." *Long Range Planning* 43: 308–25.

Zafar, Basit. 2009. "College Major Choice and the Gender Gap." Federal Reserve Bank of New York Staff Report no. 364.

INDEX

Italic page numbers indicate material in tables or figures.